PRAISE FOR CANYON

"Most visitors barely glimpse this place, and those who hike rim-to-rim tend to move so fast the Grand Canyon is a blur. With this book, Muller has filled the spaces in between. Using simple, clear language he reveals the complex geography and history that is the interior of the Grand Canyon. This is a key book for anyone wanting to grasp this place, from long-traveled hikers to those who have never even stepped to the edge and looked into the frightening jumble below."—Craig Childs, author of *House of Rain: Tracking a Vanished Civilization across the American Southwest* and *Grand Canyon: Time below the Rim*

"I love Muller's writing and have delighted in reading much of his work. He certainly knows how to tell a good story and involve the reader in every inch of his journeys."—Betsey Bruner, Arts and Culture Editor, *Flagstaff Arizona Daily Sun*

"Muller has eloquently captured the spirit of this most special place. Anyone whose heart has been touched by the Grand Canyon will love his work."—David Meyer, Manager of Phantom Ranch, Grand Canyon National Park

"Muller's story unfolds with each step into the abyss like the South Kaibab Trail itself, revealing something new around each bend. If you're thinking about taking the plunge, *Canyon Crossing* will convince you to apply for that backcountry permit sooner rather than later."— Elias Butler, author of *Grand Obsession: Harvey Butchart and the Exploration of Grand Canyon*

"Muller's *Canyon Crossing* is a deep passage through the Grand Canyon. It's a rim-to-rim journey that captures the beauty of the canyon's inner life, the burdens of trail, the ambitions of hikers, and the colorful vistas and characters met along the way."—Mark Neumann, author of *On the Rim: Looking for Grand Canyon.*

CANYON CROSSING

Experiencing Grand Canyon from Rim to Rim

BY **SETH MULLER**

GRAND CANYON ASSOCIATION

Grand Canyon Association
P.O. Box 399
Grand Canyon, AZ 86023
(800) 858-2808
www.grandcanyon.org

Printed in the United States
Edited by Todd R. Berger and Faith Marcovecchio
Designed by Vicky Shea, Ponderosa Pine Design
Cartography by Bronze Black

First Edition
15   14   13   12   11   1   2   3   4   5

Library of Congress Cataloging-in-Publication Data

Library of Congress Cataloging-in-Publication Data

Muller, Seth, 1973-
Canyon crossing : experiencing Grand Canyon from Rim to Rim / by Seth Muller.
    p. cm.
Includes bibliographical references and index.
ISBN 978-1-934656-13-6 (alk. paper)
1. Grand Canyon (Ariz.)—Description and travel. 2. Grand Canyon (Ariz.)—Guide-
books. 3. Trails—Arizona—Grand Canyon National Park—Guidebooks. I. Title.
F788.M845 2011
917.91'320454--dc22
                                2010052242

*The mission of the Grand Canyon Association is to help preserve and
protect Grand Canyon National Park by cultivating support through
education and understanding of the park.*

To my wife Jane, fellow explorer.

CONTENTS

ACKNOWLEDGMENTS

This book would not be possible without the help and advice of a number of people. I first want to thank every person who gave up some of his or her time for extensive (and in some cases multiple) interviews. Their thoughts, perspectives, and insights help make this book sing.

Behind the scenes, Grand Canyon National Park public information officer Maureen Oltrogge, Grand Canyon Xanterra general manager Jon Streit, Colleen Hyde with the Grand Canyon National Park Museum Collection, and Grand Canyon National Park librarian Betty Upchurch all proved to be of great assistance. The staff of one of the park's concessioners, Xanterra South Rim, was always cordial and offered help whenever possible. Authors Rose Houk and Scott Thybony provided sage advice for writing about one of our most beloved national parks.

I want to extend my deepest gratitude to the staff and board of the Grand Canyon Association. It excites me to no end that they saw potential in both this book and in me as its author. I loved working with such inspired professionals—particularly director of publishing Todd Berger and Helen Ranney, director of outreach and public relations. Their passion and interest in this book has been unwavering.

I would be remiss in not thanking my parents for always encouraging me to pursue my dreams. And last, I want to thank my wife, Jane. Not only did Jane join me on a number of trips shared in this book, she also endured my time away on solo trips and provided thoughts and encouragement for my writing. Her support has meant everything.

INTRODUCTION

Dusk.

April.

Indian Garden.

Three thousand feet below the South Rim of the Grand Canyon.

Four-and-a-half miles down the Bright Angel Trail.

My wife, Jane, her sister Susan Newbold, and our friends Amy and Stephen Ehrenreich relax at our campsite. I leave for my second stroll of the evening, following the same path of our earlier three-mile round-trip hike to Plateau Point.

Indian Garden is serene. The mule riders are gone. The day hikers have left. The prominent sounds are the wind rustling the paper-crisp cottonwood leaves and the trickle of Garden Creek.

I look to the distance. The sun hits the tallest buttes, temples, and mesas. It gives an orange glow to a wind-blurred contrail overhead. Around me, the light is soft. The mood is delicate. I think of the billowy comfort of my sleeping bag, of being in the tent and finding warmth against the chill of the night.

I walk back toward Indian Garden's campground. I look up to the South Rim. I see the flashes from cameras. I see the lights of El Tovar Hotel. The rim appears like a shoreline, and I am at sea. The rim and the inside of the canyon feel like two different places, as different as land and ocean.

The wind brings in cool air. The dusk is the changing hour. I take it in through my breath and my vision. I crave these Grand Canyon moments.

Within a few dozen yards of the campground, I look up one last time at the rim, before it is obscured by the campground's trees. This time, I notice something adrift. It appears to be a plastic bag caught in the thermal winds that stir at dusk. As I watch, I notice it drifts too steadily to be a plastic bag. It floats down in my direction.

It's not a bag. It's a toy paratrooper.

The paratrooper drifts down to the east of the trail. It lands in a tangle of cacti, twenty feet off the trail on a slope. I scramble up to retrieve him, finding my way between and around the spiny and thorny plants. I pull on the yellow-and-white-striped parachute and untangle the string from cactus thorns with delicate caution. I notice something about the five-inch-tall plastic green army paratrooper. Someone taped a face over the paratrooper's face. It's a black-and-white photocopy of a young man.

I look back up to the South Rim. I marvel at this paratrooper's journey, a 3,000-foot drop into hostile territory.

My mind swirls with questions. *Who threw this paratrooper off the South Rim? Why did he or she do it? Whose face was taped to the paratrooper? What was the point?*

I wad up the trooper and his parachute in my hand and carry it back to the campsite.

The Canyon Man. That's what we name him. It's the title of a song Stephen and I made up during our descending hike on the Bright Angel Trail, sung to the tune of the pop classic "Candy Man."

> *Who can make you wish that*
> *You'd never been born*
> *Your feet get all blistered*
> *Your ligaments torn*
> *The Canyon Man!*
> *Oh, the Canyon Man can . . .*
> *Who can take a trail*
> *Make it out of rocks and dirt*
> *Make you keep walking*
> *Till your knees and ankles hurt*
> *The Canyon Man!*
> *Oh, the Canyon Man can . . .*

Our silly song and the Canyon Man Action Paratrooper (the full name we christen him with) bring levity to the trip. The paratrooper shows that the Grand Canyon experience is not only about rocks, trails, viewpoints, and the wide-open natural world, but also about strange acts of humanity.

It reminds me that people by the thousands crowd the South Rim and look down at the canyon we are in. That the Grand Canyon is its own kind of theater, a performance of rock and light. The canyon challenges us to stare at it and think about it. To contemplate our own tiny lives. To become like the toy paratrooper launched into a vast chasm. The toy tossed into the unknown reminds me that human lives are mere specks against the depths of time.

My wife and I sit under the visible Milky Way at Indian Garden that night. We ponder the South Rim—seen only as a line in the darkness where the stars stop and the single bright light at El Tovar Hotel shines. For the first time, after multiple backpacking trips and day hikes, I feel the Grand Canyon as an embrace. I'm unafraid of the four-and-a-half-mile hike out, of the pain sure to result from it. I find comfort in the interior of the great gorge and along its paths.

A fleeting idea to write a book passes through my brain. I look around me, at all of the people camped at Indian Garden. I think of the two German men we saw at Phantom Beach at the confluence of Pipe Creek and the Colorado River, how they traveled thousands of miles from home to find themselves here. I think of the stories I've overheard on different trips, of people celebrating birthdays and anniversaries, of one's first view of Grand Canyon being its own life milestone.[1]

And I ponder the paths people take, made of little more than rocks and dirt and logs. The North Kaibab Trail makes its perilous descent from the North Rim and delivers people to the Colorado River. It moves from 8,200 feet to 2,400 feet in fourteen miles that coil past Roaring Springs to unfurl on the floor of Bright Angel Canyon. It follows that canyon as it leads Bright Angel Creek to the Colorado River.

I think of the Colorado River Trail, known mostly as the River Trail, blasted out of the hard basement rocks of the Grand Canyon by members of the Civilian Conservation Corps in the 1930s. They left a masterpiece in stone that could outlast the pyramids of Egypt and many other human-made endeavors.[2]

I consider the South Kaibab Trail, built as a bypass trail that plunges off a waterless ridge and barrels down from rim to river in less than seven miles. I remember the story of the trail, how it was built during an era when the battle between public versus private at the Grand Canyon raged.[3] I remember my first hike down the South Kaibab, the openness so expansive it gave me chills and a trail so steep the muscles in my legs quaked for hours after I reached Phantom Ranch.

The other main Corridor trail from the South Rim is the Bright Angel. About ten yards from our Indian Garden campsite it runs its way up to the rim. The Bright Angel emerges west of center of the most developed area in Grand Canyon National Park. It also runs its way below Indian Garden, snaking alongside Garden Creek and tacking down the switchbacks known as the Devils Corkscrew. Finally, it bumps along Pipe Creek to the Colorado River, where it connects to the River Trail.

To call the Bright Angel a trail is to call the Grand Canyon a ditch. The word *trail* barely defines the history, development, and significance of a path that finds its way into the beastly beautiful heart of the canyon. The Bright Angel dates back to the 1890s as a developed trail, and hundreds of years as an ancient route.[4] To consider it only as a trail is to dismiss the people who weigh it with deep meaning. People like Juan Martin Botero, who took the journey despite being unable to walk, and the people who helped him.[5] Or Dan Williams, a sixty-year-old who ran from the South Rim to the North Rim and back to the South Rim in fourteen hours—and still made time to photograph the flowers.[6]

Three-Mile Resthouse and the Bright Angel Trail, on the way to Indian Garden.
Courtesy of the author

A trail is a trail. The Bright Angel, delivering hikers, runners, and mule riders to the bottom of Grand Canyon, is an international icon.

Human history laces these routes that bisect the canyon, stretching from ancestors of the Havasupais who farmed at Indian Garden and hiked out to the South Rim to hunt to modern hikers wearing the latest in footwear and lightweight gear. The trails have evolved from loose, perilous routes to steady slopes on four- and five-foot-wide paths safe for mule and hiker passage.[7] Two footbridges spanning the Colorado and six bridges over Bright Angel Creek on the North Kaibab Trail also provide ease of travel across the canyon's Corridor.

Three developed campgrounds grace the Corridor trail system, spaced out from North Rim to South Rim and supplied by seasonal water—with other, developed water sources along the way. Indian Garden, Bright Angel, and Cottonwood campgrounds all offer a chance for backpackers to rest and break up the extensive trip from one rim to the other. The inner canyon becomes even more inviting with the offer of mule assistance; in addition to carrying people into and out of the canyon, mules can carry down people's gear while they hike.[8]

At the bottom of it all sits Phantom Ranch. This is a place like no other in the world. Deep inside the Grand Canyon, Phantom Ranch offers cabins, clean beds, hot showers, hot meals, cold beer, and the chance to bask in a cottonwood-shaded oasis. Mule trains carry in all of the ranch's supplies, about 1,700 pounds per day.[9] The mules also carry out the trash—and bags of letters and postcards visitors send, with the Phantom Ranch cancellation that assures they were delivered by mule from the bottom of the Grand Canyon.

The Corridor trails themselves deliver people to two developed villages on Grand Canyon's rims. The North Kaibab Trail ends at the developed North Rim, which has food, lodging, and other guest services in season and camping year-round (though winter camping is a challenge, as the only road in is closed after the snow falls and visitors must therefore cross-country ski, snowshoe, or snowmobile to reach the park). The South Kaibab and Bright Angel trails end in proximity to Grand Canyon Village, which has multiple facilities offering food, lodging, grocery shopping, and camping. The many other trails along the Grand Canyon's 277 river miles—most following American Indian routes—create a teeming trail system. Each year, the more refined Corridor trails through treacherous terrain and climate draw 80,000 to 100,000 people on overnight trips, and hundreds of thousands more on day hikes.[10] People travel from all over the country and the world for the chance to walk or run from one side of the canyon to the other—or from either rim to the very bottom on foot or mule.

For this reason, the Corridor trails suffer in reputation among avid Grand Canyon explorers and guides, who favor the park's Threshold and Primitive trails over the more-crowded Corridor routes. In the Corridor, the vexation of crowds of people is compounded by mule trains—and the dung and urine these pack animals leave along the trails.

Despite the complaints of purists, treks into the sunken heart of Grand Canyon's interior have created memorable experiences, with the added reward of providing a real sense of accomplishment. The journey etches itself into the memory of its travelers, to radiate for years. Grand Canyon guides speak of clients contacting them five, ten, and fifteen years after a trip to reconnect with their fond memories of the grandest of chasms.

⊰ ✦ ⊱

While my wife, her sister, and our friends gather at the campsite's picnic table, I sit in my tent at Indian Garden and ponder the miracle of Grand Canyon's main trails. I consider my hike out, up the 3,000 vertical feet in four-and-a-half miles. I flex my feet and remember the work they will do in the morning. I envision safe passage, and my emergence from the steep trail onto the flat top of the South Rim. The heat, the dust, and the sheer beauty of the Grand Canyon are laced into my fondest memories. I sleep and dream of the walking highway and my traveling community of canyon explorers.

I contemplate the millions and millions and millions of footfalls across the Corridor trails, day after day and year after year, of pathways pressed deep into the ground. The footfalls resound from those who carry backpacks from camp to camp. They emanate from the boots of guests hiking down to Phantom Ranch or the hooves of the mules they ride. They ring out as canyon travelers look to rendezvous with river trips. They echo from runners supremely focused on covering dozens of trail miles in a day.

I imagine the travelers, seeing the Grand Canyon for the first time or the twentieth. Together they pack out their collective experiences and the resonating power of the one of Earth's greatest landscapes.

CHAPTER 1

NORTH RIM:
Daydream Country

It is August 1973. The United States is in the final throes of the Vietnam War. The Watergate hearings dominate the news, and Richard Nixon is on his way to resigning the presidency. The spirit of the late 1960s lingers but is slipping. Young people continue to travel across the country. They try to get back to nature, and they take the time to find themselves.

They are soul-searching.

A nineteen-year-old from Pomona, California, hitchhikes through the Southwest. Wayne Ranney wears his shoulder-length hair in a ponytail under a red bandana. He sports a thin beard and wears jeans mended with patches. He catches rides by being friendly and always smiling.

In his brown exterior-framed backpack he carries a canteen, a down sleeping bag, and a long, sheathed knife, along with food and clothing. He also keeps a sign handy, to help catch rides.

He meets up with two women—one who is twenty-three and another who is twenty-five—from Lexington, Kentucky. They follow a similar kind of journey, also seeking to explore the country, its roads, and its natural wonders. He joins up with them in Mesa Verde National Park in southwestern Colorado, an ancestral Puebloan site. He slings his pack into their white four-door Datsun, and they travel to Canyon de Chelly National Monument in eastern Arizona, a de Chelly Sandstone canyon, also with ancient sites. With a second hitchhiker joining them, they travel southwest from there to Petrified Forest National Park and then on to Flagstaff, Arizona. They exchange stories and pass the time listening to whatever songs come across the airwaves.

In a strange congruence, a song often played on the radio during their Arizona travels is "Take It Easy" by The Eagles, with its line "Standing on the corner in Winslow, Arizona" and its airy country sound, a good fit for the western flair of the region's land and people.

The two women next want to travel to the Grand Canyon from Flagstaff. Before heading to the park, they stop for supplies at the El Rancho Market near the present-day intersection of East Santa Fe Avenue (Historic Route 66) and Enterprise Road, just east of downtown. Although the South Rim is 120 miles closer, they choose the route to the more secluded North Rim.

Across the sky, clouds billow. Arizona has entered monsoon season, when a seasonal shift in wind feeds unholy thunderstorms that lash the parched landscape of the Southwest. The four of them cross over the border into Grand Canyon National Park. As they arrive at the North Rim, they ease themselves out of the car and meander to the edge of the great chasm.

They walk out to Bright Angel Point, the most prominent and popular viewpoint on the developed North Rim. Ranney sees the Grand Canyon for the first time. At first, it's not the geology and topography that startle him. "I saw one of the most incredible things. . . . We were sitting there, and this single thundercloud moved through the canyon with thunder and lightning and pelting rain. The thunderstorm was level [with] or even below me when I saw it. And as quickly as the storm came in, it moved out and the sunlight was back on the rocks. This happened so fast . . . that I was blown away."

Ranney wants to stay at the Grand Canyon, to savor it. But he continues to travel with the two young women, who are ready to move on. They rumble through southern Utah and head down to Las Vegas, Nevada. They leave Las Vegas for Sequoia and Kings Canyon national parks. Ranney parts with them at Sequoia to hitch a different ride after two weeks of friendship. But along with a backpack stuffed with clothes, he carries a new passion. Seeing the Grand Canyon from the North Rim, knowing so much remained for exploration, stirred him.

"I started to send applications to work at the Grand Canyon [as a] ranger," Ranney recalls during an interview at his Flagstaff, Arizona, home. "Someone told me that if you volunteered on the trail crew in the summertime you had a better chance of getting a job. Back then, you could not get a job as a ranger. There were so many people who wanted to be rangers."

His love for the canyon deepens when he takes a geology class in 1975 at Riverside City College in Riverside, California. He travels to the Grand Canyon with the class, only to turn frustrated when a snowstorm derails plans to hike into the canyon. "And I remember I was so upset about that I marched over to the backcountry office and I got a permit for the following September. I don't know how it happened, but I kept that permit and I decided to come back, and I did my [first] rim-to-rim hike."

After Ranney finishes that hike, he finds a volunteer position that will allow him to live at Grand Canyon National Park. "I got a volunteer job at Phantom Ranch, and that started on October 6, 1975. So, through a series of a little more than two years, I went from seeing the Grand Canyon for the first time to living at the bottom of it. And Phantom Ranch was the first place I lived in Arizona. I did that for three years, and I loved it. It was just the best thing that could have ever happened to me. They did not have any money to give me for food. Other people got five dollars a day, but the supervisor had run out of money. He did have a place for me. And he apologized [to] me that it was Phantom Ranch. He did not like the inner canyon.

He was from Mississippi and he got stationed [t]here, but he did not see any value to the inside of the Grand Canyon. What he did not know is that he could not have given me a better job."

Ranney goes from a drifter who happened to catch a ride to the North Rim of the Grand Canyon in 1973 to a rim-to-rim hiker and, shortly thereafter, a resident living inside the Grand Canyon. In the years following, Ranney evolves into a well-known and admired geology educator. He earns undergraduate and master's degrees in geology from Northern Arizona University in Flagstaff, completing his master's in 1988. He writes a book, *Carving Grand Canyon*, and all along the way works as a river and hiking guide.

Geologist and author Wayne Ranney leads a Grand Canyon Field Institute trip.
Courtesy of Mike Buchheit

Through his years in and around the Grand Canyon, he develops a fondness for the North Kaibab, South Kaibab, Bright Angel, and River trails—and all of the features that make up the canyon's Corridor trail system. This, even after he has explored nearly every trail mile of the canyon, into its most remote and pristine regions.

For Ranney, his Grand Canyon passion begins with that first day at the North Rim, which likewise serves as the launching point for many rim-to-rim trips made by visitors. "I think it [is] a much different experience to see [the canyon] from the North Rim. Being a rather naive kid and not knowing how to escape crowds, I'm sure I would have had a different experience on the South Rim, with the cars and buildings everywhere. The North Rim was like a resort, far off the beaten track. It was a perfect spot for a hitch-hiking trip of discovery."[1]

To see the Grand Canyon for the first time from the North Rim, or to initiate a rim-to-rim journey there, is to start in daydream country. The North Rim stands 8,200 feet above sea level and more than a mile above the bottom of the canyon.[2] In a state famous for its arid deserts of cacti and rattlesnakes, this elevation supports a pristine alpine forest containing a mix of fir, spruce, and aspen trees, and bustling with mule deer, cougars, and the Kaibab squirrel. The Kaibab is a dark gray squirrel with striking white features and tufted ears longer than a common squirrel's. It lives only on the Kaibab Plateau, along the North Rim and in the North Kaibab District of the Kaibab National Forest.[3]

The forty-four-mile drive from Jacob Lake to the canyon rim on Arizona Highway 67 moves south along the Kaibab Plateau, a place that gets its name from the Southern Paiute words that loosely translate into "mountain lying down."[4] The road moves through ponderosa pine and into alpine forests. It passes over open meadows pocked with sinkhole ponds where the limestone formation has dissolved, creating what geologists call "a karst topography."[5] Even as late as June, the Kaibab Plateau is known to hold patches of snow in its shadows while the rest has melted and filled the ponds. The plateau receives an average of 142 inches of snow a year, nearly triple the average snowfall of Minneapolis–Saint Paul, Minnesota.[6] This is due to the 8,000- to 9,000-foot elevation of the plateau. It creates an environment people might associate more with Colorado than Arizona.

All of that snow typically shuts down access to the North Rim from late November through mid-May. The main guest services close for the winter on October 15. This quiet time leads to less human impact on the trails, soils, and plant life of the canyon's "other side." The sense of wildness feels intact, even years after the first North Rim lodge was built, in 1928.[7] The North Rim developed area receives only one-tenth the number of visitors seen on the South Rim because of the North Rim's winter closure, its limited lodging, and its greater distance from major highways and cities.[8] When the North Rim opens in May, cars and RVs line up at the park's entrance. The season brings a new flow of visitors. With lower inner-canyon temperatures in May and October, hundreds of those visitors arrive for the chance to hike down the North Kaibab Trail into the canyon's depths. It is high season for ambitious hikers traveling rim to rim in a day, and the even more ambitious to run rim to rim to rim, known by the trail-running community as an R2R2R.[9]

Hikers and backpackers traversing the canyon most often travel from the North Rim to the South Rim, as the north side's elevation rises about 1,000 feet higher than the south's. This means less elevation gain when hiking out on the south side of the canyon. To end a hike at the South Rim is also to end at a bustling transportation hub, which can make the after-hike logistics of a trek from one side to the other more easily manageable, relatively speaking.

A greater benefit is that the temperate forests perched on the Kaibab Plateau offer a chance for reflection and relaxation before plunging into the canyon's rocky and fiery heart. The lodge and its surroundings feel like a hidden retreat among the quaking aspen that stand at the edge of the chasm.

⊣ ✛ ⊢

My wife, Jane; daughter, Grace; and I arrive at the North Rim on an opening-day May visit where I will launch a solo rim-to-rim voyage. We take the epic drive from Flagstaff to the North Rim, nearly 200 miles of high desert and plateau. U.S. Route 89 ramps down from the San Francisco Volcanic Field into lowlands punctuated with scrub brush, shallow canyons, and Navajo Nation outposts. It turns into a hundred miles of reservation highway, moving through the Painted Desert and on to the radiant walls of the Echo and Vermilion cliffs. The scenic route, U.S. 89A, branches west from U.S. 89. It crosses the Colorado River at the Navajo bridges—one for pedestrians, the other for cars—passing by the road that winds down to Lees Ferry, the starting point for most Grand Canyon river trips.

The highway unfurls along the edge of the Vermilion Cliffs to the north, part of Vermilion Cliffs National Monument, and a wide plain that spreads to the south. Ahead to the west, the Kaibab Plateau awaits. The highway rides the plateau's flank with switchback after switchback and rises from the valley floor into a piñon-juniper forest. Those trees vanish, and ponderosa pines replace them. The ponderosas soon share the elevated landscape with aspen, fir, and spruce.

At Jacob Lake, the highway reaches the Arizona 67 junction—a spur road that leads across the plateau to the North Rim. The daylight fades faster than expected. We watch out the window as sunset begins its two-hour show. Mule deer congregate by the dozens along the border where forest and meadow meet.

With only a ribbon of two-lane paved road bisecting the expansive plateau, I can easily imagine the early pioneer days and initial development of the North Rim of the Grand Canyon.

⊣ ✦ ⊢

Given its closer proximity to the north side and the geographic divider of the Grand Canyon itself, Utah and its early Mormon settlers—members of the Church of Jesus Christ of Latter Day Saints—brought exploration and influence to the North Rim, the Kaibab Plateau, and, more broadly, the Arizona Strip.[10] Even through the 1970s, the North Rim seemed more connected to Utah, and the South Rim more connected to Arizona. Up through that time, North Rim workers and residents typically read the *Salt Lake City Tribune* and the South Rim population the *Arizona Republic*, out of Phoenix. Over time, the barrier softened with improved transportation and technology, making the North Rim feel more connected to its home state.[11]

That the Arizona Strip—a stretch of Arizona the size of Massachusetts that lies north of the Grand Canyon—even exists as part of the Grand Canyon State owes much to poet, writer, and Arizona historian Sharlot Hall. In the summer of 1911, she took a two-month journey there with Flagstaff guide Allen Doyle to survey the land that was initially included as part of Utah Territory. Although Utah officials wanted the state line to be drawn at the Colorado River, Hall's writings, later published as *Sharlot Hall on the Arizona Strip: A Diary of a Journey through Northern Arizona in 1911*, helped influence the idea of keeping the Arizona Strip with its namesake territory. It officially ended up as part of Arizona when Arizona became a state in 1912.[12]

The Arizona Strip's early pioneer settlement evolved during the 1860s and 1870s, following the vision of LDS church leader Brigham Young, successor to founder Joseph Smith, to colonize the region. After members of the Mormon Church migrated westward, they settled in the area that would become Salt Lake City in 1847. In the years following, Young relied on dedicated members such as John D. Lee to expand Mormon territory farther. Lee founded Lees Ferry, but was later convicted for the slaughter of pioneers passing through southern Utah, a rampage known today as the Mountain Meadows Massacre. One hundred and twenty men, women, and children were murdered that fateful day in 1857 on the plains of the southern Utah Territory near Cedar City. Eventually, Lee was caught and tried twice (the first trial ended with a hung jury), then executed by firing squad at the site of the massacre.[13]

Mormon Parley Pratt was another prominent player in the history of southern Utah Territory. He followed a trail originally known as the Old Spanish Trail. Fray Francisco Atanasio Domínguez and Silvestre Vélez de Escalante blazed it in 1776 as they looked for a route between a mission in Santa Fe, in what would become New Mexico, to another in Monterey, in present-day California. Trapper and explorer Jedediah Strong Smith followed and improved upon the route in 1826. In the 1850s, the Utah Territory portion of the route became known as the Mormon Outlet Trail.[14]

Also around this time, Jacob Hamblin, called the Buckskin Apostle for his dedication as a Mormon and his years in the wilderness, went south and east from southern Utah Territory to work among the Hopi and explore the region as the Mormon Church looked to expand. His missions to the Hopi and Navajo lands led to the development of an east–west route that allowed Mormons to move into the Arizona Territory. However, tensions with American Indians caused Mormon Church leaders to hesitate in expanding too far south and east. In the end, the Arizona Strip saw only spotty settlement in the late 1800s and early 1900s due to the area's distance from railroads and population centers such as Salt Lake City and the growing city of Phoenix, as well as its lack of water.[15]

Although remote, a few visionaries recognized the Kaibab Plateau, the Arizona Strip, and southern Utah lands as places worthy of becoming tourist destinations. Dave Rust and his father-in-law, Edwin Dilworth "Uncle Dee" Woolley, served as the most accomplished and well-known entrepreneurs of early Grand Canyon North Rim tourism. Many historians consider Rust one of a handful of men responsible for making inner-canyon tourism along today's Corridor trail system possible.[16]

Rust proved to be a hard-working and innovative man, a Mormon with pioneer spirit and grit. He served as an educator not only to school-children in Utah but also to the people he guided through canyon country. He enlightened people about the incredible nature of the Southwest while wowing them with its scenery. He, with the backing of Woolley, worked to develop a trail from the North Rim down to the river following Bright Angel Canyon. Although the trail traced a different route in its upper half than today's North Kaibab Trail does, Rust forged the north-side river access, created a camp called Rust's Camp (later renamed Roosevelt's Camp after a visit by former president Teddy Roosevelt), and spent months building and perfecting a cable system to cross over the Colorado River and connect the north side to the south.[17]

The National Park Service took over management of Grand Canyon in 1919 and steadily worked to create concessioner contracts or take control of individual ventures and claims. This edged out Rust, but his work helped establish the current Corridor trails route, which soon changed directions slightly to accommodate the development of the North Rim as a new tourist destination.[18]

In 1927 crews set out for the pristine edge of the canyon to construct the North Rim's Grand Canyon Lodge, selecting a place near Bright Angel Point, primarily to access the water of Roaring Springs directly below.[19] Architect Gilbert Stanley Underwood drafted the blueprints for a rustic retreat. He worked for the Utah Parks Company, a subsidiary of the Union Pacific Railroad. More than twenty-five years after the Santa Fe Railway's spur line reached the South Rim in 1901, the Union Pacific set out to create its own Grand Canyon offering.[20]

A Union Pacific spur line, built in 1923, carried travelers to Cedar City, Utah. From there, the railroad could load passengers into tour buses to travel to the three crown jewels: Zion National Park, Bryce Canyon National Monument (Bryce became a national park in 1928), and the North Rim of the Grand Canyon. The spur line launched a mass tourism era for the three park destinations. The Union Pacific railroad used the attractions to keep its passenger trains brimming.[21]

This development coincided with the end of one period and the beginning of another, as noted by Grand Canyon historian Mike Anderson. "I mark 1928 as the end of the pioneer period at the Grand Canyon because the park service had gained control of the park. They had set down rules and regulations. They had contracts with concessioners and [very little] of this individualist bull [remained], where people could do whatever they wanted. Plus, the park finished the black bridge [Kaibab Suspension Bridge, across the Colorado River], the North Kaibab Trail, and the [North Rim's Grand Canyon] Lodge opened. So, they had things the way they wanted them. Also, in 1928 the Navajo Bridge by Lees Ferry was completed [creating more convenient South Rim to North Rim access by road]."[22]

The North Rim was still remote and difficult to reach, and it developed at a slower pace than the southern side of the canyon. At the South Rim, the railroad pulled right up to the edge of the Grand Canyon. On the north side, passengers still had to take the 160-mile bus trip from Cedar City, and the roads were not well developed in the early days. The lodge was a welcoming place after the long journey. Its staff greeted the incoming buses and sang to the visitors as they stepped off and came into the lodge. Later in the evening, North Rim employees performed a welcome song for guests.[23]

The ponderosa-log and limestone Grand Canyon Lodge emerged as a shining example of majestic architecture in the national parks. The décor and style seemed one part Mary Colter and one part Charles Whittlesey, Underwood's contemporaries whose designs are prominent on the South Rim.[24] But in 1932, a kitchen fire spread quickly at the North Rim lodge and burned it to the ground. Despite the financial challenges of the Depression, the railroad subsidiary found the money and resources to rebuild and reopen the lodge, with the same floor plan, in 1937.[25]

The new lodge brought a return of visitors. And after World War II, the North Rim became a destination for people on road trips and family vacations. Then, in the late 1960s and early 1970s, the North Rim emerged as a staging area for backpackers descending into the Grand Canyon on rim-to-rim hikes. Prior to the 1960s, the majority of visitors entered the Grand Canyon on the backs of mules. The counterculture era and the related environmental movement of the 1960s inspired renewed interest in national parks and wilderness areas. Young people who considered themselves hippies often traveled the country and sought out natural settings for backpacking experiences.[26]

This backpacking movement coincided with a spike in Grand Canyon river running, propelled by the completion of Glen Canyon Dam in 1964.

Grand Canyon Lodge personnel in 1930 at the entrance to the original building, which burned down in 1932. *Courtesy Grand Canyon National Park Museum Collection (GCNPMC) (#00509)*

The dam created predictable water flows downstream through the Grand Canyon, with little surge and wane of the once-volatile Colorado River. However, environmentalists past and present have vilified this dam, which submerged the delicate cathedral beauty of Glen Canyon's sandstone walls and disrupted the ecosystem downstream.[27]

In the 1950s, the river runner Georgie White helped create the commercial river-running movement by bringing in large World War II army rafts, which she strapped together to create nearly flip-proof barges for large groups. The rubber rafts' ability to buckle and flex through the gnashing rapids of Grand Canyon turned river expeditions into roller-coaster rides, especially in the gnarly white water embedded in the Inner Gorge.[28]

The rush to ride the Colorado River through Grand Canyon coupled with the rush to cross the Grand Canyon by foot from one rim to another. By the early 1970s—the time when Ranney first arrived—the inner canyon had been transformed from a place few people visited to a place where thousands hiked the trails and ran the river. On one summer day in 1972, Phantom Ranch ranger Gale Burak counted more than 1,000 people sleeping at nearby Bright Angel Campground. In later interviews, Burak referred to it as "sardine-ville," both for the number of people sleeping side by side and for the stench of the visitors and their waste.[29]

"After that one day down there [at Bright Angel Campground], the park service said, 'We can't do this anymore. This is it,'" said Anderson during an interview at his home in Strawberry, Arizona. "They immediately went to work on a backcountry management plan, which they did pass, with rules, in 1972 and 1973. The rules said how many people could go down and where they could camp. And, at the same time, they passed the river management plan as to how many people could be going down the river and so forth."[30]

The park service's response through the plan and its updates and revisions, along with the ongoing operations of Phantom Ranch, have created the template for managing the modern pilgrimage that tens of thousands of people make each year.

⇥ ✦ ⇤

The journey from North Rim to South Rim on the Corridor trails begins in Roaring Springs Canyon, a side canyon of a side canyon of the Grand Canyon. Roaring Springs Canyon cuts into the Kaibab Plateau directly east of the developed North Rim. It appears on the left side of the road as visitors drive toward Grand Canyon Lodge; the chasm that holds Roaring Springs reveals itself between the ponderosas. This side canyon only hints at the looming gorge that awaits at Bright Angel Point, the prime viewpoint in the developed area.

On a visit to the North Rim on opening day, I choose to watch daylight end at Bright Angel Point. People mill and talk to each other in hushed tones. Occasionally, the buzz of a passing fly or the caw of a raven or a gust of wind breaks the silence. I think, *Always the wind at Bright Angel Point.* I sit on an outcropping of the 270-million-year-old Kaibab Formation, sea mud turned to rock. The surface teems with fossils of early marine life. Underneath me are crinoid fossils—once coral-like creatures—and the stone remnants of sponges.

I try to find a moment to myself on the usually busy point that reaches out into Grand Canyon. A mother and her adult daughter come along and talk more loudly than the others. They speak of trip logistics and how they liked Bryce Canyon better. They soon leave, and a few other people come out by themselves in search of quiet. I walk away from the point and head back when the sun hits the western horizon.

On my way back to the lodge, I let my gaze drop into Roaring Springs Canyon. I imagine myself on the North Kaibab Trail, along its first five miles—slipping steeply into the great earth. I wonder if I should skip my

Standing at the North Rim's Bright Angel Point, circa 1919. *Courtesy GCNPMC (#05439)*

plan to spend the next day out on the Walhalla Plateau, the jutting peninsula that arcs out into the canyon. Roaring Springs and Bright Angel canyons gouge out the land on its west side, and the east side marks the beginning of the slopes of eastern Grand Canyon. Walhalla Plateau invites me to explore, given the lushness of the meadows and richness of the aspen and pine forests, and the chance to wander among ancient ruins and meander around pioneer homesteads.

The North Kaibab Trail tempts me more. Its trailhead, located a little more than a mile north of the lodge, serves as a beacon. A sign marks the beginning of the ultimate path. It stands as a passageway, a portal that transports one from the sensuous forests to the scraped and tawny walls of the true Grand Canyon. I know the brutal beauty of the canyon's insides. I wonder why I would not choose to remain in the cool alpine forest and meander along a trail like the Widforss for a few miles. It stays on top of the rim and wanders through the woods. It's a trail that demands less than anything in the inner canyon.

The North Kaibab demands everything.

⌐ ✦ ¬

Two years pass, and I return to the North Rim. At 4:30 am, near the beginning of another North Rim season in mid-May, I launch my first solo rim-to-rim backpacking trip. I throw a backpack strap over one shoulder and then shift my weight to push my opposite arm through the other strap. I leave my wife, Jane, and daughter, Grace, back at the cabin.

The light is barely diffusing in the eastern sky. Most of what I see in the darkness are the trees and the indigo cast of my headlamp. The wind blows, and I hear it cutting through the pine needles. It sounds like a distant ocean.

Cottonwood Campground—seven miles below the rim—beckons as my day's destination. I start the hike earlier than needed for the trek, but I want to descend before the heat does. I choose to walk from the developed North Rim area along the Bridle Trail. It adds about a mile to my journey. I use a steady walk so I can get my blood circulating, focus my mind on the task at hand, and find a good rhythm.

This is the start of a daunting journey of nearly twenty-four miles. As I move along, I walk on a broken array of Kaibab Formation rocks. I step on pinecones that have fallen from the ponderosas. I know I will end my journey in the same Kaibab Formation on the other side.

I think of all of the moments I have experienced at the North Rim. The canyon draws me to make an annual trip, to relax and to enjoy the sense of place. And to meet my dad, who is fascinated with the North Rim too and often invites me and my family to join him here. Like Ranney, I first saw the Grand Canyon on its north side—twenty-five years after he did, in 1998. After that initial experience, I just could not stop coming back.

The trail spooks me in the dark, with only the early, thin light casting up from the eastern horizon. By 4:45 am, songbirds begin their repertoires. Roaring Springs Canyon comes into view out of the inky shadows. The half-moon shines in the southwestern sky, near Venus.

Five am and I reach the North Kaibab trailhead. The temperature hovers near freezing. I take off my pack and walk to get water. I debate putting on another layer, but realize I would not need it after a few minutes on the trail. I stop to study a sign with the image of a figure falling off the side of a cliff under a sun radiating wavy rays. I pass signs for no pets and no bicycles. Wild turkeys gobble in the distance. There is no one else here.

I pull my pack back onto my shoulders.

I clutch my hiking poles.

The trip begins with a single step.

There is enough daylight so that I can see the trail. I walk through an alpine forest. I move ever downward. I take a pause near the lip of the Grand Canyon and let myself think, *Every step down means a step up.*

I keep moving forward. I feel tempted to turn around, to go back to the cabin and be with my family. But the Grand Canyon keeps calling me back. The skeletons of aspen and their ghostly forms are replaced by leafed-out aspen farther down the trail. The wind picks up and dances around me. It happens every morning before the sun comes up. A shift arrives, and the wind begins to roll as the canyon heats in places, stays cool in others.

I force myself to take deep breaths, taking in the air. It smells of nothing, as if purified by all the trees and their oxygen. The light is becoming more pronounced, the canyon more defined.

I can feel myself tumbling deeper into the canyon, becoming increasingly lost in its beautiful madness.

CHAPTER 2

NORTH KAIBAB:
The Initial Descent

Every backpacking trip into the Grand Canyon should begin with deep considerations of nature and Earth's storied history. Few hikes on the planet reveal so much biodiversity and so much rock. The canyon is the ultimate teacher of geologic time and all its consequences. It shares evidence of long-cycling forces and changes unfolding over 1,700 million years. The Grand Canyon, while not a complete representation of the planet's geologic history, opens to reveal more than one-third of Earth's lifespan.

The layers stun the senses with varying colors, textures, and shapes. Unlike a mountain, desert, or plain—or even any other canyon—the Grand Canyon reveals ten, and in some areas of the canyon, more, prominent layers. Other deep canyons such as Copper Canyon in Mexico, Zion in Utah, and Black Canyon of the Gunnison in Colorado are made up of two or three layers at most.[1]

In the dim morning light on the North Kaibab Trail, I try to remember the names of each Grand Canyon rock layer. The formations appear from rim to river in a vertical mile.

I daydream of their colors and contrasts. They begin with the craggy gray to beige to white Kaibab, clustered with fossils from an ancient shallow sea. The Toroweap follows, with its bulbous form and gray-white stone streaked with black. The Coconino radiates yellow and gold from its blocky form. The red blush of the Hermit Shale and the Supai Group comes next. The rocks bleed red down to the Redwall Limestone—gray rock with a red sandstone dye job on its face.

I conjure the bands of Muav Limestone, with one impermeable band where the springs gush forth. And the Bright Angel Shale, seemingly tarnished copper green, eroded and broken across the Tonto Platform.

I move into the piled plates of Tapeats Sandstone followed by the fantastic nothing: the Great Unconformity. It is a gaping absence of time, a missing 1,200-million-year-old section of Earth's history.

I move on to the basement rocks—the fanged, dark, dangerous types. They appear charcoal black with ribbons of salmon and pearl, studded with glittery mica. The Vishnu Schist is 1,700 million years old. That is 1.7 billion years, more than 170 million human lifetimes. These are rocks that make human civilization seem a blip in time. The rock lies

down

at

the

bottom

of

every-

thing.

⚏ ✦ ⚎

At three-quarters of a mile down the North Kaibab Trail, I stop at Coconino Overlook. There, I sit on a lip of the mostly limestone Kaibab Formation while thinking of the layers that wait for me below. I attempt an exercise. I try to equate each layer with a part of the body.

Kaibab (bone). Toroweap (teeth). Coconino (blood). Redwall (marrow). Muav (tendon). Tapeats (vertebrae). Vishnu and Zoroaster (the brain and DNA, respectively).

I also jot down facts about the geology I want to remember. The youngest Grand Canyon layer is older than the era of the dinosaurs. The oldest layer predates any life-forms. That layer is more than a third as old as the planet itself. The layers represent the return and exit of climates over millennia. A place east of the Corridor trails shows where continents ripped apart. They make it clear that the planet is unfixed and shifting.[2]

It all begins with the Kaibab, 270 million years ago. The rock appears as broken pottery, a sift of fragments along the upper reaches of the North Kaibab Trail. As I walk across the rock at Coconino Overlook, I look at the outcroppings of limestone. I study them for signs of sponge and crinoid fossils.[3] The wonder of paleontology and geology surface instantaneously within the first steps down the North Kaibab.

To embrace the canyon is to love its rock. It's difficult to claim Grand Canyon fanaticism without at least a passing interest in geology. The canyon is blatant rock exposure, gratuitous. The layers and layers are opened to reveal sedimentary, metamorphic, and igneous rock. Many geologic forces and phenomena are revealed. Earth's history is laid bare.

Within each rock lies a past that runs deeper and richer than that of any plant or animal. For that reason, to be a geologist requires great imagination and profound thinking. Geologists must envision a world not of fixed geography, but one where oceans, continents, and topography constantly change.

Seas rise. Oceans retreat. Mountains erode. Canyons deepen. Arid regions turn wet. Rain forests go dry.

Any one point on Earth has morphed a dozen times or more. It may have been underwater, along a shoreline, a marsh or desert, and on the very top of a mountain. And all we know of this is recorded in rock.

In places of major erosion such as the Grand Canyon, stone warps and deepens our understanding of time. Anyone who considers geology within Grand Canyon is forced to deal with time on an epic level. It defies comprehension. When giving talks about the scale of time in Grand Canyon rock, geologist Ivo Lucchitta unravels a fifty-six-foot timeline. On a timeline of that length, approximately a third of an inch (roughly one centimeter) represents one million years. Early human civilization formed around one-sixtieth of an inch ago.

To think in these terms, that civilization is but a blip on a timeline, is to humble the human ego. It's difficult to fathom that our accomplishments, our advancements, and all of our creations are of tinier significance—in terms of the geologic time it took for these things to take place and in terms of their lasting permanence—than fossils in a rock layer.

Just like it did with the dinosaurs, Earth and its rock will reclaim us—and all we have wrought.

Take comfort in this, Wayne Ranney has told me. Let Grand Canyon tear down the human ego but also rebuild it. Just think, we are the first animal to understand geology, to recognize the canyon's deeper history, to hear its stories, and to appreciate its beauty.

At the top of the North Kaibab Trail, life-forms both ancient in the rock and alive in the present abound. The first two miles of the trail slide and switchback their way through an alpine forest. Spruce, fir, and aspen crowd the trail. Engelmann spruce appear as jagged arrows pointing to the sky. They stand with Douglas-fir and find their way into remote places below Grand Canyon's rim. They drink snowmelt and monsoon rain. Crowded around their bases are scrub oaks, aspen saplings, and wild currant bushes.

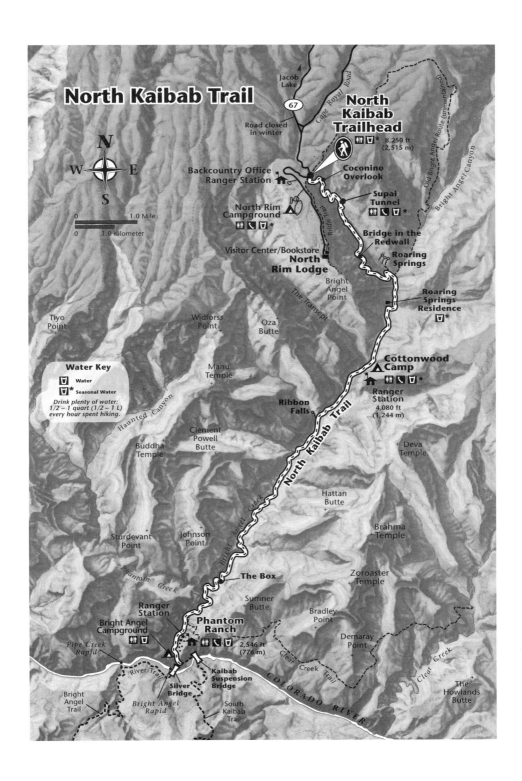

North Kaibab Trail

Jacob Lake

67

Road closed in winter

North Kaibab Trailhead
8,250 ft
(2,515 m)

Coconino Overlook

Backcountry Office Ranger Station

Supai Tunnel

North Rim Campground

Bridge in the Redwall

Roaring Springs

Visitor Center/Bookstore
North Rim Lodge

Bright Angel Point

The Transept

Roaring Springs Residence

Tiyo Point

Widforss Point

Oza Butte

Cottonwood Camp

Ranger Station
4,080 ft
(1,244 m)

Water Key

Water

Seasonal Water

Drink plenty of water:
1/2 – 1 quart (1/2 – 1 L)
every hour spent hiking.

Manu Temple

Ribbon Falls

North Kaibab Trail

Deva Temple

Haunted Canyon

Clement Powell Butte

Buddha Temple

Hattan Butte

Brahma Temple

Sturdevant Point

Johnson Point

Bright Angel Creek

The Box

Zoroaster Temple

Phantom Creek

Sumner Butte

Bradley Point

Ranger Station

Bright Angel Campground

Phantom Ranch
2,546 ft
(776 m)

Demaray Point

Clear Creek Trail

Clear Creek

Pipe Creek Rapid

River Trail

Kaibab Suspension Bridge

COLORADO RIVER

The Howlands Butte

Bright Angel Trail

Silver Bridge

Bright Angel Rapid

South Kaibab Trail

The trail along these first miles forges through plants and trees, an arboreal dreamscape. In the late spring and summer, it feels like you are entering a passageway through the greenery. The plants are joined by out-croppings of rock. At Coconino Overlook, the plants and trees part for a view into Roaring Springs Canyon and beyond.

The rim-to-rim hike in the Grand Canyon unfolds as an experience through layers. Not only do the trails burrow and snake and uncoil their way through rock types, they pass through a strata of natural life zones, from alpine forest to desert. The canyon reveals itself in a journey of miles, a journey through geologic time, and a journey through many of the conti-nent's ecosystems. Southwestern author and naturalist Rose Houk equates the fourteen-mile hike from the 8,200-foot North Rim down to the 2,400-foot Colorado River to "beginning a hike in Canada and ending at the Mex-ican border," ecologically speaking.[4]

Houk explains how the biology within the Grand Canyon sharpens per-ceptions. "The living aspect of the canyon really starts to get you to focus on the details of the canyon. I think of the color of wildflowers. The splash of color catches your attention, like a red penstemon in a desert environ-ment. It's that contrast of colors. Or finding out . . . that there's a little pocket of aspen on the South Rim near. . . . Grandview [Point] amongst the piñon-juniper and ponderosa. And then you start to learn of the [canyon's] micro-climates. With the geologic diversity and what [Clarence] Dutton calls the architectural infinity of the Grand Canyon, it creates these microclimates that allow a pocket of Douglas-fir to grow below the South Rim or a pocket of aspen to appear in a cool place where you might not expect them."[5] As Houk describes it, the living world of the Grand Canyon allows people to see it in a deeper way—with their senses. "I think when you first stand on the rim, it's a two-dimensional postcard and all you see is rock. It's a land-scape beyond people's human comprehension in size or time. Then you see a hawk coming out of the abyss and you go, 'Okay, there is life in the Grand

Canyon.' You go from seeing this immensity that's hard to comprehend and you start to see the color, life, and movement of a living thing within it. And you realize it's more than this two-dimensional thing you see."

Although microclimates abound, the descent into the canyon results in one ecosystem steadily yielding to another. Aspen and ponderosa give way to juniper and piñon trees, usually stunted, bushy, and craggy. Ferns yield to high desert succulents and sagebrush. Farther down, cacti and century plants thrive in the heat and aridity. Bushy-tailed squirrels and nearly silent mule deer in the forests and meadows of the Kaibab Plateau are exchanged for whiptail lizards, scorpions, and Grand Canyon rattlesnakes. But a different category of animals and plants and trees thrive along the ribbons of water that emerge from the canyon walls and make short courses to the Colorado River.

The first two miles of the North Kaibab Trail through Roaring Springs Canyon flourish with mixed and intersecting ecological life zones. In the arid, sun-battered climes of northern Arizona, how often the sun reaches the ground dictates what grows. This leads to a realm where ponderosa pine trees stand a few feet from spiny yucca and cacti. The south-facing canyon appears like a banana belt in places, as plants that thrive in warmer environments climb up to meet the forest and enjoy the southern track of the winter sun.

The differences in temperature, sunlight, and soil support a bevy of wildflowers in warmer months. The purple flair of dwarf lupines, the fine-petaled radiance of desert blazing stars, and the red strokes of scarlet gilia and common paintbrush dot the edges of the trail. The bulbous flowers on narrowleaf yucca plants join them, along with the dangerous and mysterious sacred datura, a common plant in the Grand Canyon.

The datura, producing five- to seven-inch-long white blooms that are the largest of any flowering plant in the park, offers an alluring scent. In *Cannery Row*, John Steinbeck wrote that "the flowers smelled of love and

Sacred datura, a common wildflower in the inner canyon. *Courtesy of the author*

excitement, an incredibly sweet and moving odor."[6] But the datura is poisonous and sometimes used to induce hallucinations. An East Coast species is often called jimsonweed, its name derived from the name of the Jamestown colony in Virginia, where soldiers in 1676 boiled down the plant to eat it and spent many days in a "frantick condition."[7] In the Grand Canyon, datura sometimes offers a temptation to curious backpackers and river runners, who may prepare it because of some recipe they found only to end up panicky, blind, and delirious.[8] It can also prove fatal.

Along with wildflowers, early morning starts down the North Kaibab Trail often mean crossing paths with a half dozen or more mule deer. Wild turkeys might slip across the pathway, while songbirds emerge from their elaborate nests and greet the warming day. The wind in the Grand Canyon morning stirs aspen into quaking life, their leaves brushing together, sounding like a watery cascade. Even below the rim, the forest spills off the plateau and makes for a relatively lush start in life zones that overlap in some places and recede and give up ground in others, depending on the spot on the slope and the intervals of shade and sun.

The northern beginning of the rim-to-rim passage through such delicate natural shifts and balances serves as an early testament that the Corridor trail route will be a diverse and engrossing journey.

⊰ ✛ ⊱

The North Kaibab Trail drops into Roaring Springs Canyon a mile north of Grand Canyon Lodge. The trail exists here because of the lodge and developed area's need to access the perennial waters of the springs five miles below the rim. The original rim-to-rim route descended into the canyon about ten miles to the east. There, a U.S. Geological Survey crew led by François Matthes in 1902 first followed a path through upper Bright Angel Canyon.[9]

Matthes arrived at the Grand Canyon to survey it after mapping much of the West's great mountains and terrain, but the canyon confounded him. "The writer next found himself commissioned with the survey of a hole in the ground. Not a mere depression of moderate extent, but a horrible, ragged rent, a chasm two hundred miles long," he wrote.[10] Matthes crossed the canyon on the North Bass and South Bass trails, thirty miles west of the developing Grand Canyon Village on the canyon's South Rim.

On the Kaibab Plateau, Matthes and his survey crew spent two summers and, as part of the expedition, went down upper Bright Angel Canyon into Bright Angel Canyon proper, and down to the river. They sketched out a rough trail on this route, but they came a dozen years after the first known rim-to-rim passage made by Dan Hogan, a trapper and prospector who crossed in 1890.[11]

Behind Matthes came Dave Rust, who followed the same route to the river and developed it as a trail. He and his father-in-law, Uncle Dee Woolley, arrived with ambitious plans to create a backcountry adventure for

Workers on the Francois Matthes U.S. Geological Survey take measurements at Cape Royal on the North Rim. *Courtesy GCNPMC (#04453)*

tourists to travel to the edge of the North Rim and descend into the canyon. He and his crew spent several months between 1906 and 1907 constructing a trail suitable for stock. Woolley would later host trips down the trail as part of his Grand Canyon Transportation Company.[12]

The National Park Service took over trail construction and maintenance on the trail in late 1920—one year after it took over management of the Grand Canyon from the U.S. Forest Service. It took most of eight years for the work to finally arrive at the fork of upper Bright Angel Canyon and Roaring Springs Canyon. With the development of the North Rim and a pump house at Roaring Springs, the crew turned west instead of east, blazing a different route than the one Rust used. Despite the steep cliffs of the Redwall Limestone in the constricting canyon, the crews created a trail that met park standards set during construction of the South Kaibab Trail, completed three years before work on the upper section of the North Kaibab Trail began. This included a four- to five-foot-wide thoroughfare suitable for hoof travel, grades reduced to less than 20 percent.[13]

The trail in the Redwall Limestone was "literally hewn from solid rock in half tunnel sections" using explosives, portable drills, and jackhammers.[14] The trail clings to the 500-foot cliffs of the western wall of Roaring Springs Canyon. Along with the blasting and hammering used to construct the Redwall section, crews blew out a twenty-foot-long tunnel through an outcropping of Supai Group rock. On the west end of the tunnel, the workers established a rest stop, with water piped from Roaring Springs.

In 1927, workers for the Union Pacific Railroad began work on the foundation and infrastructure for the North Rim developed area. To expedite their work, they installed a cable conveyor system from the rim down to Roaring Springs. It replaced mules that had initially carried equipment for the trail work, and the conveyor system helped with finishing the route.[15] In 1928 crews completed the final length of what has become the main route from rim to rim. The narrative of the trail's nomination for the National Register of Historic Places notes, "Few if any major alterations have been made to the North Kaibab Trail since its completion . . . but the entire trail has demanded continuous maintenance due to frequent landslides and floods."[16]

⊰ ✦ ⊱

More than eighty years after the completion of the trail, I walk its mostly unaltered path. I take the journey tens of thousands have taken before me. And possibly hundreds are taking it now, as I do. A little after 6 am I reach the entrance to Supai Tunnel and the rest area to the west. The twenty-foot portal in the red rock glows in the morning light that pours into Roaring

Springs Canyon, making its way to the canyon floor where breaks in the forest allow. A ribbon of warm air wafts up from the canyon. It disappears, replaced by a cool breeze flowing down from the rim. I've missed breakfast, and I set up my camp stove to boil water for instant coffee. I bask in the awe of the moment. I've passed through an eastern woodland–type forest crowding the red dirt trail on the approach to Supai Tunnel. The light reflects off higher points, filling the forest with its glow. I meditate on the passage that brings forward memories of places I hiked in my college days, mostly in the wilderness areas of West Virginia.

I draw a spark from a lighter, and the camp stove hisses with blue flames. The coffee ritual begins. I spoon instant coffee into my cup, pour in boiling water, and inhale the aroma. Morning erupts across the canyon around and below the rest area. Four hikers stop for two minutes to rest. They wear light-colored shorts, long-sleeved shirts, and running shoes, with small backpacks holding water bladders, the umbilical-like tubes near their mouths. "Supai Tunnel," a fit, older-looking woman says to the others. "We're making good time." She sips from her bladder and stands with her hands on her hips. The others look winded, but the fit woman nods and they pass through the tunnel, disappearing before I take my first drink of coffee.

A middle-aged couple follows them. They stop to get a drink, but the faucet at the rest area doesn't work. I get up, open the small door at the base of the spigot pipe, and tinker with the plumbing. I find the valve and the lever. I turn on the water. The sound and sight of it inspires us all to take a drink. A man of retirement age ambles down the trail toward us and then up to the restrooms. Before I stopped, I didn't pass anyone on the trail. After ten minutes of rest, people catch up with me and then continue down the path. A running couple passes by the rest area without hesitation. They arrive and depart in seconds. Onward, into the abyss.

The early traffic on the North Kaibab Trail will pick up through the morning hours. With the North Rim lodge open, the rim-to-rim journeys flow. Most of the people moving from north to south are backpackers, rim-to-rim-in-a-day hikers, and Phantom Ranch overnighters. The runners going rim to rim to rim in a day, most of whom start at the South Rim, are already beginning their journey. Today, the mid-May Sunday of the North Rim's opening weekend, a backcountry ranger will count more than 400 people passing through Cottonwood Campground.

At Supai Tunnel, a different kind of traveler will soon arrive. The North Rim offers mule rides to the tunnel and back, a two-mile trip each way. This mule ride is significantly shorter than the ride offered from the South Rim, which heads all the way to Phantom Ranch on the Bright Angel, River, and North Kaibab trails. On the north side, the Supai Tunnel trip offers visitors a chance to descend into the canyon by mule. It remains a long-standing tradition at the Grand Canyon, and even a four-mile round-trip offers a taste of adventure for visitors.

As I pack up my camp stove and finish my coffee, another retired man with a round face and continuous smile says hello. He points to my backpack. "I see you have a friend traveling with you," he says. He's indicating the raven stuffed animal that's strapped to my pack. The raven belongs to my daughter and his name is Emery, after the Kolb brother. The two Kolb brothers—the other being Ellsworth—arrived at the Grand Canyon from their Pittsburgh, Pennsylvania, home in 1902. They photographed tourists on the Bright Angel Trail and embarked on various Grand Canyon adventures. "The raven makes for a good mascot," I say as I pull my backpack onto my shoulders and clip the straps. I also ready my hiking poles for the descent. "They're more resourceful than we are."

He nods, still smiling. "Perfect day," he says. I want to note that the temperature is higher than expected in May, close to fifteen degrees above average. The temperature only feels comfortable now, at 6 am, in the trees. Scorching heat awaits us later in the day, at lower elevations. Phantom Ranch will, on our journey, reach triple-digit highs equal to those normally not experienced until June. We will need to consider all measures to avoid direct sunlight.

Instead, I look around and nod. For Grand Canyon lovers, any day inside the gorge is a perfect day.

He gestures for me to walk ahead of him, to pass through Supai Tunnel and out the other side. I step into its glow and pass through into the next phase of the North Kaibab descent.

⊰ ✦ ⊱

The construction of the top section of the North Kaibab Trail—and the completed, better-developed connection from the North Rim to the South Rim—coincided with the end of an era. As historian Mike Anderson mentioned, 1928 could be considered the end of the pioneer era at Grand Canyon and the real beginning of Grand Canyon National Park. This shift led to a significant reduction in mining, lumbering, and resource extraction within the boundaries of the park, replacing much of the commerce in commodities with tourism.[17] The North Kaibab Trail and its involved construction also sealed the Corridor's destiny as the principal route from the North Rim to the South Rim. In the earliest days of Grand Canyon tourism development, a rim-to-rim route that crossed the canyon twenty miles downriver from Bright Angel Canyon and thirty rim miles west of the would-be site of Grand Canyon Village gained traction as the possible principal transcanyon passage. "In the 1880s, there [was a] good . . . possibility that the central trail corridor might have been out in the Bill Bass area," notes Anderson. He speaks of a route that runs down South Bass Canyon to the river, then crosses over to the Shinumo Creek drainage and follows it up to the North Rim.

In 1885 Bass created a tent camp on the rim that served as the beginning of his tourist enterprise. He offered tourist trips informally until he improved roads and trails in the early 1890s. The Indiana-born Bass chose to live in Arizona to improve his health, and when he looked to the Grand Canyon area for work, he saw fortune in the possibility of tourism. He met one tourist in particular, a New York woman named Ada Lenore Diefendorf, who caught his attention. They married in 1895. Ada Bass turned out not to be a typical stay-at-home mom, but rather a woman who maintained the day-to-day operations of the camp during her husband's long absences, often attributed to his drinking problems.[18]

In the ensuing years, with the help of his wife and family, Bass launched work on an inner-canyon trail system that went down South Bass Canyon to the river and up to the North Rim along Shinumo Creek, then broke west from Shinumo and continued up the route carved by White Creek.[19]

"Bass had the first rim-to-rim trail corridor," Anderson explains. "What stopped that from [becoming the main trail corridor] was simply that the Grand Canyon Railway arrived where it did on the South Rim of the Grand Canyon in 1901. That of course produced Grand Canyon Village. A lot of people don't know that it really ties into the history of the American West— that wherever the railroad builds a depot, the town grows up. Flagstaff, Williams, Ash Fork, and Seligman are examples. All of these were railroad depots. The same thing happened at the Grand Canyon. The railroad arrived in 1901. So, that's where the village erupted."

Despite this, Bass continued to improve his route and attempt to draw tourists to his part of the Grand Canyon. He used mining claims both bogus and legitimate to secure his place in the canyon. And, in 1906, he installed the first river crossing with a two-line, one-car cable system. In 1908 he upgraded it to a four-line configuration, which still carried one cable car across the river but made the crossing both safer and more stable. Around that time, Rust built his cable system across the river at the mouth of Bright Angel Canyon. Rust tapped into a better circumstance: he connected with the Bright Angel Trail and its origin in burgeoning Grand

Canyon Village, catering to tourists brought to the canyon by railroad.[20]

That the train arrived where it did on the South Rim had more to do with mining than it did with tourism. "The primary reason the railroad took the route it did [was] for the mining claims," Anderson says. "The man behind the railroad on the South Rim [was William] "Buckey" O'Neill. You see a lot of newspaper reports through the late 1880s and 1890s of people wanting to build a railroad to the rim from either Flagstaff or Williams. . . . O'Neill knew about these mining deposits in an area called the Francis Mining District, [from] Rowe Well south and through [the copper mining camp of] Anita. A lot of little mines. Buckey O'Neill bought up those mining claims. [O'Neill] had a vested interest. The mines are not much good unless you can get the ore to smelters, so building a railroad up from Williams made a lot of sense. They looked like they would be very good copper deposits. It turns out they weren't."

The first passenger train arrives at the South Rim, September 17, 1901. The train tracks' endpoint near the head of the Bright Angel helped focus development on the Corridor Trails. *Courtesy GCNPMC (#02435)*

Anderson continues, "He was thinking in terms of shipping ore from the mining district as well as the tourism. He built his cabin at the South Rim . . . while he was doing the railroad planning, and it is still there today. In 1898, [O'Neill] died in the Spanish American War. The Bright Angel Hotel took over his cabin. Still, the railroad company had the capital, and it laid track as far as Anita before it went bankrupt. The Santa Fe [bought] the company out of bankruptcy when they were twenty miles from the rim. They completed it in 1901. How [the railroad] came to end up where it did on the South Rim was principally because [O'Neill] wanted it there. He knew the Bright Angel Trail was there. He knew inner-canyon tourism was something. And it just made sense to continue up Bright Angel Wash. It made for an easy route with low grades to get up [to] the rim. He could have gone in any direction up to the rim from Anita, but the direction he took up Bright Angel Wash was the most favorable for building the railroad, and it was the shortest [route] to the rim."

When the railroad arrived, it launched the construction of El Tovar—one of the finest hotels in the country at the time of its completion—and bought and refurbished an already existing Bright Angel Hotel. El Tovar opened and the Bright Angel reopened in 1905. "After that, any other tourist business along the rim was dead," Anderson notes. "It couldn't be done. The stagecoaches stopped running from Flagstaff to the Grand View Hotel [located a dozen miles to the east of the village near the present-day Grandview trailhead]. There was hardly any way you could get to Grandview. The writing was on the wall. Pete Berry [who owned the Grand View Hotel at Grandview Point] was going to be out of business, and Bill Bass was going to be out of business."

With this, the Corridor route began its rise to prominence as the most developed and popular inner-canyon access.

⊣ ✦ ⊢

As I move deeper into the canyon, I find I can never take for granted the route a trail follows, the decisions its builders made regarding its alignment, and the history that created it. I also never take for granted the work it takes to negotiate a trail into the Grand Canyon, as every descending route rails against topographic lines.

More than three miles down the North Kaibab Trail, the Redwall Limestone reveals itself. The solid, sheer walls of this rock layer create one of the canyon's more formidable barriers. Walls tower 500 to 1,000 feet and stand sheer and uncompromising. The North Kaibab crosses a wooden-planked footbridge known as the Bridge in the Redwall. Instead of continuing downhill, the trail takes a steady climb uphill. Perched on a limestone ledge on the east side of Roaring Springs Canyon, it returns to its downward angle, following a route blasted into the rock.

With the descent, Roaring Springs Canyon deepens east of the trail. The path loses elevation steadily while the floor of the canyon quickly drops from sight, an abyss the only view from the trail. Height fears are triggered along this route. A wrong slip sends stones underfoot bouncing and echoing in the chasm below. The trail remains four to five feet wide and promises safe passage, but stepping off the trail carries with it a risk of falling. The sign at the trailhead with the image of a figure plummeting off the side of a cliff warns of sections of trail like this.

During a previous day hike on the North Kaibab Trail, my wife, our friend Fred Calleri, and I push the outer limits of day hiking from the higher-elevation North Rim into the chasm. It's August, and we've gotten an early start. We pass the Redwall section and feel the temperatures spiking higher than normal, even for late summer. We reach a point in the canyon, though it's barely later than 9:30 am, where furnacelike heat builds up between the walls. Fear nips at my thoughts, as I know that once we reach our turnaround spot at the Roaring Springs picnic area, we still need to hike five miles out. Our plan, even though we intend to hike out shortly after our hike in, proves a poor one. The sun rules. The shade is gone. Heat dominates.

We keep going. We follow the path carved and blasted from the Redwall Limestone. We move down steadily along that western wall. We pass the four-mile mark of the descent. Then we hear it. The sound of water.

On the eastern wall, Roaring Springs gushes and cascades out of passages in the rock. It tumbles nearly 500 feet to the canyon floor, which we can finally see stretched before us downstream. Wondrous circumstances of geology allow water to surface here. The permeable rock layers above trap precious precipitation and it seeps down through them, exiting at Roaring Springs as it reaches harder layers. In the side canyons to the north of the Colorado River, the springs burst through with more bravado—as though Earth has sprung a leak in places such as Vaseys Paradise in Marble Canyon and Thunder River and Deer Creek near the midway point of a river trip through Grand Canyon. The Little Colorado River and Havasu Creek tap similar aquifers on the south side.

The north side of the Grand Canyon unleashes more water from its walls for three reasons. The North Rim stands 1,000 to 2,000 feet higher than the South Rim, allowing it to wring more moisture from passing storms. Also, this portion of the Kaibab Plateau slopes southward, so precipitation that falls on the North Rim heads south toward the canyon and not north off the back slopes of the plateau. Groundwater south of the Colorado River generally flows southward, away from the canyon.[21]

That relative abundance of water also creates long side canyons that recede farther from the center of the Grand Canyon. This leads to longer trail approaches when traveling from the North Rim to the river. The North Kaibab Trail, at fourteen miles, is the longest rim-to-river hike in the Grand Canyon. By contrast, the Bright Angel Trail and South Kaibab Trail, both dropping down from the South Rim, are nine miles long (including the River Trail section) and seven miles long, respectively.[22]

The cascades of Roaring Springs—still nine hiking miles away from the river—mark a new realm. The water appears in glimpses as it tumbles through a carpet of greenery clinging to the rock and feeding off the springs. Where the perennial waters meet the canyon bottom, trees and plants flourish. The sound of the water and the sight of Eden in the high desert excite us. It also tortures us. We see water. We hear water. But the canyon separates us from the water while we suffer in the building heat. I also suffer regret of the foolish choice to hike so far down into the canyon in August. The notion goes against all National Park Service warnings.

My wife, Fred, and I walk faster. We sense a new and watery beauty—a whole other realm like a lush and hidden garden—that rewards the travelers who make the descent closer to the bottom of the Grand Canyon and its majesty.

CHAPTER 3

ROARING SPRINGS:
One Family's Adventure

In the Grand Canyon, the presence of water changes everything.

About four-and-a-half miles down from the North Rim, a spur trail breaks northeast from the North Kaibab Trail. The quarter-mile trail cuts along a slope and eases its way down to the Roaring Springs day use area. Here, the thunder of the springs is more prominent, with its source only a few hundred yards to the south. Other springs contribute to a burbling stream flowing along the canyon floor near the end of Roaring Spring Canyon. Here, Cottonwood trees tower overhead. Smaller mesquite trees and shrubs create a habitat different from the raw and open areas I've just passed through in the unrelenting sun.

Songbirds flit from branch to branch as they hunt for seeds and insects. If I don't look up or much beyond the branches, the Roaring Springs area could be any inviting stream habitat in any locale. That it's nestled in the Grand Canyon makes it a miracle.

Roaring Springs creates a behemoth water source in a parched landscape. An estimated 4.85 million gallons a day flow out of the springs. The water diverted for the developed North and South rims is anywhere from 300 to 700 gallons per minute. One hundred gallons per minute go to the

In 1966 severe damage to the nearly completed pipeline meant to bring higher volumes of water to the South Rim was destroyed along with large sections of the North Kaibab Trail. The pipeline wasn't rebuilt and operational until 1970. *Courtesy GCNPMC*

North Rim in season, and most of the remainder goes to the South Rim along a pipeline completed in 1970. Small amounts siphoned from the pipeline supply Phantom Ranch and Indian Garden.[1]

Between 1927 and 1929, the Utah Parks Company created the infrastructure for the North Rim developed area. The company's crew built a water and power system that cost $500,000 (in 1920s' dollars) to service fewer than 10,000 visitors. The basic system, though upgraded, continues to satisfy the needs of the North Rim's developed hub. The centerpiece remains the Roaring Springs pipeline and water plant. Utah Parks Company workers ran a 3.5-inch-diameter pipe up 4,000 elevation feet and pumped water up to a 50,000-gallon holding tank on the North Rim. A hydroelectric plant built beside Bright Angel Creek housed two one-hundred horsepower turbines that powered the pump house. To build all of this, the company installed a 10,000-foot-long tramway to deliver supplies to the site.[2]

Because of relatively little available surface water on the rims, National Park Service officials wrestled with how to bring water to the South Rim. They searched for a new plan as the demand for water outstripped the water supply that came from a system pulling water from Indian Garden. That system was built in 1931 following years of bringing water to the South Rim by train. By the 1960s, the amount of water pumped up from Indian Garden could not keep up with the expansion of tourism.[3] In 1965, the park service embarked on a plan to build a pipeline from the lush flows of Roaring Springs, down Bright Angel Canyon, across the Colorado River via a bridge—later to become known as the Silver Bridge—and up to Indian Garden, where a pump house could pump the water up to the South Rim.

A severe flash flood destroyed the nearly finished pipeline in December 1966, and the reconstructed pipeline was not completed until 1970. Once in place, the waters of Roaring Springs and the new system could deliver 190 million gallons annually to the South Rim while still providing water to the North Rim and allowing the remaining water to continue its flow to the Colorado River.[4]

⊣ ✢ ⊢

On my solo rim-to-rim hike, I return along the spur trail from the Roaring Springs day use area to the North Kaibab Trail. The sun dominates the landscape. The North Kaibab, here made of shale pounded to powder, winds through ancient juniper trees that could be 700 or more years old. Their limbs arthritically twist and gnarl as they fight to grow in the parched soil. Only a few hundred feet below courses the water ejected from Roaring Springs on its way to join Bright Angel Creek. I imagine it, cool and clear, leaping and bouncing down through the boulders.

Although the trail begins to bottom out from the big descent, it stays higher than the riparian area surrounding the creek and river. It moves through desert land, though lushness reasserts itself below. The living world along this stretch is austere, but it's only a short distance from a place where life is gratuitous. "The Grand Canyon reminds us how important water is to humans and, of course, natural diversity. We learn from biologists that the diversity at places such as [the Grand Canyon's] Thunder River and Elves Chasm . . . have 500 times the biological diversity of the immediate desert," notes southwestern author and naturalist Rose Houk.[5] The morning sun is finding its focal power. I daydream of the water. I ignore how much I am sweating. Ten, then fifteen minutes pass, and the trail makes a steady descent toward lush green boughs of cottonwood trees. They shade the Roaring Springs residence, a place situated just before a steel girder bridge crosses over the waters of Bright Angel Creek and transfers the trail to the east side of the waterway.

An open plot of bunchgrass has been crushed flat under the shade of the trees. Here, I see a dozen hikers and backpackers who've passed me during my rest stops higher on the trail, although a few are hiking up from Phantom Ranch. They take turns at a water spigot, filling Nalgene bottles and CamelBak water bladders.

Among them are Kim and Neil Silcock of Fullerton, California, whom I meet for the first time here. They wrap up their break and prepare to hike down to Bright Angel Campground near Phantom Ranch. I want to talk more extensively to them once I learn it is their first trip into the Grand Canyon. But I also want to keep moving to get to Cottonwood Campground before the heat builds, and not slow their progress down to Phantom Ranch for the same reason. They look to be experienced desert backpackers: both wear light-colored clothing, including white hats with flaps covering their ears and necks. They have relaxed faces and a quiet confidence. Neil is quick with a smile and conversation. More than anyone I've seen on the trail, they look to be enjoying themselves.

Others taking a break at Roaring Springs are clearly nervous. They fidget with water bottles and drink with big, sloppy gulps, allowing water to run down their shirts. One man, a solo hiker in his late twenties, checks his watch four times in two minutes. He quickly leaves.

The Silcocks say they have a permit for two nights at Bright Angel Campground. I tell them I will find them when I get there. Although I took a break at the day use area, I allow myself a few more minutes at this stop, commonly referred to as the ranger residence.

The home was initially built for the crew needed to maintain the Roaring Springs pump house. The job became particularly important after the construction of the transcanyon pipeline, which, as noted, brings water to the South Rim. A job opening in the early 1970s attracted one particular man and his family. He became a famous canyon artist, and his family, living in the inner canyon with him, a curiosity to visitors passing by their home each day.

≒ ✦ ⊨

Bruce Aiken and his brother Rick drove from New York City to Phoenix in 1969. There, the brothers visited their grandparents and the place where their mother was born and raised. Then they traveled to the Grand Canyon and stood on the South Rim. Aiken had first visited the Grand Canyon as a child, in 1954, at the age of four. But the canyon did not truly impact him until he saw it as a man. He remembers how it moved him: "I saw the Grand Canyon for the first time as an adult (I had been there twice as a kid). I was thoroughly impressed, just like everybody else. It does not matter if you're six, nine, nineteen, or one hundred and eleven, this canyon can do nothing but impress you."[6]

After another year back in New York, Aiken felt called to return to the Southwest. When Aiken made it back to Phoenix, he stayed with his grandparents. He met Mary Shields while he was a student at the University of

Arizona in Tucson. The two fell in love and married in Phoenix in 1972. They rode a motorcycle up to the South Rim that same year. Aiken decided he could not leave. In July 1973, a month before geologist Wayne Ranney would first see the Grand Canyon, the Aiken family arrived at the North Rim. Aiken, his wife, Mary, and their one-year-old daughter, Mercy, set off down the North Kaibab Trail. They hiked down to the place that would become their home.

Aiken took a position at the Roaring Springs pump house, eager to hold a job that required he live inside the Grand Canyon. He arrived as a burgeoning artist. Raised in New York City, he received formal classical art training. He began his life at the canyon as he was searching for the ultimate subject to paint.

He found it.

For the family, the move initiated an adventure. Mary Aiken didn't know how it would work. She struggled to keep up with her husband on that first hike down. When she reached the bottom, pained from the hike, she wondered if she could ever get out. "I was just like, 'Where in the hell is this guy taking me now?' I thought it was really amazingly beautiful, but in the back of my mind I was thinking, *We won't be down here very long,*" Mary recalls with a laugh during a 2007 interview. "I didn't know how it was going to work, with the baby and all. Bruce was going to be one of the three guys down there working at the [Roaring Springs] pump house. We had one bedroom and this baby, with two other guys working [and living] there."[7]

Aiken went to work operating the pump house and painting. He struggled with his art in the early years, overwhelmed with the fortune of living inside of his subject. It would take him close to five years to truly "see" the Grand Canyon as an artist—to recognize its real colors and capture them on canvas. He spent his days off on long wanderings and explorations, always watching how the light changed and interacted with the great gorge. After tens of thousands of brushstrokes and hundreds of paintings, his style evolved and soon became his signature. In later interviews, he compared the process to how a rock band might hit on a particular sound that everyone loves, and the band then sells a million or more records.[8]

The Aiken family's arrival brought more than a new artistic vision to the Grand Canyon. Interior canyon locations such as the Roaring Springs pump house, the ranger stations, and Phantom Ranch typically attracted

Bruce Aiken sketching on the rim. *Courtesy Janie Blanchard*

single people or couples. The Aikens found themselves to be the only inner-canyon family, a family that soon grew with the addition of two more children. Shirley and Silas Aiken's first memories are of Roaring Springs. Mary hiked out of the canyon to give birth to Silas on October 8, 1977. She was nine months pregnant and wearing a bikini top, capturing the attention of everyone she passed on the trail.[9]

Mary worked to manage the household in a place where groceries arrived from more than seventy-five miles away and were delivered via helicopter. It made the simple act of buying food an epic journey. "The food was a big deal because we had to go up on Bruce's four-day weekend; he worked ten days on, four days off," Mary explains during our 2007 interview. "In the beginning, we used to go up to Utah and shop and then we'd pack it in on mules. Then the park service started flying a helicopter all of the time. So then we would just coordinate [with] a flight because we figured it would be more convenient for everybody. We'd hike to the North Rim, drive to Flagstaff, shop, drive up to the South Rim, and weigh it . . . because we'd go to three or four stores and spend $700 or $800. And then we would drive back to the North Rim or hike in from the South Rim. At the very least, it was a two-day affair."[10]

The food supply also came from a garden well tended by Mary and her children. As for education, the Aiken children were taught by their parents, park rangers, the Grand Canyon, and the natural world. Only later did the Aikens send their children to school on the South Rim. "Down in the canyon, it felt like camp," Mary notes. "We'd bake bread, go hiking and swimming, and in the evening we would break out the guitar and sing songs."[11]

The family lived and played in an isolated and potentially dangerous place, but they encountered relatively few problems. Because they did not attend public school in the early years and they interacted with a limited number of children, the younger Aikens caught few major illnesses. Mary also never worried about her children playing in traffic, and the inner-canyon's permanent residents were all people the family knew and trusted.

However, a few injuries and emergencies gave the family some scares. When three-year-old Shirley suffered a nasty scorpion sting, it turned into a traumatic event. "Shirley woke up screaming in the middle of the night," Mary remembers. "It was one of those blood-curdling screams . . . . I thought she was going to die. You couldn't even count her pulse, it was so high. She had convulsions and had bit her tongue, so there was blood everywhere. And I was just holding her and praying." By morning, she had fallen asleep and seemed to have recovered, but the doctor highly recommended she leave the canyon for medical attention, and Shirley was lifted out in a helicopter.[12]

Shirley, so young at the time, doesn't remember the incident. "I just remember waking up from what felt like a long sleep and walking into the living room. Everyone started clapping."[13] The episode didn't faze the young girl, but her mom grew concerned. "After the scorpion bite, I started to think, *Am I a responsible parent? Should I get them out of the canyon?* But Bruce talked me out of it. He said there were dangers everywhere. There're always dangers," Mary recalls.

One might imagine the Aikens as some kind of modern-day Swiss Family Robinson, marooned in a remote place and left to figure out how to make home and family work. One would think being the only family living in the Grand Canyon could lead to delayed social development for the children. Or that such an unconventional upbringing would make for a difficult transition as they left the canyon for society beyond.

Shirley Aiken remembers it much differently. "Being a kid growing up down there, the friendships with [backcountry rangers and Phantom Ranch employees] were very important. Once we went out to visit people on the rim or . . . friends and different people, and we would realize that we had a different situation. . . . We would talk to our parents a lot about it.

They tried really hard to give us a natural, normal upbringing. They tried to implement conventional qualities to our upbringing, with a schedule and a routine—making sure we had social contact by inviting people down. We had friends coming down, and friends of friends, and cousins. Hikers we knew from before and friends of those hikers. It was a huge web of people who visited us. . . . People expect me to have grown up socially awkward, as if I lived in a cave. In fact, it was the opposite."[14]

⊱ ✢ ⊰

All three children moved away from Grand Canyon at first. Silas attended college at Northern Arizona University in Flagstaff and moved to Phoenix to teach physical education. But the canyon called him back. At age thirty-one, he took a leave of absence from his teaching position.

"We [Silas and his father] happened to have planned a trip to Roaring Springs," Silas recalls. When they arrived, they found the home at Roaring Springs relatively unmaintained compared to when they lived there. "My dad had really gotten the lawn and house so green and lush. It occurred to me that someone needed to be there full-time, and that someone needed to be me. I wrote the superintendent a letter. I know the guy [former Super-intendent Steve Martin]. I know he cares about that place. I told him, 'Hey, someone needs to be there and I will do it, even if I have to volunteer.'"[15]

Martin agreed. So, Silas returned to his childhood home at Roaring Springs as a VIP, or Volunteer in the Park. During an interview given in Flagstaff, Silas speaks of his first time returning to the canyon, to where he grew up, as a VIP. "It was better than I even thought it would be. I had all of these expectations. I have such a great memory of the place. And the things I missed the most and the things I wanted to see the most were the extra blue of the sky against the red rock and the perfect puffy clouds and the smell of the riparian area mixed with the hot canyon air. And it delivered better than I remembered. It's really a spiritual place. You cannot deny the spirituality. I slept outside in the breeze and by the sound of the creek all but one night [during his first shift in the canyon], and that was because it rained one day. I was closer to God than I had been in a long time."[16]

The house at Roaring Springs remains Silas's favorite place in the canyon. "I feel like it's the best way to experience the Grand Canyon for anybody. Going down the river or going to Havasupai might rival it. But people coming to visit got to experience the folklore of what my parents did and got to eat well and have a good time. . . . I also like hiking up to Roaring Springs itself. You can drink water straight from the springs and sit in this paradise that does not look like it's of this world."[17]

Though Silas returned, Shirley and Mercy have continued life mostly beyond the canyon. Mercy moved to North Carolina, and she has spent most of her adult life working with Christian ministries and Bible-based teaching programs, and on Christian Web sites. Although she and her family grew up in a location far from the doors of a church, she embraced God throughout her childhood.

"I think growing up in the Grand Canyon really helped us to have our own connection with God," explained Mercy during an interview held while she was visiting her parents for the holidays. "We would read the Bible together. So our faith was there more on a daily basis. Because we were so remote, we could not be part of a regular church. I think it helped me. [Religion] was more organic and real and part of our everyday life."[18]

Mercy often thinks of her time in the Grand Canyon as her time in the ultimate church, an infinite place of worship with infinite lessons. "I remember looking at the Grand Canyon, thinking about God, thinking about time and space and the history of Earth. God has spoken to me a lot through the canyon. I think about how he knows everything about the canyon. I remember having moments like that where I could feel the presence of God powerfully. I love [poet Alfred Bryan's] quote that the Grand

Canyon is 10,000 cathedrals rolled into one. It makes me realize I grew up in the greatest of cathedrals."[19]

Bruce and Mary Aiken finally left the canyon in 2005, but they did not wander far from it. They made a new home in Flagstaff, Arizona, where Aiken set up a studio that overlooks Heritage Square downtown. He continues to paint his canyon landscapes, but also works on abstract canyon art and human figures.

He has a cadre of collectors. His most popular work shows the canyon in representational form, but with a slight abstraction that appears like small ripples in water. His paintings often depict the rich blues of reflected light. The buttes and temples dominant in many of his works appear sentient, commanding attention.

Aiken also paints from the river, capturing on canvas the constantly changing interface of water and rock. From his river paintings, he moved into complete abstraction, basing his next phase of work on the colors and forms in rocks he picked up along the trails and other places in the canyon. With each passing year, Aiken has found new ways to explore the ultimate grand subject.

Along with raising a family and creating his artwork, Aiken found himself interacting with a fascinating string of people who entered the canyon and crossed it rim to rim via the Corridor trails. Living in the only family home along the trail, the Aikens met all manner of hiker, backpacker, and "canyon head," a widely used term for people who are passionate about the canyon and keep returning to it.

A standing group of people came back repeatedly. They came to know the Aikens and always looked for them. "They are the visitors who love the Grand Canyon," Aiken says during an interview in his Flagstaff studio. "They absolutely love it. They crave it. They get back home, and when they're back in Long Island or Boston or Dallas they're thinking about Ribbon Falls or that stretch of trail between Indian Garden and the river. . . .

They think about this one rock they sit on between the top of The Box and Asinine Hill. And they love this rock, that's where they always sit. Things like that. There are parts of that trail that become familiar to them. It makes them feel included. They become part of this thing that's so much greater and bigger than them. And therefore, it makes them feel uplifted. They feel better about themselves."[20]

⊰ ✛ ⊱

All rim-to-rim hikers filter past Roaring Springs along the passage of the North Kaibab Trail. The home where the Aikens resided sits less than a hundred feet from the trail.

People who had the privilege to stay with the Aikens found a cozy ranch-style home with a full kitchen and bar, a living room with a land-line phone, a full bathroom, and all of the amenities of any American family's residence. However, guests would have spent most of their time under the roof of the back porch, which faces out to the large concrete helipad and takes in the sounds of the creek below. Once the sun disappeared behind Roaring Springs Canyon's western wall, they would have moved out to the small stretch of lawn between the helipad and the house, lounging on patio furniture and sipping wine while the sunset painted the sky above them.

On most nights, they would have been invited to sleep on the helipad, one of the best night's sleeps in the Grand Canyon. The orientation of Roaring Springs Canyon draws a steady and cool breeze from the higher elevations on most nights. The sound of the creek fifty feet below the helipad creates a soothing white noise that lulls people to sleep. For those who stay awake, the helipad gives an unobstructed view of the night sky, rendered flawless with the lack of light pollution.

Roaring Springs is a place of convergence. Roaring Springs Canyon meets Bright Angel Canyon. The waters of Roaring Springs feed into Bright

Angel Creek, which from there turns into a churning waterway. The North Kaibab Trail goes from steep and relentless between the North Rim and Roaring Springs into a steady, more gradual nine-mile descent from Roaring Springs to the river.

The trail changes character.

The canyon changes character.

The habitat undergoes its set changes.

The Grand Canyon reveals another layer to its magic.

CHAPTER 4

COTTONWOOD:
The Middle Ground

My first ambitious hike into and out of the Grand Canyon takes me to Cottonwood Campground. I consider the hike a rite of passage following my relocation to northern Arizona. I plan to hike down to Cottonwood, spend the night, and hike out the next day.

At the North Rim's Backcountry Office, I request a permit to camp. The ranger points out that there are a handful of open sites for the following night, but then I look at a printout of the weather forecast posted in the office. The ranger station staff posted two printouts, one for the North Rim and the other for Phantom Ranch. Each forecast features seven windows of sky for the seven days. My hike-in day shows high winds. My hike-out day notes a twenty-degree temperature drop and a slash divides the window, with rain on one side and snowflakes on the other.

I change my mind about the overnight trip. I want a different kind of experience for my first trip into the Grand Canyon, one without a cold front. Instead, I choose a day hike to Cottonwood—fourteen miles round-trip, a longer day hike than the NPS recommends. I had previously hiked similar distances in Buckskin Gulch near the Arizona–Utah border and in Zion National Park. I note the added benefit of lower-than-normal October temperatures. I plan to begin early and end late.

I don't have a reservation to camp at the North Rim that night, so I drive out of the park and into the adjacent Kaibab National Forest, which is open to dispersed camping. I sleep along the Arizona Trail and wake to a frosty dawn and a campsite surrounded by piles of deer pellets. I shove my tent and sleeping bag into my pack with numb fingers and drive back into Grand Canyon National Park. The blue of night fades between pickets of spruce trees as I roll toward the North Kaibab trailhead.

I follow the snaky trail down, down, down into the canyon. Distances feel longer to me than the mileages noted in *The Guide (North Rim)* newspaper that the National Park Service distributes. This I attribute to the challenge of the trail. I want to turn around for my ascent back to the rim early, but I make good time and know I can rest for three or four hours at Cottonwood. Finally, after all of the walking, wishing I had stopped at Roaring Springs or somewhere farther back, I arrive at Cottonwood Campground.

Feelings of desolation and disappointment move through me. Cottonwood does not make a good destination point. It serves primarily as a place to stop halfway between rim and river. The campsites stand empty. They appear sad and beaten to me, openings in the chaparral. The stunted trees give little shade, with some sites having no shade at all. Picnic tables at each of the sites appear weathered and shaky. The campground's namesake trees huddle in one place, south of the campground near the ranger station.

I walk past the grove of cottonwoods to see if the campground continues, but the trail rolls out of it. I turn around, investigate some more. I find a bench built of planks and juniper logs. It looks out on Bright Angel Creek and faces downstream. I sit there with replenished water and a freshly opened tin of cashews. I daydream the rest of the creek's journey, seven miles down to its delta where it spills into the waters of the Colorado River.

I know I cannot sit at Cottonwood Campground for three or four hours, given my restless nature. Instead, I allow myself an hour to observe, write, and rest my legs. I hear voices, nearly breathless, of people I suspect are heading to Phantom Ranch to camp or stay in the cabins or bunkhouse. I hear people who stop and rest for three to five minutes and move on. No one makes it out to the benches by the creek, where I feel hidden.

I leave Cottonwood and head up toward Roaring Springs. Clouds slide over the canyon. The sky is muffled in gray. I suspect my photographs—on film, not on a memory card—will appear murky because of the overcast day. The wind turns shifty and uneasy. At Roaring Springs, I wait twenty or thirty minutes and begin the hike up through the Redwall Limestone. I take small breaks along the ascent, then a larger break at the Bridge in the Redwall. I move up next to Supai Tunnel, where I finish out my snacks, including all of the cashews, fruit leather, and two granola bars.

Halfway between Supai Tunnel and the North Rim, my insides go wrong. Sharp bursts of pain in my abdomen cause me to double over. Agony radiates from my middle back. Tears stream down my face. I stop to rest. An itchy thought causes me to wonder if I am dying from something, right here on the trail. I've felt similar pain a couple of times before, but dismissed it as worse-than-normal indigestion. This dysfunction steps into a new arena. I imagine that a hole has opened up in my stomach.

I fight the pain and keep walking. I tell myself I can rest at the top. Panic tells me to get out. I move a step at a time despite the pain. I pass a group of people, buoyant day hikers probably going to Supai Tunnel after a late-day arrival at the North Rim. I hide my agony but go back to wincing once they pass. I feel like I cannot breathe. I go two steps, stop. Two steps, stop. Two steps, stop. I judge the nature of the forest and know I am close to the end. I keep going. For the last half mile, I see no one. I am surprised to be alone.

After I reach the trailhead, I get inside my car, recline the seat, and curl into the fetal position. I wonder if a park ranger might find me dead in the car. But the pain eases, a receding tide.

If I make it home alive, I tell myself, *I will go to the doctor.*

Six weeks later, a surgeon removes my gallbladder—emergency surgery the day after Thanksgiving. It is a satchel holding a dozen stones.

⌐ ✦ ¬

When I pass the Roaring Springs residence and cross the bridge during my May solo hike, I fall into a beautiful rhythm. Off my right shoulder, Bright Angel Creek serves as my new companion, one that is always talking and full of forward momentum. I watch as the creek—voluminous by desert standards—rolls its way through its canyon. It begs me to follow, like an excited dog that has discovered something ahead.

The trail has uncoiled and relaxed from its bound form trussed into Roaring Springs Canyon. It has straightened and taken on a new character—a path of steadier elevation change. Here, I feel my legs recover from the recoil. For five miles, they bore the weight of me and forty pounds of gear in a backpack, enhanced by gravity. I use hiking poles to arrest my progress and take some weight off my knees. Their clacking sound on the stone of the trail becomes part of my rhythmic sound.

But my legs still bear the brunt. The muscles ease as the force of gravity lifts.

Gravity is no longer the foe. The heat building at the lower elevation and the rays of sun serve as the new enemy.

To my back the canyon walls climb to the rim. The trees cling to the upper slopes and, from 4,000 feet below, look like thick hairs. I think of the people on the North Rim, content to fall into rocking chairs and meditate on the canyon's nature. I think of the fine dining in the lodge, with silverware and napkins, iced tea, fresh salads, and the aroma of the food wafting from the kitchen. I think of the two canyon experiences: the civil and the edge of the uncivil. Straight above my right shoulder is the rocky outcrop of Bright Angel Point. I imagine people looking out into the canyon, across it and not into it. I marvel at being in it, bisecting it.

Still, feelings of desolation nudge at me again as I arrive at Cottonwood Campground, the same feelings I had the first time I saw it. It is 10 am. The heat reigns. I look at the needle on the thermometer, in the shade of the kiosk. It sits at a hair below a hundred degrees. In response to seeing it, I blink the sweat out of my eyes, lift my hat, and wipe my head and face with a bandana.

I am alone with six or seven hours to fill before sundown. The heat of the sun feels violent on my skin, as if it could redden me to the point of pain in five minutes. I will need to spend most of the time in the shade, trying to make friends with fellow hikers, passing the time with conversation. I hope to swim at least once—erasing the edge brought on by the weather.

I drop my pack at a campsite. I kill my first hour scribbling in my journal in the shade alongside the ranger station. At 11 am, I eat a lunch—a salt bagel with mustard, lettuce, and cheese and a bag of barbecue potato chips. My body craves the salt. I scrape out every flake and crumb in the corners of the potato chip bag, lick my fingers, and wish for more. I step back out to the trail in search of conversation. In the breezeway of the ranger station, positioned between two buildings, I see a ranger. I introduce myself. I recognize his name; he is a longtime inner-canyon presence.

Bil Vandergraff nods and shakes my hand.

He does not step into the sun, but gestures me into the breezeway.

By this time, the thermometer reads 102 degrees in the shade.

"You'll notice that in the summer, rangers lay real low during the day," he says. "We stay out of the sun and heat as much as possible. We don't do much between 10 am and 4 pm. It's just too hot. We're saving our energy for that big emergency or problem that might hit later in the day."[1]

The heat prompts Vandergraff, who began as a backcountry ranger in 1990, to talk about the hikers and backpackers.

"I think the challenge of doing a rim to rim is what draws the majority of the people here," he notes. "The less time people spend down here, the more challenging it gets. But the people who maximize their time here are in it for the beauty and the remoteness of it."

As we look out beyond the breezeway to the blanched-out scene of rock, tree, and trail, Vandergraff shares his favorite piece of advice for hiking or backpacking the Grand Canyon.

"Don't do it in the summer. . . . This time of year, you don't want to be in the sun. There's a saying that only two kinds of people hike the Grand Canyon in the summer: fools and rangers. The rangers are there to save the fools." He makes a comparison to hiking in the summer in Phoenix. "You wouldn't want to walk for twenty-three miles in downtown Phoenix in the summer. Why would anyone want to do the same thing here?"

We watch as people move up and down the trail under the blast of sun. Vandergraff shakes his head. It closes in on noon, and his radio starts to crackle. He listens in. He hears a report of a medical problem at The Tipoff, a rest area four-and-a-half miles down the South Kaibab Trail from the South Rim, at the edge of the Inner Gorge. "I tell people to avoid the South Kaibab in the summer. There's no water and no shade. What starts as a physical challenge becomes a physiological challenge. I say hike down Bright Angel. It's two miles longer, but it is less steep. It has water. And, it has shade."

The heat keeps us hunkered down, and we talk for nearly two hours, with occasional interruptions from hikers asking questions and looking for advice. "How much farther to Phantom Ranch?" is a common one. The reply: "Seven miles, but stop now and rest in the shade until dinnertime." When I check later, no one to whom he spoke waited. "Do you know the temperature?" The answer: "Too hot." And Vandergraff has questions: "Are you drinking plenty of water?" "Are you resting?" "Are you eating snacks?" "How does your stomach feel?" Some people complain of nausea or dizziness, or just not feeling right. "That's how we all feel down here in the summer," Vandergraff quips. "Welcome to the club."

A young woman who works at Phantom Ranch stops for a break and some conversation. "How are you doing, miss?" Vandergraff asks. "Are you okay? Do you feel like you're going to throw up?" She laughs. "Maybe." Vandergraff scolds her for hiking in the middle of the day, tells her she knows better. She admits to a late start because she had some morning duties, but she's trying to get out of the canyon before dinner. Her face is flush and she's sweating.

The three of us talk for twenty minutes. He tells us he sat out with a counter the day before tallying hikers, backpackers, and rim-to-rim runners. The number exceeded 400. The added presence of day users stripped the campground toilets of toilet paper, and some of the people on the trail did not bother using the designated bathrooms at all. It's opening weekend on the North Rim, and people are taking advantage of the rim-to-rim access before the heat of summer hits. But the temperatures are spiking anyway, ten to fifteen degrees above normal.

The young woman from Phantom Ranch returns to the trail. Vandergraff shakes his head.

We have more time to pass, so I ask him about his day-to-day ranger duties. "Well, in a typical day at Cottonwood, I clean toilets and do a lot of maintenance. This place is a maintenance hog. It has a lot of housekeeping. That work is mixed with providing public safety. We are law enforcement. We are EMTs [emergency medical technicians]. In the morning, we're running around and doing quick patrols and picking up trash."

The talk of maintenance reminds him of some work he wanted to do, fixing a water trough at the old corrals north of the campground. Despite the heat, we head up there. As we walk up the trail, the radio on his belt

The refreshing waters of Bright Angel Creek course through boulders near Cottonwood Campground. *Courtesy Grand Canyon Association*

crackles and hisses. We hear more talk of medical problems called in from emergency phones along the trails or reported by hikers who have returned to the rims. Vandergraff turns to me. "Fools and rangers."

After returning to the breezeway and more than two hours of talking, Vandergraff realizes he needs to make some phone calls. I walk back out into the blare of radiation, the insanity of the sun's rage at midday—the temperature in the shade at 105. I decide to soak in Bright Angel Creek, its water temperature lingering around sixty-five to seventy degrees. The creek rolls and churns and pours over rocks. Its volume swirls and pushes and cuts down into the canyon. It changes the scene. The Grand Canyon loses its hostility. The threats of heat and dehydration recede with water present.

Here, before Bright Angel Creek, the Grand Canyon feels like sanctuary.

I stand on the east bank of the creek, near the Cottonwood Campground ranger station. It's 2 pm. Water pours over a four-foot drop created by boulders. The sound hypnotizes. It lures. Two people, a young man and woman, mill in the creek. Four others sit on the bank with their feet in it. I survey the flow and find an entry point. The water on my feet triggers a chill. The sensation stuns. I climb the boulders to find deeper water and discover a spot about two feet deep.

I plunge into it, up to my rib cage.

My body throws itself into shivers.

I give myself a few minutes to get used to it, but it takes all of my will. I scoot along the bottom to the west edge of the creek and find refuge under the shade of tamarisk trees. I ponder the water's origin, birthed from passageways of ancient rock, as I soak in the water of Bright Angel Creek for half an hour.

I close my eyes and focus on the sensations of hot and cold. Mary Aiken compares sitting in Bright Angel Creek on a summer day to becoming the human version of a hot fudge sundae—cold on the bottom and hot on the top. Some of her best memories involve soaking in the creek while staring up at the cliffs baking in the summer sun. She would follow her soak by lying on a hot rock and—after the numbing sensation of the water—enjoying the sun again.[2]

I reach a point when the creek's coolness nudges down my body temperature. I climb out, and chills whip through my body. The dryness of the air and power of evaporation create transevaporative cooling. I did not bring a towel or change of clothes. I rush back to my campsite. My body shivers and my teeth chatter. I walk past people who are red-faced and sweaty.

I strip and pull on dry clothes, including a light polar fleece pullover and fleece hat. I lie directly in the sun in an attempt to warm my body. After a one-hour recovery, I feel normal again.

The swim levels me somehow. I sit on the shaded stone steps of the ranger station and feel content to watch the stir of the cottonwood leaves. I listen to a raven chortle and click from a nearby branch. I make conversation with the people who stop, spend time with others while they wait for the ranger.

Four o'clock arrives, and the day begins to feel different. Shadows lengthen. Breezes dance. Heat lingers, but the sun feels as if it's losing power. The campground fills. Cottonwood begins to feel more welcoming to me, more lively. A new party arrives, and one of the men announces that only three spaces are left of the twelve in the campground. The steady stream of day hikers and rim-to-rim runners recedes. The few who did take a long break under the cottonwood trees are gone. Runners, for the most part, should be finished; day hikers are on the last leg of their trip.

⊰ ✦ ⊱

We move into the settling hours. The canyon traffic is quieting. Everyone has reached their destinations.

It is in this moment that Veronica and Juan—visiting from New York and New Jersey, respectively—arrive at Cottonwood Campground.[3] They wear small backpacks and carry their sleeping bags. She holds a water bottle and wears a floppy, dark brimmed hat and tennis shoes. In their late twenties, attractive and filled with positive spirit, they've planned to hike the fourteen miles from the North Rim to the river in a day and camp at Bright Angel Campground. Then they look to spend the night at Indian Garden before ascending to the South Rim.

"Is there a ranger around?" Veronica asks me.

"He's in there," I say. "It sounds like he's on the phone."

She knocks. Vandergraff calls out, "I'm on the phone."

"Where are we?" Juan asks me.

"Cottonwood Campground."

"How much farther to Phantom Ranch?" he asks.

"About seven miles. This is the halfway point between the North Rim and the river," I say.

"Wow," he says.

"Yeah, we're supposed to camp there," Veronica notes.

"You should ask if you can stay here tonight," I suggest.

Vandergraff steps out of the ranger station. He makes small talk with the couple. "Are you tired? Nauseous? You should be. It's hot. You've been walking for seven miles in it." He suggests they hold off for another hour before starting the second half of their hike. "Wait until the sun gets a little lower; you can hike in the shade most of the way." Then he offers another alternative. "I could let you stay here at Cottonwood for the night. But you'll want to get up early, before the sun is up. Out of here by 5 am at the latest. Really. Don't wait around. Get down to Phantom Ranch early and lay low there for the day, hike up to Indian Garden in the evening."

"I would do that," I offer. "You can hang out in the air-conditioning at the Phantom Ranch Canteen, drink lemonade, and wait out the heat. You'll have a good night's rest here, a good day of rest at Phantom, and break up your hike better. You'll hike twelve miles tomorrow—seven to Phantom and almost five to Indian Garden—but you can really break it up."

Veronica looks to Juan, her mouth pursed to one side in thought. "What do you think?" she asks him.

"At the very least, you should wait here an hour," Vandergraff says. "Think it over. It's really up to you what you want to do."

In thirty minutes, Veronica and Juan set up camp in one of the last two vacant sites. Their tent soon falls into shadow, along with all the others as the sun drops behind the western cliff wall. Within moments, the air feels more comfortable and the indirect light creates soothing tones. In summer in the canyon, the disappearance of the sun deserves celebration. I hear elation in the voices of the campers as the last ray of sunlight retreats from the campground.

⊣ ✦ ⊢

As campers settle in for dinnertime and relax in the absence of the heat at Cottonwood Campground, a man named Andreas from San Francisco deals with his twenty-three-year-old son, Eric, who is having a medical emergency. He has suffered *two* dislocated shoulders. He fell while walking through Bright Angel Creek. First, he dislocated one shoulder. Then he dislocated the second trying to take care of the first.[4]

After more than an hour, Eric fixes his left shoulder with the help of his father and fellow campers. The right shoulder proves difficult to realign. As Vandergraff makes the rounds to check on camping permits, he is summoned to the site of the emergency. The ranger grabs a bucket of water for Eric to hoist. Eric seethes in pain, sucking air through his teeth. After thirty minutes of trying, his shoulder does not budge.

Eric faces the possibility of spending a painful night at Cottonwood Campground, and will not be able to carry his pack to hike the seven miles out. Vandergraff gives the father and son an option—a flight out by helicopter for Eric. But daylight is falling and they only have a half-hour window to decide. Andreas chooses to have his son life-flighted out.

Vandergraff calls for the helicopter. I help by clearing debris off and around the primitive helicopter pad just west of the campground. I also notify campers near the landing site—including Veronica and Juan, who are the closest—to secure their belongings because of the rotor wash. A little before 7 pm, we hear the thrum of a helicopter. It flies around and over the campground. The mechanical buzz fills the side canyon. After circling twice, the helicopter's skids touch down on the landing pad. The blades slow, and a woman wearing a helmet and yellow jumpsuit exits the helicopter.

She escorts Eric onto the helicopter, holding his backpack. She slams the door. In two minutes, the blades begin to turn.

Eric is gone. The helicopter disappears into the fading-day sky.

Vandergraff invites Andreas to stay at the Roaring Springs residence for the night, as it puts him a mile and a half closer to the North Rim for the hike out the next morning. I accept an invitation to accompany Andreas and Vandergraff up to Roaring Springs. We follow the North Kaibab Trail under the glow of headlamps.

I find myself sitting outside the Roaring Springs residence and former home of the Aikens, taking in what happened over a couple of beers Vandergraff offers Andreas and me. He also drags out two-inch-thick sleeping mats before heading inside the house, where he will sleep. We'll sleep on the helipad. As we relax and decompress, we sit on mesh patio chairs and breathe in the cooling air. My nerves unwind as the alcohol enters my bloodstream. The emergency causes me to flash back to the gallbladder attack I had during my long day hike to Cottonwood the fall before. I remember that feeling of things going uncontrollably wrong and the swirl of uncertainty.

"This trip was a gift to him," Andreas explains. "One year ago, he lost his left eye."

Andreas tells the story of how his son, who worked as a logger, was warming himself by a fire, unaware that someone had thrown a spray paint can into it. "He was an innocent bystander," Andreas notes. "The paint can exploded and took out his left eye. He had some bone damage as well."

"That's some bad luck," I say. "First that, then he's flown out of the Grand Canyon with a dislocated shoulder."

"This is good, though," Andreas tells me. "He needs to get surgery, to fix the problem [with his shoulders]."

Inside the ranger residence, the phone—the old style, with an internal bell—rings. The purl of the ringer sends Andreas inside. His wife, Eric's stepmom, is calling back. She gives him all the details of Eric's admission into Flagstaff Medical Center, where they have reset the shoulder and administered medicines. Andreas returns to the helipad. "He's going to be fine." But the situation reminds me of how a common medical problem in the Grand Canyon can elevate to a scenario requiring evacuation.

The light slipped out of the western sky hours ago. I see the Big Dipper hanging upside down when I look up.

Andreas put his hands on his hips and scans the outline of Roaring Springs Canyon. Tomorrow he will walk out, back to the truck he left at the North Rim, and then on to Flagstaff to be with his son.

⊰ ✢ ⊱

I awake to the electronic beep of my watch alarm: 4:15 am. I sit up in my sleeping bag, get my bearings, and recall that I am on the helipad at the Roaring Springs residence. This is important to remember, as the pad is surrounded by ten- to fifteen-foot drop-offs. I switch on my headlamp and look beside me to see a man in a sleeping bag. It's Andreas. I wake him, as promised. Within a minute, we go to work packing our gear. The light inside the Roaring Springs house flicks on. Vandergraff is in the kitchen. I shoulder my backpack and notice the pale first light in the east. It begins to eat the stars. Otherwise, it is dark. All I can hear are my footsteps and the rush of the creek.

I know Andreas will head in the opposite direction. Vandergraff, with a light pack and duties waiting at Phantom Ranch, will pass me at some point. I know I'll see Veronica and Juan at Phantom Ranch and will catch up with Kim and Neil Silcock, whom I met the morning before, watering up here, at the Roaring Springs residence. In a day, I have discovered members of the community traveling the line, hikers and rangers alike, a tribe interconnected by days in the canyon.

I reach Cottonwood Campground in the blue light. Campers stir. I smell coffee and oatmeal. I hear the hiss of camp stoves. From Vandergraff's perspective, these campers have fallen behind schedule. I stop to eat a granola bar and some dried mango. Vandergraff arrives. He offers me a banana. I decline, and he leaves to get some supplies from the ranger station. I think to wait for him, but decide to go.

I leave Cottonwood as a cool breeze drifts across the trail. In hours, the day will turn hostile with heat. The weather report added a few degrees to the Phantom Ranch temperature. But the timing of my passage into the open land beyond Cottonwood and then into the closed walls of The Box promises a cool, placid experience.

CHAPTER 5

COTTONWOOD CAMPGROUND TO PHANTOM RANCH:
Quietude and Chaos

The seven miles of trail from Cottonwood to Phantom Ranch can feel like the most isolated miles in the Corridor. The central section of the route, these miles fall farthest from the rims. They seldom see mules or stock animals and feature few specific stopping points, save for Ribbon Falls. And in the winter, with the closure of the North Rim, only a trickle of people venture along the North Kaibab Trail beyond Phantom Ranch, compared to the continual flow of people during rim-to-rim season. This length of trail is divided into two realms. The first, south of Cottonwood Campground, reveals a shallow canyon, more like a ravine. Its boulder-strewn sides—bristling with yucca and agave—slope at thirty- and forty-degree angles. Here Bright Angel Creek cuts its way through soft tissue of sandstone and shale as it follows the Bright Angel Fault. The fault line makes the passage possible and allows the creek to slice deeper.

Then, in a sudden change, Bright Angel Creek reaches the Zoroaster granite and Vishnu Schist. It goes from cutting soft tissue to cutting bone. The passage turns into an incision: The Box. Dark walls close in and vault toward the sky. The creek bends and twists, gouging a path where it can find one in the seldom-compromising stone.

The sound of Bright Angel Creek echoes through the chamber. The flow finds its way among moss-covered boulders. In some places, where sun hits water, a light show dances on the rocks. The Box reveals itself as yet another canyon inside a canyon. The ancient rock, older than most life-forms, appears as dark and jagged teeth veined with ripples of pink Zoroaster granite. The whole of Grand Canyon extends and radiates beyond.

The narrowness of The Box shifts one's focus from large to small: this is a place of canyon walls and water. When topographical mapmaker and surveyor François Matthes first made his way through the constricted passage of Bright Angel Canyon, he recorded that he and his men needed to make ninety-four crossings of Bright Angel Creek.[1] In 1920, less than twenty years later, crews with the National Park Service began work on these lower three-and-a-quarter miles of what would become the North Kaibab Trail. Long, steady work eliminated more than forty of the crossings reported by Matthes. That work and the easier-to-complete miles between Ribbon Falls and The Box—done in two trail-building phases—took about six years to finish.[2]

Ongoing work to reduce creek crossings continued shortly after the initial work. The park service crews elevated the trail above the canyon floor and routed it in such a way that the number of creek crossings was reduced to six within The Box. Counting one more at the mouth of Manzanita Creek near Roaring Springs, there are now a total of seven Bright Angel Creek crossings.[3]

From that point on, little work occurred to change the route or significantly improve the trail, save for infrastructure development in the late

1960s associated with the transcanyon pipeline, which was under construction at that time.[4] Workers added stone retaining walls, drainage structures, and sturdy metal bridges. At a place where the trail rounds a bend, a twelve- to fifteen-foot-high retaining wall formed of cemented rock protects the trail from flooding.[5]

These cement and metal structures and retention walls inform hikers of the watery violence that can pummel through the canyon. The biggest floods spread the creek toward the canyon walls and scour whatever lies within the narrows. Flash floods—where the water rises rapidly, moves swiftly, and recedes within hours—stand as one of the great threats in the Southwest's canyon country.[6] These floods have threatened, and in some cases killed, hikers throughout the Grand Canyon, though Bright Angel Canyon requires a major influx of water to pose a danger to the North Kaibab Trail and its travelers.

When not swollen by floods or roiled by spring runoff, Bright Angel Creek brings comfort to the Draconian-looking passage. It passes through dark rock twisted by endless millennia of force, heat, and pressure. The water sings to the walls, offering solace in a land dominated by waterless stretches. And it moves to its final destination: the river, near a place that offers civilization in an oasis beneath shady trees.

I open my eyes on a December backpacking trip to a morning breaking softly over buttes and ridgelines. The Inner Gorge remains in shadow. The early reflective light casts the deeper part of the canyon in subtle, dreamy tones. The sun reflects against the towering rocks above. I walk back to Bright Angel Campground from the river after taking pictures in the golden hour—thirty minutes before and after the 7:24 am sunrise. The fog of dreams burns away and reveals reality.

My friend Stephen Ehrenreich emerges from the tent and slides out of the door as if being born. We fire up the camp stove for coffee and oatmeal. We stare at a line of cliffs to the north as they soak up the sun. He and I fill our daypacks and relish the thought of not having to break down our camp. We planned two nights at Bright Angel Campground near Phantom Ranch, with a day off for wandering. We carry an ambition to hike up and back to Ribbon Falls, almost thirteen miles round-trip. But we also want to relax in the afternoon before hiking out to the South Rim the following day.

We stop at the Phantom Ranch Canteen for bagels, a second breakfast. We head north from there, passing the junction for the Clear Creek Trail—a nine-mile route that travels east from the North Kaibab. He and I walk toward the closed-in part of Bright Angel Canyon known as The Box. There, the dark walls of Vishnu Schist and Zoroaster granite create a narrow passage. Stephen and I remain in shadow as we gaze up at the high points on buttes and cliffs, the only places yet reached by light. We walk more than a mile without seeing anyone else. I breathe in the faintly musky aroma of the creek, which chugs in the opposite direction.

We pass Phantom Canyon, a smaller drainage that comes in from the west. It gives Phantom Ranch its name. When cartographers worked to map the Grand Canyon, they accidentally left Phantom Canyon off. As I stare into a gorge 300 yards wide with thousand-foot cliffs and a perennial stream, it reminds me of the scale of things in Grand Canyon. A formation the size of Phantom Canyon was lost. In other parts of the country, Phantom Canyon would likely serve as a state landmark.

We fall into a good pace. Stephen sings the chorus to Johnny Cash's "Get Rhythm." We twice cross Bright Angel Creek on steel-frame bridges with asphalt walkways. We pass a pile of search-and-rescue gear stashed along the trail.

I suffer a cramp in my neck from the cold—and from looking up. I pull out my notebook and write down the words that come to mind. The first word I write: *Passage.* I look to the top of Bright Angel Canyon and see the taller buttes and cliffs that loom all around us. Their presence feels so solid and unmoving. They stand like sentinels. I skip word association for a moment to write this sentence: *We find passage through a land of stone giants.*

Our momentum slips as we contemplate what nearly thirteen miles round-trip means, especially after a hike down into the canyon and a need to hike out.

We emerge from The Box.

We cross a bridge that goes over a wetland area—Willow Marsh—fed by trickling springs. Cattails and tall sawtooth grasses crowd the trail. It's another one of those unexpected Grand Canyon places—a marsh in the high open desert. I spot little movements in the grass and hear the tiny chirps of small birds.

I draw in the earthy smell.

I hear the trickle of water.

I know life-forms proliferate here.

After two hours of walking north, still guessing we need to hike at least another thirty minutes to reach Ribbon Falls, Stephen and I stop. We want to save our legs for the hike out the next day. After all we have seen this morning, Ribbon Falls does not feel like a requirement.

We slide off our day packs and fish out some food. We perch on a slab of rock and take in the open expanse outside The Box. I stare at an extended peninsula of rock studded with ponderosas in the distance. The North Rim.

Above us, the sky, marbled with thin clouds, slowly clears. I shell roasted and salted peanuts. I want to sit on the rock all day and stare. I hear the churn of the creek. I study the slope of rock before me, the cliffs all around. The temperature in the sun is perfect, upper 50s with no wind. I let myself feel satisfied, happy to turn around and return to Phantom Ranch, following the trail for nearly five miles in a dreamy state.

A distinct movement across the canyon stirs me. I watch a bird take flight from a boulder on the far slope. Too big to be a raven. Too small to be a condor. And, I see a flash of white.

A bald eagle.

"Stephen! Look!" I point and he stands up.

"Man!" He knows what it is right away.

We watch the eagle flap and glide, flap and glide up the canyon, away from us. We watch until he disappears. We know it came to Arizona for the winter, as many bald eagles do. We wonder about the nest, full and thick with brush with a jettison of large and shiny feathers scattered around it. Eagle feathers. Sacred objects.

With the eagle sighting a highlight of our trip, we turn and head back. It feels as if the bald eagle is what we hiked up for all along. We move back into the closed place, to be held again by the towering walls of The Box.

On the walk back, the sun is in our faces. As we enter the depths of the side canyon, the scene alters from direct sun to shadow, a perfect dichotomy. I feel as if I'm dying and being reborn each time I cross from light to dark.

In the shadow, the terrestrial world returns to view when my eyes adjust. For a second, the walls of the canyon look like two wings fully raised.

I walk between them.

I dream of returning to the passage, of making it back to Ribbon Falls on a sunny, warm day to be swallowed by the oasis. To be enamored of a place that has moved so many others, a place that proves there are intimate corners inside an unfathomable canyon.

⊱ ✦ ⊰

The verdant alcove that harbors Ribbon Falls is a popular day hike from Phantom Ranch (thirteen miles roundtrip) and Cottonwood Campground (two miles roundtrip). *Courtesy Grand Canyon Association*

Surveyor and topographical mapmaker François Matthes gave Ribbon Falls its name because he thought the water flaring in the sunlight resembled ribbons turning in the breeze.[7] In *Brighty of the Grand Canyon*, Marguerite Henry describes the falls as "a white jet of water that shot gaily out of the rocks above, washed down the face of a jutting ledge and joined forces with the creek."[8]

The enchanted alcove that enshrines the falls is located a mile's walk south of Cottonwood Campground or a six-and-a-half-mile hike north of Phantom Ranch, making it one of the longest—but still popular—day hike destinations from Phantom. The main access to Ribbon Falls is located north of the section of trail nicknamed Asinine Hill. The hill is a steep climb up and down the side of a slope, which seems pointless on a trail that otherwise follows the creek and remains level.

A short walk on a side trail across a bridge over Bright Angel Creek leads hikers back to a partial rock enclosure. The 300-foot walls of Shinumo Quartzite rise from the floor of the alcove. From a slot high at the back of the recess, Ribbon Falls plunges 120 feet. For ninety feet, the water falls freely. Thirty feet above the floor it strikes a cone of travertine. To the right, a grotto has formed in the travertine deposits. The constant flow and splash of water leads to an explosion of plant life. Maidenhair ferns—delicate-leafed greenery that speaks of a lush microclimate—yellow columbine, and monkey flower proliferate here. All are southwestern plants, but all need that constant pulse of water to thrive.

"I send a lot of people down there in the [early evenings during] the summer while people are staying at Cottonwood," ranger Bil Vandergraff notes. "It's cool back there. You lose twenty degrees being by those falls. But I have to warn people who stop there on the hike down to Phantom Ranch not to stay too long. While it stays cooler back there, it's getting hot on the trail."[9]

David Meyer, manager at Phantom Ranch, often suggests a hike up to

Ribbon Falls when the weather is right and guests have the time and energy to make the thirteen-mile round-trip trek. "If you are hiking the Corridor trails, or if you have time to hike up from Phantom Ranch, Ribbon Falls is not to be missed. It is just so beautiful, with the vibrant greens, the sound of the falls. And, if you go, you have to walk behind the falls. It's just an amazing place."[10]

While the hike up to Ribbon Falls from Phantom Ranch leads you through The Box, another hike from Phantom offers an alternative with wide and expansive views. This antithesis to being in the swallowed depths becomes a required investigation—at least for a mile or two—for anyone trekking the Corridor trails who has the time.

⊰ ✦ ⊱

Remember where you are. This serves as a favorite Grand Canyon mantra. I repeat the sentence in my head. A three-second looped tape that becomes an affirmation. As in, *Remember where you are*: in the Grand Canyon, the Inner Gorge, at the center of the real and raw divine—before the greatest of earthly displays.

People plan their whole lives to travel here, I think to myself. *Many will consider it a highlight of their lives.*

Remember where you are. I repeat the mantra to the tempo of my footfalls as I ascend the Clear Creek Trail on a tepid February afternoon. The trail tacks its way up a steep slope from the trailhead a half mile north of Phantom Ranch.

A Civilian Conservation Corps project in the mid-1930s, the Clear Creek Trail provides a nine-mile one-way adventure to the next perennial-water canyon to the east of Bright Angel Canyon. The CCC planted cottonwoods that shade three campsites not far from the stream. Clear Creek tumbles for five miles from the campsites before it reaches the Colorado River.[11]

When building the Clear Creek Trail, the Civilian Conservation Corps built a rock bench. The trail offers spectacular views of Phantom Ranch, the Colorado River, the Kaibab Suspension Bridge, and the South Kaibab Trail on its final descent to the river. *Courtesy of the author*

My ambition takes me only to a place about a mile and a half to two miles from the North Kaibab Trail. It offers the broad view—an open perspective on the canyon and the river traveling through it. To get to that point, I work my way up the switchbacks, and Bright Angel Canyon's floor drops away. I step along a straight part of the trail. Below me, the slope features the result of runoff: bushels of green shrubbery among the grayish rock. I brush by cacti and Mormon tea. I study the mush of fiber from a decayed agave. I admire rock walls stacked and fitted into cliffs to protect the trail, built by the skilled hands of the CCC workers.

I reach a bend in the trail at three-quarters of a mile. It offers a chance to look down at Phantom Ranch more than 500 feet below. I see the winter skeletons of cottonwoods, roofs and chimneys and trails. Dots move around—I know them to be people. I take a break at the CCC-built stone bench. Not a bench of wood or concrete, but one made of large flat stones that nearly blend in among the shelves and outcrops of schist.

I follow the path up another long incline. Isis Temple appears to the west. A cloud hovers around its summit. The trail breaks east and moves out of Bright Angel Canyon. But not before it reveals a small segment of the North Rim and a slope directly below it. The face of rock is buried in white with the season's snow.

Remember where you are.

I find the vantage point I want. To the south and below is a God's-eye view of the South Kaibab Trail and the Kaibab Suspension Bridge. The South Kaibab slants and notches its way up the slope to The Tipoff. When viewing it from a distance, it suggests a near impossibility—a relentless climb out of the canyon that is in fact only one-third of the South Kaibab's total ascent.

I move a hundred yards up the Clear Creek Trail to look upriver and into the sacred heart of the Inner Gorge. The Colorado, a thick soup red-brown with late-winter runoff, reflects the diffused sun. I see rafts, specks in the water undistinguishable in my photographs when I get the film developed back home. Rarely is the river running red. Rarely is the snow as deep as it is on the South Rim, or as deep down in the canyon as it appears, three or four rock layers below the rim. Rarely is the winter light so beautiful.

Remember where you are.

I revel in the chance to steal a moment on the Clear Creek Trail, a brief interlude away from the Corridor. I take in some of the soul-altering views. I breathe and watch the plants shake as curls of wind pass by. A red-tailed hawk circles to the west, a good 1,500 feet up, with a snake dangling from its talons. It drops the snake, and I smile as I wonder if it might land on a surprised hiker below. I watch the hawk tilt and turn and ride a thermal above the canyon. It is a little higher than me, but looking at the South Kaibab, the Inner Gorge, the higher buttes and walls, and up to the rim, I believe we share similar perspectives.

Remember where you are.

⊣ ✦ ⊢

After passing the junction for the Clear Creek Trail while heading southbound on my solo rim-to-rim hike in May, I move out of The Box and its shadows. I emerge briefly into the sharp angles of morning sunlight. I pass two runners in white shirts and white hats. They also wear small Camel-Bak water packs. They move at a steady jog. I know they will discover the heat of the day on their ascent of the North Kaibab. I try to imagine it, pushing my body and will to make good time against physiology, terrain, and searing heat.

My experience is different. Within minutes of the sun reaching my place in the canyon, I move under the canopy of cottonwood trees and walk into the sanctuary of Phantom Ranch. Small pangs of tension—from carrying pack weight, from traveling solo, and from knowing a horrible heat would soon arrive—melt away. I am in the welcoming place. A place of comforts in the hostility of the canyon.

I take it in.

The wonder of being here.

Phantom Ranch.

CHAPTER 6

PHANTOM RANCH:
Life at the Bottom

During a late October backpacking trip with my wife and our friends Amy and Stephen, we walk up the trail from our campsite under a low blue-gray sky. Drizzle pecks at our arms and faces. The rain of an autumn cold front surges and recedes. The four of us walk the quarter mile from our campsite to Phantom Ranch. We accepted an invitation from David Meyer, the manager at Phantom Ranch, to enjoy dinner at the 5 pm seating.

We follow a side path of what becomes the North Kaibab Trail. We walk past the mule corral and into a circle of cabins. In the center of them stands the Phantom Ranch Canteen.

The canteen appears modest, especially given the architect who designed the place. Mary Colter conjured a series of masterpieces on the South Rim, the most prominent and accomplished being Desert View Watchtower. The seventy-foot tower resembles those built by ancestral Puebloans throughout the Southwest. Colter even created the remains of a fallen tower next to Desert View. Inside, Hopi artist Fred Kabotie painted a set of murals that depict Hopi lore.

The Watchtower joins Hopi House and Hermits Rest as places that tell stories. Hopi House appears to be an ancient pueblo at the edge of the

Visitors relax outside the original Phantom Ranch lodge, circa 1925. *Courtesy GCNPMC (#04970)*

canyon. And Hermits Rest looks like a loosely constructed hideaway at the western edge of the developed South Rim. Colter even put soot and cobwebs around the fireplace to make it appear as if it had been there for a hundred years.

Phantom Ranch carries a more-subtle mythology when compared to Desert View, Hermits Rest, and Hopi House. Phantom Ranch features Hopi and other American Indian iconography, notched and painted on the beams and by the windows in the canteen. In the cabins, visitors might find such imagery as the face of the sun painted on the floor near the cabin's entrance.

But despite all these magical touches, much of the aura of Phantom Ranch lies in its location. The cabins, canteen, and bunkhouses sit at the depths of the Grand Canyon. Visitors wonder how the buildings and materials made it down, and how the down-in-the-chasm accommodations operate. Mostly, Phantom Ranch's construction relied on the backs of mules. The lumber, glass for windows, and other building supplies were all packed down. Today, food and daily supplies still arrive by pack mule, save for relatively rare transports of large items such as major appliances, which reach the canyon floor by helicopter.[1]

The four 1922 cabins at Phantom Ranch were the first built.[2] To cut down on the amount of materials that needed to be transported in, the cabins' walls and chimneys were built from stones found in the canyon. Other walls were made of a mixture of yucca plant fibers and plaster. The 1928 cabins, which went up shortly after the Kaibab Suspension Bridge was built to replace an inferior, less-stable suspension bridge, feature more-conventional stick-frame construction.[3]

I look at the row of cabins closest to Bright Angel Creek as we wait outside the canteen for dinner. The staff has locked the door, and diners gather in the drizzle. Employees are preparing the place for a feast. I imagine the visitors over the decades: honeymooners, longtime friends, families, and people from all over the world. Meyer even told me the story of stepping out of his cabin one day to learn that a man with a dog was in the canteen. As he approached the man, Meyer realized the visitor was blind, and his canine was a Seeing Eye dog.

Those of us gathered in front of the canteen in the rain have accomplished our own feats. We all made it to the bottom of the Grand Canyon. We arrived on foot or on the back of a mule. The only other option to get here is to travel by boat.

The gathering includes people of widely different ages and backgrounds. I see families with early teenagers. I see retired couples, including one newly retired man who could not stop smiling. I hear the soft, fluid tones of a couple speaking in French to each other.

We are a community united in place, shared accomplishment, and food. The sound of the door unbolting catches everyone's attention. One of the Phantom Ranch staff members opens the door. We line up. One by one, she takes our names and we find our seats at four long tables prepped for forty-four people.

The aroma of steak and potatoes and corn fill the room. We stare at the baked potatoes, wrapped in foil. Sticks of butter sit next to heaping bowls of sour cream. Crisp salads and creamy and tangy salad dressings take up any remaining space on the tables.

The staff members trot out steaks and, for vegetarians, lentil loaf. Twice I wipe drool from the corners of my mouth as we pass around bowls of steaming vegetables, corn, corn bread, more salad, butter. Around it goes. I fill up fast, but eat more. I opt for iced tea while my wife and friends drink Tecate beer.

I know this will hold a place as one of my favorite meals. My first dinner at Phantom Ranch ranks with some of the best holiday and celebratory dinners in my life. To eat such an elaborate home-cooked meal at the bottom of the Grand Canyon feels like a beautiful extravagance. A baked potato never tastes as good as it does at Phantom.

The meal ends with a hunk of chocolate cake, slathered with chocolate icing. I nearly fall into a coma as I finish the cake and drink some hot mint tea. Bogged down with calories and carbohydrates, we waddle back to our campsite. The rain softens. The clouds thin in places. We see the half-moon through the veil. As we near camp, a small break in the clouds reveals the moon in full light. Wet rocks shimmer from nearby canyon slopes. We study the inky blue light as we cross the footbridge over the creek that leads to Bright Angel Campground, our bodies sated, our minds lost in the moonlit scene around us.

⇥ ✛ ⇤

Phantom Ranch creates an oasis retreat in the Grand Canyon unlike anything else in the world. It remains the only developed commercial accommodations in the inner canyon, located a vertical mile and nearly seven traveling miles below the rim on the shortest trail. Run by a private company, park concessioner Xanterra Parks & Resorts, Phantom Ranch offers both cabins and beds set up in four bunkhouses. It serves breakfast, packs and sells bagged lunches, and offers steak, stew, and vegetarian dinners.

Other national parks feature isolated hike-in lodges, such as LeConte Lodge in Great Smoky Mountains National Park. LeConte is open March through November and is supplied by pack llamas. But unlike most of these lodges, many in mountainous areas, Phantom Ranch and all of its services are available 365 days a year. This allows about 25,000 visitors to stay at Phantom annually, 3,500 of them arriving by mule. The rest of the guests arrive after a hike into the canyon, while a small number of guests will stay as part of a river trip.

The ten available guest cabins include two cabins with five sets of bunk beds that sleep ten people. Six cabins have four beds. The remaining two cabins are sometimes referred to as the honeymoon suites, with one queen bed offering room for two. The rooms each have a toilet and sink, but no showers. A bathhouse provides three shower rooms, as well as toilets and sinks. Also, Phantom Ranch features beds in four bunkhouses, two each for male and female visitors. An individual bunkhouse can house up to fourteen people. Typically, people make reservations for accommodations as much as thirteen months in advance, when the concessioner opens the dates for booking.[4]

During a winter's retreat, I hike down to Phantom Ranch with the promise of a warm room with a bed and a hot shower—an incentive that makes the trudge through snow, ice, and slush more tolerable. I will miss the airy joys of camping, the brisk air, night sky, and all of the sensory experiences that come with it. But I learn of a chance to upgrade to a cabin from my space in the bunkhouses and revel in the thought of staying in a Colter-designed abode. I stay in number ten, behind the canteen and a dozen paces to the west of the place where pack mules are tied up during deliveries.

The time I spend in the four-bed cabin gives me a chance to meditate on the pleasure of accommodations in the depths of the Grand Canyon. I note it particularly on the first night, as a rare heavy rain pummels Phantom Ranch. I watch it from my door frame while clutching a mug of hot tea. I study the cabin's accents and color schemes. Welded horseshoes form the bases of lamps. The concrete is painted earth red. The window trim and tables are painted southwestern sky blue. I know this blue. Colter used it at the Painted Desert Inn at Petrified Forest National Park in northeastern Arizona.

The small cabin in the southwestern wilds makes me think of Zane Grey, the author of Westerns who holed up in cabins like this to write novels and steep himself in atmosphere. I sit at the desk and write. Each of the sets of windows frames a Grand Canyon scene: the western slope of Bright Angel Canyon; the path north out of Phantom Ranch turning into the North Kaibab Trail; the other buildings and cabins of Phantom Ranch. I nestle in my corner of the rustic setting.

At the center of it all, the canteen serves as the dining room and gathering place. It offers two breakfasts for dining guests only. By 8 am, the staff opens it up to general use. People sit at the tables and fill out postcards, eat snacks, or drink lemonade, beer, or other beverages. In the summer, the air-conditioned canteen—usually much cooler than the air-conditioned but poorly insulated cabins—attracts guests who escape the triple-digit heat outside and pass time playing cards or board games.

Beyond the dining room, the canteen features a full-service commercial kitchen, complete with two Vulcan ovens and ranges; a walk-in refrigerator and freezer, the latter nicknamed "The Montana Room" for its chilliness—and its temptation to employees as an escape on hot days; a separate, smaller dining area for the Phantom Ranch staff; and a commercial-grade automatic dishwasher.

The kitchen remains stocked with sixteen-ounce containers of herbs and spices, from anise seed to Chinese five-spice to dill weed. The dried baking staples at the ready include five-pound canisters of everything from baking powder to cornmeal.

Along with the canteen and its stocked kitchen, cabins, bunkhouses, and bathhouse, Phantom Ranch has a laundry building, an extra set of bathrooms adjacent to the canteen, the only pay phone in the Grand Canyon, and housing for employees. Beyond the immediate boundaries, the Phantom Ranch area includes a ranger station, ranger residences, a sewage treatment facility, and mule corrals. All of the buildings receive electricity via a power line that runs parallel to the water line up to the South Rim. For backup, Phantom Ranch has a generator.

Phantom Ranch represents more than a collection of buildings and facilities at the bottom of the Grand Canyon. It forms a community of workers

The bucolic, cottonwood-canopied grounds of Phantom Ranch are an oasis for rim-to-rimmers, mule-riding "dudes," and river runners. *Courtesy Grand Canyon Association*

who serve a community of visitors. At Phantom Ranch, the employees must work as diligent multitaskers and must support one another as a team. Few moments of the day capture this notion like the process known as dinner reset.[5]

What happens between the 5 pm steak dinner and the 6:30 pm stew dinner is a mastery of fast work and choreography. It shows how the employees at Phantom Ranch work collaboratively to handle a multitude of duties required to maintain services at the remote site. The staff members working one October night—Ross, Brandy, Jessie, and Mike—begin snatching the plates and bowls off the tables. Ross carries out pitchers six at a time. Brandy and Jessie bring out a dishwashing tray to load glasses. They work to make the four banquet tables feast-ready for the next diners. According to the schedule, forty-four people will eat the stew dinner tonight.

The four of them move quickly. Other members of the kitchen staff push out of the swinging door and step into the dining room to help. The volume of the stereo in the kitchen is turned up. The Violent Femmes' "Blister in the Sun" plays, the frantic pace of the music a good match for the cleanup process. The next song, "Is This Love?" by Bob Marley, is slower. But the employees keep up the brisk pace.

Within minutes, the four tables are clear. Ross and Mike wipe down the tabletops in quick and vigorous strokes. Next, the white bowls for the stew are placed down one after another, staff members balancing stacks of bowls as they move around the room. The bowls are followed by napkins and knives and forks.

The speed of their work seems comically fast, as if they're competing to break some kind of land speed record for setting tables. But as Ross said, "We don't try to break records or make a good time or try to outdo each other. We just keep a good flow going and get it done."

Outside in the fading light, two dozen people wait by the door. It's twenty minutes until the seating, but without television or other ways to pass time, many people choose to wait outside for dinner. The staff finishes setting the tables by 6:15 pm. The smell of the stew and vegetarian chili lingers in the room. Suddenly, "Superfreak" by Rick James blares through the kitchen speakers. The kitchen staff sings and dances. It's a four-minute fun break before the frantic—but purposeful—dinner service. Brandy will do most of the announcements, such as explaining to guests how the seating for the dinner works, and will then wait on the tables.

The dinner bell rings, echoing off the cliffs and through the cabins of Phantom Ranch.

These cycles and rhythms play out every day, in a fragment of civilization pocketed in a great expanse of the natural world.

Not far from the confluence of Bright Angel Creek with the Colorado River—the place where Bright Angel Campground and Phantom Ranch sit—dirty blond sand created from pummeled sandstone and shale covers the ground. Floods carried it, slackening at the delta, and dropped it there. The sand has built up as benches on the banks. Relatively flat, they create the property for Phantom Ranch on the east bank of Bright Angel Creek and Bright Angel Campground on the west bank.

Wild grass flanks the trail. Prickly pear cacti lobes nestle in the grass, their spines hidden. Lizards scurry. Rock squirrels and mule deer move at a slow pace. They show little concern for the hikers and the mules. The deer munch on the grass and use the trails to move from one patch to another.

Mule trains arrive in the morning and afternoon. They stir clouds of dust on the trail. The dust takes five to ten minutes to settle. It clears to show the rock walls, dark gray veined with salmon-colored ribbons of granite, injections of magma forced into metamorphic rock. When the sun strikes the cliffs, embedded mica sparkles.

The canyon cradles this place. It's unlike the environment of the rim in many ways: geology, biology, climate, population of staff and visitors, history, presence of flowing water, aura, remoteness, lack of roads and cars, makeup of the community, physical topography, spiritual topography, access via trail or river, and the challenging exit.

The existence of Phantom Ranch—of a place to sleep and dine and relax at the bottom of the Grand Canyon—traces back to Dave Rust and his father-in-law, Uncle Dee Woolley, and the first decade of the 1900s. Rust grew up not far from another location later designated a national park, Capitol Reef. There, he grew into a hardworking, resourceful, and well-read man. In his early adult years, he worked in various jobs, from a gold-mining operation near Glen Canyon to positions within local school systems.[6]

He ended up in Fredonia, in present-day Arizona, in the fall of 1902, where he took a job in the school system. But by this time, he had discovered an unshakable passion for the landscape around him. He channeled this passion into a guiding service, leading people into uncivilized territory for a glimpse at the divine. He took clients up Navajo Mountain, into the high country of what would be Zion National Park, all across the Arizona Strip, and to vistas on Grand Canyon's North Rim. He worked with Woolley, who incorporated the Grand Canyon Transportation Company in 1903.[7]

Woolley championed the idea of developing tourism for the North Rim to bring prosperity to southern Utah and the Arizona Strip. He witnessed the boom of the South Rim once the railroad arrived in 1901. He daydreamed of road or rail service to the North Rim so it, too, would evolve into a popular destination.[8]

Woolley financed his son-in-law's construction of a cabin at the North Rim, blazing of a trail to the river, and operation of a camp—Rust's Camp. Rust's involvement with the camp was not direct much of the time—he had obligations at home with his wife and family; at school and later as a newspaperman; and in his community, to answer the call to better Kanab and other towns in southern Utah. He served in the state legislature for two years, where he battled to improve transportation from Salt Lake City to the southern part of the state.[9]

The camp persisted for a dozen years, until around the time the National Park Service assumed jurisdiction of the Grand Canyon, in 1919. A year later, the Fred Harvey Company became the first official concessioner at the park. "[The Fred Harvey Company] had already been there eighteen years, but the park service signed an official agreement with them," notes historian Mike Anderson. "It was a twenty-year contract stating that they would provide the principal services for Grand Canyon National Park. . . . The contract included what the [concessioner] would do. . . . Things they would invest [in], services that they would offer, things like that."[10]

During negotiations, the park service and Fred Harvey Company agreed that they would keep facilities and accommodations centralized. Instead of building hotels and restaurants all along the rim, they planned to keep all of the hotels and restaurants in one area. The park service also made long-term plans to limit future inner-canyon development to the central Corridor.

With concerns about access and ownership of the Corridor trails, particularly with the Bright Angel Trail privately owned and operated at the time the park was established, the Fred Harvey Company set up operations with an inner-canyon facility called Hermit Camp. Located fifteen or so miles west of Grand Canyon Village and the Corridor route, the camp, opened in 1912, was supplied by a cable-car system, and featured dining services and tents on foundations. Guests rode mules down the Hermit Trail and took trips to the river by following an established trail along Hermit Creek.[11]

"They continued to run Hermit Camp until 1930, but consistent with keeping things centralized, they decided they would build there along the Corridor," Anderson says, noting that the idea of constructing visitor facilities in the Corridor first came up during negotiations for the 1920 agreement. "They already knew that Rust's Camp [then known as Roosevelt's

Dave Rust at the terminus of his cable car for crossing the Colorado River, circa 1910. The cable car was discontinued with the completion of the first Kaibab Suspension Bridge in 1921. *Courtesy GCNPMC (#16001), David Rust Collection*

Camp] was there. Rust had planted cottonwood trees and willow trees. It was a pleasant place, but they immediately realized they needed a better way to get across the river. A cable gauge was not going to do it. The park service spent a goodly chunk of their congressional appropriations of their budget to build a bridge in 1921."[12]

Meanwhile, the Santa Fe Railway and Fred Harvey Company invested $20,000 to build what the companies initially named Roosevelt Chalet. This played off the name Roosevelt's Camp, a moniker the rustic site along Bright Angel Creek near the Colorado picked up when the former president visited in 1913. Rechristened Phantom Ranch by Colter, it opened in 1922. Six years later, the Kaibab Suspension Bridge created a better connector between the south-side trails and Phantom Ranch, located on the north side of the river. During the 1930s, the Civilian Conservation Corps arrived and made their own improvements. They worked to create a camp that later became Bright Angel Campground. They also excavated and built a swimming pool at Phantom Ranch. The pool remained an attraction for years, but soon proved difficult to maintain. In 1972, the park service decommissioned the pool and filled it in.[13]

Along with the business of Phantom Ranch, the National Park Service and other government entities began constructing buildings and facilities a half mile up Bright Angel Creek from its confluence with the Colorado. In the same year Phantom Ranch opened, the U.S. Geological Survey installed river-gauging equipment. This included a fifty-foot-high transmitter tower used to relay data and a four-hundred-ten-foot cable sixty feet above the river, still seen upriver from the Kaibab Suspension Bridge. A residence was soon constructed nearby for the hydrographer, who measured the water depth, volume, and velocity of the Colorado River.[14]

In 1926, the park service constructed its first permanent structure at the creek delta, a single-room residence called the Rock House. When the CCC arrived, a few more buildings came along. The corps built the Packer's

Cabin, known currently as the River Ranger Station. The CCC also built bathrooms for the developed Phantom Ranch area. In the 1940s, the U.S. Geological Survey built other facilities, including a lab that burned down in 1966. The USGS later built a larger lab and residence. Today, that building serves as the Phantom Ranch Ranger Station.[15]

While the government constructed various buildings closer to the river, Phantom Ranch has received only a few other upgrades since the days of the CCC, namely infrastructure improvements. Because of its history as a small area of development in the mostly unblemished land of the canyon, Phantom Ranch has proved a curiosity and a great draw over the decades. Its existence on the map tempts the curious to drop off of the rim and into the maddening beauty to spend a night, a few days, or a week inside the Grand Canyon.

Still others arrive and stay for years.

☲ ☩ ☲

It is 1 pm at Phantom Ranch on a day in May with near-record-breaking heat. I sit on the back porch of the Phantom Ranch Ranger Station, with just enough shade to avoid the oppressive, dangerous intensity of the sun. The temperature is 105. It threatens to climb a few degrees higher before the day is out. I sit with Sjors (pronounced "Shores"), a volunteer who has worked for the National Park Service for more than two decades, receiving only a fifteen-dollar daily food stipend and housing in exchange for his work. Sjors does not want his last name in print. There's no need for it to be. Canyon regulars simply know him as Sjors.[16]

Sjors arrived at the Grand Canyon in 1986 after he volunteered on an environmental study that examined the impacts of Glen Canyon Dam on the Colorado River below the dam. For his first time in the Grand Canyon, he took a boat trip from Lees Ferry to Hance Rapid, a level 7–8 rapid on the Grand Canyon's 1–10 rating system (10 being reserved for the most difficult). He spent eighteen days at Hance observing how the fluctuating water levels coming out of the dam affected the rapid and how river runners ran it.[17] Sjors left his good-paying job as a television repairman and returned to the Grand Canyon in 1988 to work as a volunteer. After a few years of volunteering, he had winnowed his needs down to the base necessities: food and shelter, the latter a modest-sized bedroom at the Phantom Ranch Ranger Station. He keeps few possessions.

Sjors volunteer work with Grand Canyon National Park began on the North Rim and included filling in for Bruce Aiken at the Roaring Springs pump house. Within a few years, he ended up at Phantom Ranch and soon became a permanent resident. "When I first got here, I felt like I fit right in," Sjors notes. "I ended up here at a time when the weather was more extreme. My first two summers here were extremely hot and my winters here were extremely cold. And the number of [medical emergencies] here in the summer was unbelievable. . . . My two first summers here, it reached 119 on the official thermometer. If you walked around here, you could get readings of 123, half the temperature of boiling [water]."[18]

Such extremes might drive a person out of Phantom Ranch, but Sjors embraced living and working in the Grand Canyon. He even considers summer the best time of year. He enjoys the heat and watching how high the mercury can climb. "It is almost comical how hot it gets here," he says. "I love it."

Sjors spends most of his days maintaining the thirty-three-site Bright Angel Campground and interacting with and assisting visitors. "If there are no medical emergencies, I usually go into the campground and pick up garbage. I repair bubbler systems [water and irrigation], and I look at the trees. If I see one dying, I'll try to figure out why."

As part of his visitor interaction duties, he conducts what is known in the park as Preventative Search and Rescue, or PSAR. It involves asking visitors a series of questions to assess their mental state and physical health. From there, rangers consider the visitors' supplies and preparedness and offer advice to keep situations from becoming medical emergencies.[19]

This coincides with another important task for Sjors and other Phantom Ranch park service staff: counseling visitors. "What we do more than [medical emergencies] is relieve people from the stress and the worry," Sjors says. "You have to work with them through the psychological things. A lot of visitor reaction is 'I barely made it in here. How am I going to get out?' What they are looking for is a way out in their mind. They're looking for hope. I tell them all of the good things to help get them out. That has been my goal. . . . [I] give them hope."

Sometimes, interacting with visitors requires strategy. "Each person you have to analyze and figure out what angle you are going to take," Sjors tells me. "With the runners, I will say, 'You guys look really fit. But you know if your body runs cooler, you will be more efficient and you'll make a better time.' And I'll convince them to get themselves wet and stay that way."

Beyond this day-to-day work are Phantom Ranch's tragic and bizarre moments. Two weeks before my interview with Sjors, National Park Service crews responded to the death of a mule from an apparent heart attack on the Kaibab Suspension Bridge. They dragged the mule to the center of the bridge where a helicopter lifted the 900-pound animal from it.[20]

Sjors recalls similar problems with mule deaths. During his early years at Phantom Ranch, the helicopters could not bear the load of a whole mule. This meant cutting mules in half in order to haul them away. "We cut them in half with a knife and a little saw. You get a good-sized blade that's very sharp and cut [the mule] in the middle. When you get to the spine, you use the little saw. It's not as bad as it sounds. It's not as gross as you think. Other people have done it, trail crew and other rangers. It happens."

Sjors and others also deal with the darkness of human deaths at Phantom Ranch. The beginning of the month during which I interviewed him,

Sjors had assisted in the recovery of one of three boys' bodies. All of them drowned trying to swim in the turbulent Colorado River. "The worst is when people pass away. Of course, this is both for the people who lose their lives and those who are survivors of this person [sometimes on the trip with them]. The most difficult ones at Phantom Ranch had to do with people I know getting hurt. We had two people working at Phantom Ranch who fell off a cliff. One did not make it and then another one fell and injured [himself]. That's much harder to deal with. . . . We're a tight-knit family down here, so it's a big loss."

Sjors does think that people are typically smarter when they hike and explore the Grand Canyon today compared to past years, which has helped to reduce medical emergencies and the number of deaths. "Most hikers know when to hike in terms of time of year and time of day. They know what to bring. They are taking advantage of getting themselves wet to stay cool. They seem to be taking more responsibility for their own safety. Even the rim-to-rimmers are doing a lot better than they ever have. Of course, there's always room for improvement. And we're here to help."

⊰ ✢ ⊱

Ranger Matt Slater walks the path from the Phantom Ranch Ranger Station to Phantom Ranch, a few hundred yards to the north. He wears a park service uniform with shorts and sport sandals, his long hair pulled back into a ponytail. He is young, loves to talk, is quick to laugh, and is often smiling. He says hi and asks a question or two of everyone he passes on the trail.

Slater reaches a canopy of trees with benches arranged underneath. Here he will give the 4 pm ranger talk, one of two evening programs the rangers give, with the second one at 7:30. He admits that his program is a way for guests of Phantom Ranch to pass the time while they wait for the 5 pm dinner bell. "There is no television down here. So I really try to entertain them with the programs. These people are on vacation, and they're looking to have fun."[21]

Through his entertainment, he hopes to educate people about being smart and safe, and to inspire them about the Grand Canyon.

Slater, along with other interpretive rangers at Phantom Ranch, gives talks on geology, the river, California condors, and nocturnal wildlife as common topics. They also play games such as a version of *Jeopardy!*—but involving questions and categories centered on the Grand Canyon.

For this particular May program, Slater opts for a game called "Ask a Ranger," but Slater calls it "Stump the Chump."

"And, as it turns out," he says, "I'm the chump."

He challenges the visitors to ask him any question about the Grand Canyon, and he tries to answer it. Given the kind of people who travel down to Phantom Ranch, and given the experience they are having, the questions are often intriguing.

"When you're up on the rim, you play 'Ask a ranger' and the questions are 'Where's the toilet?' and 'When do the buses run?' But the people down here have a lot of questions about search and rescue, wildlife, how many people have fallen off the edge." He smiles. "People are twisted down here."

Fifteen visitors gather for Slater's ranger talk. A family of five with two teenage daughters and a preteen son take up two benches up front. Three college-aged girls linger toward the back. A middle-aged man sits by himself off to one side, clutching a walking stick. Four men traveling together take up two other benches. A couple that looks to be close to retirement rounds out the group.

Within minutes of playing "Stump the Chump," one of the two teenage daughters of the family throws up her hand. "Has anyone died falling off the mules?"

Slater feigns shock. "I can't believe you'd ask such a morbid question. Jeez! I guess if you want to talk about death, that's fine. But I hate to disappoint you, 'cuz people just don't get killed on mules." He goes on to explain mules' sure-footedness and how, during more than a century of people riding them into the Grand Canyon, only a few incidents have occurred.

"I mean, don't get me wrong, people die down here. . . . They even wrote a whole book about it," he notes, referencing the book *Over the Edge: Death in Grand Canyon* by Michael Ghiglieri and Tom Myers.

"I saw that up at one of the bookstores," notes the man who is by himself.

Slater ticks off a few examples of how people die: medical problems that turn fatal, flash floods, drowning in the river, lack of preparedness in the backcountry, and occasional falls. It gives him a segue to discussing prevention. He talks about eating and drinking, about hydration and hyponatremia—too much water without enough nutrients—transevaporative cooling, and taking advantage of the cool waters of Bright Angel Creek. "Really, you need to put yourself in there," he says of the creek. "You won't regret it."

Slater tells a story of how he decided to hike up and along a remote trail on what is known as Mormon Flats. He didn't take enough water. The temperatures spiked and he turned delirious. He stumbled back into Phantom Ranch physically drained and mentally eviscerated by dehydration. Another ranger had to talk him into getting into Bright Angel Creek and lead him into the water, as if performing a baptism.

≒ ✛ ╞

Slater has worked only a few years as an interpretive ranger at Phantom Ranch, so he doesn't have as many stories of strange and weird moments as Pam Cox; she logged more than a dozen seasons at Phantom. The stories involving her visitor interactions have lingered long after she left the canyon; they still come up in conversations with rangers at the inner-canyon ranger stations and the Backcountry Information Center.

In an interview from southern Utah's Cedar Breaks National Monument, where she took a temporary position, Cox tells me the bizarre tales. "I did a search-and-rescue ranger talk for a while down there. I talked about people [making] wrong choices. The whole goal was to [encourage people to] make good choices. I talked about the heat-related problems. I talked about how they're all preventable. I talked about hyponatremia and dehydration. If you talk about too many symptoms, people think they have that, but I wanted to give them an idea. Then, in the middle of one of these search-and-rescue talks, I had a person sit up perfectly straight and projectile vomit, a fifteen-footer. I said, 'Dude, what's going on here?' Sure enough, in answering my questions I knew he had hyponatremia. I told the folks at the program that I was going to take him to the ranger station, and I cut the program short."[22]

Later that evening, she returned to Phantom Ranch to make sure she hadn't left anything behind and was shocked to see a crowd waiting for her. "There were seventy-five people sitting there. I asked why they were waiting, and some guy said, 'We heard you had really cool special effects!'"

Along with unusual occurrences at ranger programs, Cox recalls a number of times she has helped upset visitors who make it to Phantom Ranch but are certain they will not make it out. After finishing an afternoon program one day, Cox was approached by a husband, wife, and their three children—two teenagers and a ten-year-old. She guessed the husband weighed at least 300 pounds. The wife was also heavyset, as was their youngest child.

"There was a lot of distress on the woman's face," Cox remembers. "I turned to say, 'How are you guys doing today?' They said they had a problem. Usually, it's a mental thing like fear and apprehension. I wasn't too concerned because they were upright and breathing. So we started to talk, and I spent the next two hours convincing these people they were not going to die. They heard there was a possibility to hike to Phantom Ranch when they were up on the rim, that there were five openings [at the ranch]. [They had] no idea of what they were getting themselves into."

The husband said he could not hike out because his knee had swollen on the trail. Cox examined the knee and it appeared fine. She spoke to the family in a calm voice. She tried to reason with them. But the wife grew insistent. "She says, 'We can't hike out! Look at him! There's no way he can hike out!' Each time I tried to inject a positive message, she would come up with something else."

Cox started the conversation over. She developed a strategy for them to hike out. She tried to get them to imagine getting to the top, how thrilled they would be that they had hiked the Grand Canyon. "But the woman [was] just crazed. She burst into tears. She said, 'But . . . but, I have a blister!' I comforted her. I said, 'I know you're scared. We're going to take care of that blister and you'll be fine.'"

Cox loaded them up with a bunch of food and a second, larger backpack to supply their hike out. The next morning, the family left on their big adventure out of the canyon. "All day long I was listening to the radio," Cox says. "I called the Indian Garden ranger. Ranger never saw them. But, in the end, they did get to the top. They returned the backpack [when they reached the rim]. They left a little note that read, 'Thank you for your help. We had the time of our lives. We can go home and say we were able to hike the Grand Canyon.'"

Cox sometimes reflects on this family, along with others she has helped along the way. "I wonder if it changed their lives."

⊰ ✣ ⊱

On one hot day in May, campers and Phantom Ranch guests hide from the sun, duck into the canteen and stay for a beer, relax in a cabin with a struggling air conditioner, or soak in the creek. The 106-degree day drives everyone into coping behavior. Shade, water, air-conditioning, and icy drinks offer salvation. A dozen people sit in Bright Angel Creek, in one- and two-foot-deep pools created by previous visitors who built small rock retaining walls in the stream.

As the clock moves past 5 pm and on to 6, the sun drops behind the cliffs, and Bright Angel Campground and Phantom Ranch begin to fall into shadow. The sun strikes the buttes, temples, and mesas above. As the difference between what the sun finds and what it does not increases, I know that on the North and South rims camera shutters are clicking tens of thousands of times to capture the scene.

Throughout Bright Angel Campground, conversation and activity begin to flow. Every campsite is full. Red and green and blue and yellow tent domes have been erected at two-thirds of the campsites. The remaining campers have skipped tents, bivouacking as an efficient alternative given the weight of a tent and the lack of necessity for one in the canyon during the dry part of summer. Sleeping outside promises fresh air without the stuffiness of a tent. The forecast calls for an overnight low of seventy-two degrees, room temperature.

Going down the path through the cottonwood trees, past the restrooms, I see people ignite their camp stoves. The heavy whisper of gas turns each stove into a small rocket of blue flame. Water boils in minutes. Hints of curry, onion, and spices linger in the air. Two college-aged women spoon pasta from cook pots while sitting at their picnic table. An older couple and two teenage children eat from bags of once-freeze-dried food now hydrated and cooked with boiling water.

I walk past most of the sites and move toward the southern half of the campground. There, I find Kim and Neil Silcock, the couple I first met at Roaring Springs on my descent. They eat a dinner of cheese and tortillas and watch the sky above for the recession of the sun, the way its light plays notes on a streak of clouds.

The husband and wife, on their first backpacking trip in the canyon, talk of other ambitious hikes they've taken, such as route-finding ascents up various peaks and following unmaintained trails for more than a dozen miles. They've embarked on hikes requiring GPS units and topography maps. For them, the Grand Canyon does not stir even a flicker of fear or anxiety. They both call it a fun challenge. "The trail is an easy trail, apart from being steep," Kim says. "It's well groomed and easy to follow. The heat has been the worst of it."[23]

The Silcocks originally decided to backpack in the Grand Canyon after Neil latched on to the idea after reading a newspaper article. "The reporter had taken a trip rim-to-rim in the canyon. And I thought, *That sounds interesting.* And that's really where it started. That was two years ago. And I thought, *If I do it, I'm going to do it before I'm sixty.*"

He turned sixty shortly before the dates he secured for the trip, but the effort of what lay before them hardly fazed him.

Neil talks of his first visit to the canyon, a number of years before, when he looked at it from the rim. "The Grand Canyon was . . . the first place I ever looked at and thought, *This is way more amazing than I ever imagined it.* I think the only place I have seen that came close since was [Utah's] Bryce Canyon [National Park]. I think the Grand Canyon is just spectacular. I stood up there at that time and wondered, 'What is it really like to go down there?' Having come into the canyon now, I am even more impressed with it."

After our conversation at the picnic table, I move around the campground in search of other conversations, other people's stories. A desire overwhelms me to know the backgrounds, passions, and thoughts of the nomadic community threading its way through the Grand Canyon with me. I meet with Dennis and Pat Sheidler of Bluffton, Ohio. They sit at the picnic table at their site. Dennis has made a chicken stew, and he is trying to get Pat to eat it, but it's too salty. They relax in the cool wind lightly drifting through the campground.

I ask them a handful of questions. The Sheidlers explain how they are not on a rim-to-rim trip, but instead will return the way they came and go back up to the North Rim. The backpacking is part of a monthlong southwestern road trip to visit all of the places they missed—or places where they spent little time—on a previous trip. "We had been out West, but we had never [been to the] North Rim of the Grand Canyon, Zion, Natural Bridges, Capitol Reef, Bryce Canyon, or Canyonlands," Pat explains. "We have a truck camper, and we've made our way around."[24]

We tell jokes, stare at the creek, and look all around us. Dennis shakes his head. I do not ask, but I think I know why. He cannot believe he is eating his too-salty chicken stew in the belly of the world's greatest gorge. Pat looks up toward the South Rim. "Most people see the Grand Canyon from the top, but getting into it is a whole different thing," she says.

I rise to leave in search of one more conversation, one more connection with the traveling show of Grand Canyon backpackers. I have one more party I want to meet: a group of three people led by Omar Martinez. He works for the Four Seasons guiding service out of Flagstaff. On this trip, his clients are Sue and Mike McDermott of Waterloo, Nebraska, and Michelle Lin of Chicago.

Guided trips—led by a variety of businesses and organizations—represent yet another way people experience the Grand Canyon. Lin and the McDermotts chose a guide for their canyon trip for their own reasons. The McDermotts, on the trip in honor of their upcoming sixtieth birthdays, explain why they made the decision: "First of all, we didn't know anything about the canyon, and we felt like a guide could help us there. And, using a guide service allowed us to show up without a lot of equipment, get great input about the canyon, and relieve anxieties about being in a place so unfamiliar to us."[25]

Lin notes that she wanted her first Grand Canyon visit to include a backpacking adventure. "I always had in my mind it was not worth the trip because you just viewed the canyon from the top, and there were too many tourists," she explains.[26] She then read a book called *Classic Hikes of the World* by Peter Potterfield, who included the Grand Canyon Corridor in the book. The entry intrigued her. This led Lin to find a guide to help lead her into the depths.

They all agree that Martinez hosts a great trip. He sets the tone. He keeps them relaxed and well fed. And, in their moments at Bright Angel Campground, they take their time to absorb everything. Martinez and his group spend two nights at the bottom, with a whole day at the center of the trip to enjoy the area around Phantom Ranch.

"I think it's really important to take time to just *be* while on the trip and not get all wound up in the pace of the hike and the miles and the heat," Sue McDermott explains. "The canyon has a lot to offer, and you miss it if you're too focused on doing."

⊣ ✢ ⊢

As light retreats from the sky, I walk to Phantom Ranch. After spending time with the transient community of hikers, I want to meet with one more member of Grand Canyon's more permanent community. I wander past the canteen and the bathrooms. I find the small path that leads to the cabin of Laura Tibbetts, the assistant manager of Phantom Ranch. She first arrived at Phantom in 1994.

Instead of asking her to trace the full path of her experiences, I find myself intrigued by one event in particular after hearing it referenced by Sjors and two others. We get to talking about it at length as we sit outside her cabin. I want to hear about what happened—a story to shake my notion of Phantom Ranch as a sanctuary, a safety zone.

On March 5, 1995, a flood came—one of the biggest floods ever registered in Bright Angel Canyon and at Phantom Ranch. Several feet of snow had blanketed the Kaibab Plateau and North Rim during the course of that winter, considerably more than the area's already formidable 142-inch average snowfall. A warm, wet storm system churned up from Mexico. Historic weather reports show the storm dumped five inches of rain on top of the snowpack—this in a month that averages 1.4 inches of precipitation—and melted much of the winter's snow. This 1995 flood is well known among longtime river guides for the debris flow it pushed from Prospect Creek farther downriver, then deposited in the already treacherous Lava Falls Rapid, permanently increasing the rapid's intensity.

During the course of a day, Bright Angel Creek swelled into a muddy, cranked-up torrent. The floodwaters reached the riprap, a shored-up area of rock near the edge of Phantom Ranch. The creek went from running a typical 73 cubic feet per second to peaking at 3,000 cubic feet per second, according to USGS measurements.

"Later in the evening, the creek was huge," says Tibbetts, who had arrived at Phantom Ranch only months before. "We'd find out later this was a thirty-year flood."[27]

As night descended, Tibbetts and four other Phantom Ranch employees walked along the raging creek to its confluence with the Colorado River. "We wanted to see what it looked like when it hit the river," she remembers. "We were enthralled. So we walked down there to check it out. We did not stay very long."

In the time it took for five people to walk to the river, the flood changed. "We were all disoriented with it being dark and only having our headlamps. We tried to walk back the way we came, but the creek was there. Then we turned around to find the creek again. It took us a while to see what was happening, to figure out that the creek had split and we were trapped between the two parts of the creek and the river."

Although the creek split in two, dividing its power, it was raging on both sides and had become impassable.

The five stranded people spotted four others, Phantom Ranch employees who had come to look at the flood too. The newcomers saw the five and realized what had happened. "From there," Tibbetts says, "it became a series of misadventures."

Park service rangers arrived and threw a rope across. They used the rope to send the stranded employees a two-way radio to establish a line of communication. Tibbetts noted that everyone was fine, but that the tension grew among the people on the other side. The rangers needed to figure out how they were going to rescue Tibbetts and her group. Uncertainty remained as to whether the flood would strengthen or recede. A worsening flood had potential to erode the ground on which the five employees stood.

In the previous year at Phantom Ranch, staff members had mourned the loss of one of their friends, who had fallen from a cliff and died—an event Sjors described in my interview with him. Fears of losing other employees escalated during the flood. "Having just arrived at Phantom Ranch a few months before, I didn't really know much about flash floods in the canyon or what they could do," Tibbetts recalls. "So it didn't scare me as much as it did the others, especially the people on the other side. I think it was more frightening for them."

At first, the rescuers planned to pull each of the five across the flooding creek on the rope. But it looked too dangerous to try. Instead, they used the rope to shuttle gear—tents, life jackets, and clothes—to prepare the five for a night on the newly formed island.

After an hours-long ordeal, the morning light of March 6 broke over a receding flood. Though still not reduced enough for the five Phantom Ranch employees to get off the island, the shifting flood left more room to land a helicopter. Each of the five people took a short flight to safety. "It ended up being an overnight adventure," Tibbetts says. "Maybe if I had known better, been down here longer, heard other stories, I might have

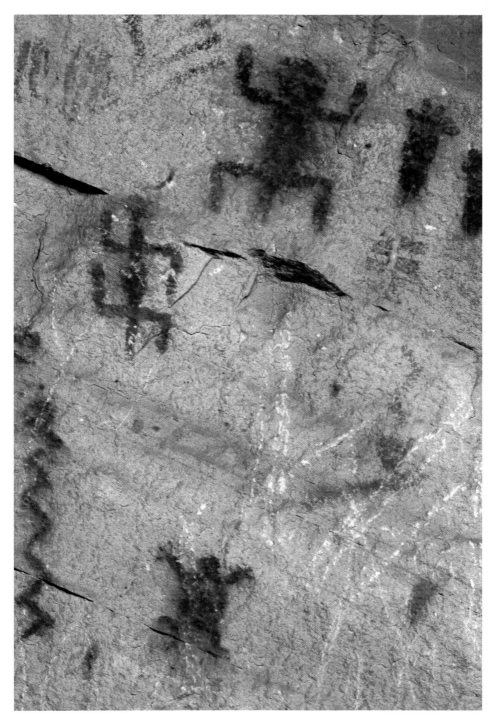

Pictographs on a rock wall not far from the Bright Angel Trail. *Courtesy of the author*

The author takes a predawn look at the canyon from Coconino Overlook along the
North Kaibab Trail. *Courtesy of the author*

Prickly pear cacti become more and more prevalent as you descend the North Kaibab Trail. *Courtesy NPS*

For hikers, river runners, and mule riders, the Phantom Ranch welcome sign greets like an old friend. *Courtesy of the author*

Mule and rider cross the North Kaibab's Bridge in the Redwall. *Courtesy Grand Canyon Association*

One of the bridges over Bright Angel Creek in the Box section of the North Kaibab Trail. *Courtesy of the author*

A lone hiker on the South Kaibab Trail. *Courtesy of the author*

Hikers in the Redwall Limestone on the North Kaibab Trail. *Courtesy Tim Berger*

Plateau Point at sunset. The point, about 1.5 miles from Indian Garden, offers spectacular views of the Inner Gorge of the Colorado River. *Courtesy of the Grand Canyon Association*

A private river trip takes a break at Boat Beach, not far from the delta of Bright Angel Creek near Phantom Ranch. *Courtesy of the author*

A group of hikers descend to the Bright Angel Trail to Phantom Ranch to join a private river trip. *Courtesy of the author*

Cooling off at Ribbon Falls, a short hike from the North Kaibab Trail. *Courtesy NPS*

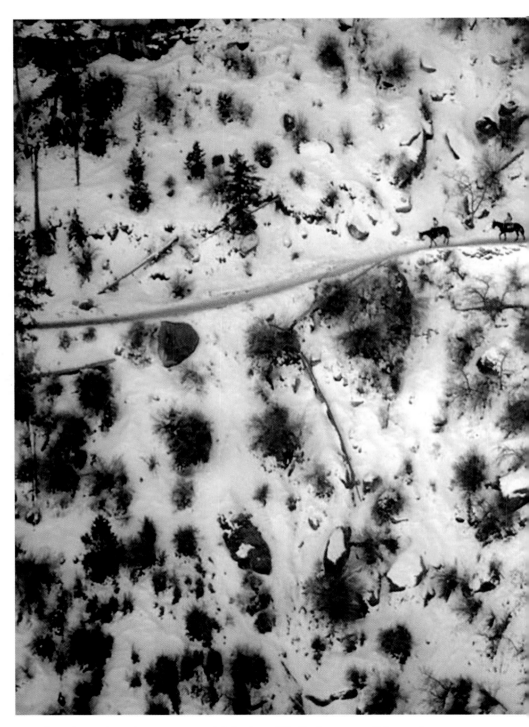

A mule train snakes along a snowy Bright Angel Trail. *Courtesy of the author*

The mail bag at Phantom Ranch collects letters and postcards to be marked as being delivered by mule from the bottom of the Grand Canyon. *Courtesy of the author*

been more scared than I was. Even today, a lot of people still consider that flood and the rescue a big deal."

⊣ ✢ ⊢

A few hours after my conversation with Tibbetts, I stretch out on the picnic table at my campsite. Bright Angel Creek sounds tame. The sky appears equally docile. I try to imagine the creek so violent that it rips in two and traps people in the middle. I try to think of the desert sky dropping that much rain on top of that much snow, altering the arid canyon and sending brown waves crashing down washes and drainages. Although I have seen the canyon in deluge, I still struggle to conjure it that way after so many hikes in fair weather, under a cloudless blue sky.

The evening air carries warmth, with heat radiating from dark rocks that spent hours in the sun. But the creek, about twenty feet away, exhales small breaths of coolness. I lie on top of my sleeping bag. Streaks of clouds recede to show the winking stars. As minutes pass and the light of day fully vanishes, stars appear en masse. With barely a hint of light pollution, the sky above Grand Canyon reveals the Milky Way and hundreds of faint stars never seen in cities, towns, and suburbs. I spot Cassiopeia, the Big Dipper, the Dog Star in Canis Major, and what I guess to be Venus—Ishtar—appearing in the southeast quadrant of the sky.

The bustle of people around the campground fades to quiet conversation in a couple of corners. The lights of headlamps occasionally bob along the trail as someone heads to the bathroom. An out-of-nowhere breeze kicks through the campground then, just as quickly, slips away.

All around me at Bright Angel Campground and up Bright Angel Creek at Phantom Ranch, I imagine cherished memories forming among people nestled for a short time inside the Grand Canyon. I conjure this as I begin my fade into sleep. The constant swish of the creek relaxes my thoughts, takes my mind downstream, away from the ache of muscles and mild sunburn. Tomorrow, I will walk away from the centered oasis and into a new day that takes me closer to the rim.

CHAPTER 7

THE BRIDGES AND THE RIVER:
Intersection Point

I **wake to the** swish and gurgle of Bright Angel Creek and the flickers of birdsong. I sleep in my tent and my friend Fred Calleri sleeps outside during a November backpacking trip. He covers himself with a thick blanket, his only protection against the cool night air. As I stand over him, I wonder which end is his head. I expect I will need to nudge him awake soon.

I slip past the spot where he sleeps. I cross the main path through the campground. I walk to the bank of the creek. I drop into a crouch and balance, perched on the small slope, in my sandals and thick wool socks. I dip my hands into the icy water and splash my face. I am in the waking world.

I look downstream to watch a mule deer doe. She takes delicate steps toward the creek. She twitches her ears.

I wonder how she made it—or how her parents or grandparents made it—to the bottom of the canyon. I guess it was the same way I did: down the trail.

The canyon gives few other options.

She walks farther downstream, through small trees and high grasses. She disappears.

After watching her, I ponder the animal world of the Grand Canyon. Looking at it from the rim, the craggy cliffs and buttes and high-desert openness suggest inhospitality. Instead, the canyon bristles with life. Mule deer, desert bighorn sheep, wild turkey, ringtails, beavers, squirrels, chipmunks, coyotes, mountain lions, and all manner of birds—ravens, California condors, owls, hummingbirds, blue herons, songbirds, and more.

The Grand Canyon is arid.

And water is life is water.

But the gorge is lined and dotted with oases and springs—dozens of side canyons with perennial water. And down the canyon's spiny middle runs the largest river in the Southwest, the Colorado. So, animals thrive. And, as writer and naturalist Rose Houk suggests, they give the canyon perspective. They take a landscape that looks nearly two-dimensional from the rim and give it an added depth.

I wake Fred. He mumbles, finds fuller consciousness, and pulls on his boots. We stroll to Phantom Ranch along Bright Angel Creek. We go for breakfast, not wanting to fuss with making ours in the cold. I load up on pancakes, orange juice, and coffee. Morning brings tempered blessings. We bask in the joy of eating a hot meal at the bottom of the Grand Canyon. It is fuel we need to hike out, to return to civilization.

I follow Fred back to camp. He stretches out his long legs and prepares to travel. We pack our gear into our backpacks, trapping with it the earthy smells of camp. I swap my sandals for boots and lace up. I draw the air into my nostrils. I steel myself for the day's journey—nine miles up the Bright Angel Trail, all the way to the top. A near-mile of elevation gain in a day.

At the start of the hike, I think of its sections and stages: crossing the Silver Bridge, following the River Trail, turning south into Pipe Creek Canyon, walking up the canyon to the Devils Corkscrew, the corkscrew itself, and walking along Garden Creek to Indian Garden. That's the first half. The second half is 3,000 feet of elevation gain with two rest areas.

I take in another deep breath to smooth the edges of my nerves. I nod to Fred. He says, "Let's do this."

Compared to others who stayed overnight in the campground, we are late starters. It's close to 9 am. All but three other campsites stand vacant. We will barely hike a quarter of a mile before running into people who ran down from the rim. The Grand Canyon favors the ambitious, or the ambitious favor the Grand Canyon.

Fred and I walk over the Silver Bridge, which spans the roiling waters of the Colorado River. We see it under our feet through the grated walkway. As we walk to the center, the rhythm of our stride makes the bridge bounce.

I keep my attention on the river.

I look upstream and down.

I imagine myself on a river trip, with its own rhythm.

I consider the wisdom of the river and the rock it cuts. In the gorge, we experience nature and its different clocks. The age of geologic time and the time it takes for water to cut the rock. The ancient cycles, the rituals of erosion—water and gravity versus the resistant stone.

We cross to the other side. It gives me a feeling of progression. Part of me wants to turn back. Part of me wants to go on, to be home. All of me knows I will be back in the canyon soon, drawn to the bottom.

The air warms into the fifties after the first few hours of light. It will hit the seventies by the afternoon. The temperature varies by as much as forty degrees between the North Rim and Phantom Ranch. In November, the Inner Gorge furnace is shut down. The sun tracks at an angle, dipping to the south. Its light comes later and leaves earlier, offering more shade and only a slim chance of triple-digit temperatures.

I cast my gaze to the buttes and temples. The sun lights up their easterly sides.

Fred's legs carry him ten to fifteen paces ahead of me. He rounds a bend in the River Trail. I let myself enjoy the temporary solitude.

As I walk, I hear some small rocks skitter from above. I look up and see nothing. I keep looking, interested in the tone of the sky.

A desert bighorn sheep peers over an edge of rock about twenty-five feet up.

We stare at each other.

For several seconds, we each consider the other.

The sheep has thick horizontal lines for pupils and fur that blends white, gray, and brown into a drab but beautifully earthy pelt.

"Seth!" Fred calls with a frantic whisper from his place on the trail. "Quick! You gotta see this!"

Fred's voice breaks my stare-off with the bighorn. I look down the trail. I glance back up at the bighorn, but he has disappeared.

I lumber as fast as I can with my pack. I turn the corner of the trail. Another bighorn sheep stands on the path.

"Check him out!" Fred says. The bighorn is between Fred and me. He climbed down onto the trail after Fred passed.

I admire the animal. All muscles and sinewy parts. The bighorn sighting brings magic to the morning. It's not any wildlife encounter, but a close one with one of the largest animals to roam the Grand Canyon.

I take out the lightweight camera I brought for the trip, a point-and-shoot digital that also takes short video clips. I switch it to video.

As I point the lens at the bighorn, adrenaline pours into my system. I realize the bighorn has found itself between two humans.

The bighorn chooses to walk toward me. I keep the camera on him but walk backward.

And then he breaks into a run.

My panic spikes.

The bighorn runs in my direction but cuts from the trail a few yards before he reaches me. He makes a swift-footed dash down a slope off the trail and back up it.

He disappears around the trail bend.

"Man!" Fred calls out.

I walk over to Fred and we watch the video on the camera's playback. We want to confirm what happened. Fred and I smile.

Such an animal encounter turns into an honor. It becomes the first thing we will tell everyone about our trip.

As we hike along the final stretch of the River Trail, I become more aware of my surroundings. I look in all directions for bighorn sheep. I expect one around every corner.

Each animal encounter alters my perception of the canyon's craggy interior. I think of the animals that live here, of the ones I have seen before. I've spotted beavers in the river. Ringtails on the perimeter of a campsite. Coyotes trotting across the Esplanade. Condors, ravens, and swifts on the wing.

In these thoughts, the canyon loses some of its desolation. It becomes a land of the living.

Fred and I follow the River Trail and stop before it turns into the Bright Angel Trail and heads up Pipe Creek Canyon. We contemplate the river, which stirs into a small rapid near a place called Phantom Beach. The river draws more people. They ride the artery down through as many as 210 miles of the 277-mile canyon, coursing through scores of major rapids, falling in tune with the pulse and rhythm of the water for days and weeks.

The river, too, is another approach to Phantom Ranch and the Corridor trails. It reaches that pocket of civilization after nearly ninety miles of desolate canyon, below the launch at Lees Ferry. It becomes another way to know the canyon. Another way to cross paths with the Corridor.

⊰ ✦ ⊱

It is early May, two seasons before my late fall hike with Fred. The Inner Gorge swallows our bleary eyed tour group whole. We motor slowly along the Colorado wearing rain gear and stupid grins. The rain gear protects us from the waves of the rapids. But the rapids are behind us.

In minutes, our river trip will end. It's a three-day upper-canyon motor run with the Canyoneers, one of the park's river-running concessioners. Marc Perkins, our lead guide, slows the motor to a crawl. The thirty-foot rig shimmies along a ripple in the current and moves out to flat water.

The Kaibab Suspension Bridge appears around a bend. It signals the inevitable end of our trip. Beyond it, on river right, our destination nears. We will arrive at Boat Beach shortly before 11 am.

The river trip includes sixteen passengers—a group whose members come from all over, brought together by an ultimate adventure. One couple is from Florida, the husband the mayor of their midsized town. A father and his teenage son hail from New Jersey. Four of their friends join them. They all go to the same church. Originally, the entire river trip was going to be made up of members of the congregation.

We all find a way to get along—to bond, even—over the course of three days. The journey leads us through Marble Canyon and to our first camping spot, near the mouth of a side passage called South Canyon. We travel on to Redwall Cavern and the Little Colorado River, where we swim.

The trip feels hurried as we motor through stretches of the gorge. I try to stay present and focused, but the pace of the trip at times moves us past views and vistas faster than I can absorb them.

The second night on the river brings an anniversary party for my wife, Jane, and me. Marc the guide makes a fruit cobbler in a Dutch oven for dessert. He places candles in Jane's and my cobbler to celebrate our two years of marriage. He cajoles everyone into singing a happy anniversary song to us. Jane and I savor our celebratory dessert as dusk falls. We sift the fine, cool sand with our toes and watch for the emergence of stars, and bats.

The day after our second anniversary, Jane and I leap from the inflated bow of the boat onto Boat Beach's wet sand. We pull our packs and boots out of rubbery dry bags and grab our walking sticks from a compartment in the floor of the boat. We will need them for the next day's hike out.

We experience the odd moment of exchange with members of the lower-canyon trip. As we end our upper-canyon journey at Phantom Ranch, they have just finished hiking down to start their lower-canyon journey. Our meeting displays emotional incongruence. They all look anxious, arms folded. Jokes are met with nervous laughter. One teenage girl bites her nails. We talk openly and laugh freely, and there is feeling of relief in the air. The sadness of the trip ending has not really set in. We remain in the canyon and still have the rest of the day today and a hike out tomorrow to savor. Jane and I plan a day hike, too, after we settle at Phantom Ranch.

The temperature climbs into the mid-nineties. We walk a half mile along Bright Angel Creek to Phantom Ranch. Jane and I learn that we are staying in Phantom Ranch's bunkhouses, divided into male and female quarters.

We toss our packs onto our respective beds and set out for some walking. But not before stopping in at manager David Meyer's cabin for a visit. After we catch up and express the appropriate amount of envy for his cabin inside the canyon, we set off for our hike.

The river trip did nothing to satisfy our legs, heart, and lungs. For most of the trip, we sat in a boat, passive passengers moving through a landscape usually requiring sweat and muscle. With all of the snacks, breakfasts, lunches, and big dinners, we had serious calorie gain. The trip made Jane and me cagey. We need to move and explore.

We initiate a hearty hike up the North Kaibab Trail and use the time to ourselves to reflect on our river experience. A commercial motor river trip turned into a strange endeavor for us. Everyone else traveled from far corners of the country to do it. We make our home nearby, in Flagstaff. Mark the guide lives two blocks away from us.

But we took the trip for the same reason many other people do: because the river called to us.

I longed to see places such as Redwall Cavern, to walk into its gaping mouth and feel its sand, as soft as flour, on my toes. When I do, my thoughts turn to John Wesley Powell, the first person to describe the cavern in writing. How it was like an amphitheater. How it could hold 50,000 men standing side by side.[1] Jane and I run to the back of the cavern and sat where the ceiling vaulted out and up from us.

I also savor, for the first time, seeing the Little Colorado River's blue-green waters, emerging from a spring sacred to the Hopi and eventually spilling into the Colorado River. I want to see other places, too: Vaseys Paradise and Stantons Cave and that mile where the river first moves into the darker walls of the Inner Gorge.

At Phantom Ranch, we ponder these river moments and the ninety miles it took us to get here. Those ninety miles are only one-third of the

Participants and river runners in a Grand Canyon Field Institute Colorado River trip in the mouth of Redwall Cavern, along the Colorado upriver of Phantom Ranch. *Courtesy Mike Buchheit*

river through Grand Canyon. The river stretches and coils for another 187 miles before the cliff walls drop away beyond the Grand Wash Cliffs and the river pools up behind Hoover Dam to form Lake Mead.

We wish we did not have to get off the boat at Phantom Ranch. Too many other adventures await down the river. The upper-river run only gives us a taste of it. We want more.

With a little more than an hour before dinner, Jane and I wander back to Boat Beach. We sit in the sand and stare upstream. The water from our vantage, given the time of day, takes on a darker metallic-green color. Above, the Kaibab Suspension Bridge casts its shadow on the river.

As we sit on the sand, I contemplate the waterway before us. The Colorado River is significant by desert standards. It is responsible for deepening the canyon and carrying away sediment and rock eroded from its walls. The river also stands as a lifeline, the most important groundwater source in the Southwest when its reservoirs are counted. It once carried the snowmelt from the Rocky Mountains to Mexico and the sea. It is a magnificent living beast, a roiling snake that drops from mighty mountains into thirsty desert.

To some river lovers, it is no longer a river at all. The many dams keep it in check, slacken it in places, and tame its wildness. A beast domesticated for human benefit. Activist and writer Katie Lee curses what she calls the ugly blue water that comes out from the dam, no longer muddied by the silt that once made the river an earthy red.[2] Dams or no dams, the Colorado is considered one of the siltiest rivers in the world. Predam, it could carry annual sediment loads on par with the longer, heavier flowing Mississippi River.[3]

Whether running green or red, with or without dams, the river is not even close in size to the top twenty-five largest rivers by water volume in the United States.[4] Major East Coast rivers, northwestern rivers, midwestern rivers, and southern rivers have more-generous sources, lose much less to evaporation, and are fed by skies producing moisture much more steadily. Still, the Colorado is a river running through parched country, and it is one of the most relied-upon sources of water in the West. It has been noted that if the Colorado stopped flowing, in four years its reservoirs would be depleted to a point requiring the evacuation of most of Southern California and Arizona.[5]

Although it does not top the list of American rivers in terms of flow, the Colorado is a major river-running destination. Commercial river trips carry as many as 27,000 people down the river annually as guests of sixteen approved outfitters.[6] However, private trips navigating the Grand Canyon carry a whole other breed and culture of people, many of whom visit Phantom Ranch and hike Grand Canyon's Corridor.

⊰ ✦ ⊱

I watch the river from the last half mile of the South Kaibab Trail during one of my many hikes to the bottom. I hear its white noise. I turn switchback after switchback as the trail uncoils to its end point. As I near the river, I hear catcalls and cheers. I look to the river again to see eight rafts floating by in a steady drift. Their vibrant yellows, blues, and reds bounce on the green water.

Even from a distance, I see the boats packed and stacked with gear. I know it to be a private trip, not a commercial one, mainly because of the time of year. It's winter, early December. Another telltale sign: one boat flies a leopard-print flag, a possible homage to leopard-print-bathing-suit-wearing river runner Georgie White.

True river rats do not live like normal people. The kind of people who gravitate toward rivers—who run rivers until their bodies cannot take it, who bond over harrowing stories, who run the Colorado and its sunless stretches in December, like the people I see below—do not operate like most humans.

River rats live as vagabonds with poets' hearts. I first met them in college through my friend Kevin Prickett, at the time a river-rat-in-training. He worked for a river guide company that ran the Gauley and New rivers in West Virginia. He and the other guides lived in a house that had dirt floors. Some of them slept in an old school bus abandoned in the yard. They made little money. They ate leftover lunches from the guided trips, whatever the customers did not eat.

I know, in spirit, the river runners who pull into Boat Beach as I near Phantom Ranch. To run the Colorado in winter, river water must have found its way into their blood. Such river runners thrive in the cold turbulence. They crave the thrust and pull of the rapids. If they carry any of the traits of the river runners I have met, they drift along, live for the season, find winter jobs in ski towns, or live in the desert until river spring training, known officially as the Guides Training Seminar. River runners call it the Big Kahuna.

One friend of mine, Shelby Earls Wohleber, has long lived for rivers. She pines for the loamy aroma of a riverbank. She dreams of the sound of rapids, ponders the currents and eddies. She unfolded her river philosophy to me over more than a dozen conversations. She talked of reading water, of knowing hydraulics. Of rivers as arteries filled with lifeblood. Like all river lovers, she knows wild rivers carry water brought writhingly alive, animated by gravity. She knows they represent movement.

They bring passage.

They cut through rock and land.

They are restless.

The river runners at Boat Beach spring from their boats and tie them off as I finish out the South Kaibab Trail hike and approach Bright Angel Campground. They come up behind me on the trail, on their way up to Phantom Ranch.

After I drop my pack at camp and set up, I walk to the Phantom Ranch Canteen, where I plan to have dinner that night. When I reach the canteen, I walk around back to the bathrooms. The river runners gather in front of the restroom building. They take turns making phone calls from the pay phone. They also prepare letters and packages to send from the only mail pickup and drop-off inside the canyon—save for the village of Supai on the neighboring Havasupai Indian Reservation, which is a ten-mile walk one-way from the river.

For most river runners, Phantom Ranch is their one intersection with civilization. Further downriver, some will hike those ten miles from the river to Supai, but most do not take the time. Yet some private trips are known to pass Phantom Ranch completely, unyielding in their desire to skip any interaction with civilization.

For the trips that stop, Phantom Ranch offers a moment to indulge, to engage. I listen to a grizzled-looking guy—stringy blond hair, flip-flops in December—talk in a hushed voice on the pay phone. He also wears a som-brero and shorts, with no caution for a shady winter canyon and frigid river. He nods often, says he is being safe. I guess he's talking to his girlfriend or wife, or possibly his mom.

I approach one of the older guys on the trip. He wears a full beard speckled with gray and a brimmed hat that looks a hundred river trips old. I ask him about the trip. Seven days in. Mostly cold, with no problems run-ning rapids. But the river level is dropping, which has made a couple of rap-ids dicey. "Worried about Horn [Creek Rapid]," he notes of the rocky rapid downstream from Phantom. The rapid is 8 on a scale of 10. At low water, it forms rough waves and menacing hydraulics that make it one of the wick-edest runs in the canyon.

The runners come together, a mix of people mostly from Montana and Colorado, with a few Californians thrown in. All are united by a private permit draw for the winter run.

I return to camp with plans to finish setting up, but I wander to the river instead. I want to watch the river trip depart. I drop onto the cool sand and observe their steady progression. The boaters wander back to their rafts, stacked and stuffed with ammo cans and dry bags. The oldest-looking man, in a yellow raft, pushes off and drifts upstream on the current of an unseen eddy. He stands up and stares at the river he just came down from beneath the Kaibab Suspension Bridge.

The others board their rafts, either one or two people per raft. They are rigged up with one boater on double oars. As I watch them, they study the steady crumble of a small ledge in the sand. They see the river level dropping before them.

"Horn Creek's gonna be rough," one of the guys calls to the other. I realize that the guy who says this is the same older man I talked to earlier. I watch as each of the boats breaks from land and floats off. The boaters line up their rigs like taxiing planes. One by one, they catch the main current and slip through the small rapid created by Bright Angel Creek's run-off. After a few hours of buildings, phones, access to mail and provisions, the river runners return to their walled-in solitude, moving deeper into the canyon they simply call The Grand.

I walk quickly to the Silver Bridge before the last two boats catch the currents, in hopes of standing over them as they pass on the river below.

⊰ ✣ ⊱

The river that runs under the two Corridor trail bridges—the Kaibab Suspension Bridge and Silver Bridge—roils with current. I imagine the unseen currents and hydraulics. The waters pass through a channel of their own carving, confined by schist, gneiss, and granite walls. In the distance, the TV-static-like sound of a rapid echoes downstream.

I consider the immensity of the Grand Canyon and the crossroads where terrestrial travelers meet water travelers. The two most popular routes through the canyon—the Corridor trails and the river—intersect at the bridges. The Kaibab Suspension Bridge serves as an overpass. It and the Silver Bridge connect the land route.

The journey from rim to rim in the Grand Canyon centers on these safe, high crossings above the Colorado River. The river is not one for swimming, with its wild currents, swift flow, and—after the completion of Glen Canyon Dam—near-constant temperature of forty-seven degrees. Aside from a bridge, the use of a boat or ferry is another option, but a bridge creates a constant passage.

The first means of crossing above the river on the Corridor came when Dave Rust and his crew constructed their cable system. It involved bringing a 500-foot-long cable and a 1,500-pound cable car down the trail. Transporting the supplies proved easier than stringing the cable across the river with a rowboat and properly balancing the cable car to attach it.[7]

In September 1907, Rose Evans and Lida Bilveal became the first tourists to cross what would be the Corridor's first river-crossing system. It could only bring people across in small numbers and required an operator. Theodore Roosevelt arrived on the south side of the river en route to a Kaibab Plateau hunting trip in July 1913, only to encounter a misunderstanding by Rust and company of the day of his planned arrival. Someone needed to row a boat across the river to bring everyone else across on the cable system. Roosevelt—though so intrigued by the cable system he insisted on cranking some of his party across himself—was angry at Rust for the miscommunication.[8]

When plans for Phantom Ranch were under way, in 1921, the National Park Service decided to spend $17,000 on a swinging suspension bridge. The bridge proved an inadequate and, to some, frightening experience. Only one mule could cross at a time, and the mule and its passenger caused the bridge to swing. In addition, high winds that moved through the canyon could flip the bridge.[9]

A hiker sets out across the Kaibab Suspension Bridge over the Colorado River.
Courtesy of the author

With the completion of the South Kaibab Trail in 1925 and the growth of Phantom Ranch and the developing North Rim, park service officials realized that they would have to replace the swinging bridge with a sturdier one. They drew up plans to construct a cable-supported suspension-style bridge and set aside $48,000 to build it. Crews began work in March 1928.[10]

To build a load-bearing bridge that could support a train of mules and all of their riders proved daunting—especially in a time with no helicopters to haul supplies. Logistics and rough rapids prevented use of the river for transport. So, National Park Service mule pack trains with three packers and more than forty mules hauled approximately 122 tons of steel, support cables, concrete, sand, and equipment to the base of the South Kaibab Trail on multiple trips. Another twenty-six tons of steel came down on pack trains operated by the Fred Harvey Company.[11]

The mule trains could not carry down the 548-foot-long main bridge cables. Instead, a team of forty-two men—mostly Havasupais—carried the eight cables for more than six miles along the South Kaibab Trail. The men were spaced out along the cables so they each carried about fifty pounds' worth of cable on their shoulders. Each of the eight trips required two days.[12]

A foreman and nine skilled laborers then went to work on the bridge, and the park service added eleven more workers during its construction. They worked for six months, mostly at night during the summer, to complete the bridge. The bridge work also required the excavation of a 105-foot-long tunnel—ten feet high and six feet wide—blasted from schist and granite. The size of the tunnel allows for passage of mules with riders.[13]

The southern approach through this tunnel when coming down the South Kaibab Trail creates a feeling of passing through a portal from one phase of the journey to another. The entry and exit of the tunnel are not aligned, so to walk into the tunnel from one end is to walk into darkness. Once in the tunnel, light from the other end reveals itself. With each step, the domain of bridge and river grow closer until the tunnel ends at the wooden planks of the bridge's walkway.

No crews or projects have significantly altered the Kaibab Suspension Bridge since its completion in August 1928. It stretches 440 feet long, and the walkway is five feet wide. According to reports from construction supervisor J. H. Lawrence, it is a bridge that can "support all the live load that can be placed on it." The total cost of the bridge project was $39,500, much less than its $48,000 budget. At the time of its completion, no other bridge spanned the Colorado River for 385 miles to the south and 370 miles to the north. But Navajo Bridge at Marble Canyon, about eighty-five miles upstream, opened to cars in January 1929.[14]

About forty years later, the Corridor trails received a second footbridge across the Colorado River, though one that required less work and came with less ceremony. In the mid-1960s, the park service initiated work to build the transcanyon pipeline from Roaring Springs to the South Rim. Crews nearly completed the project in 1966 when one of those thirty-year floods destroyed it. They went back to work and completed the pipeline in 1970. The second bridge, known as the Silver Bridge, was built to accommodate the water pipeline over the river. A metal grate walkway was placed over the pipeline to allow hikers to cross, but mules won't cross on the grating.[15] They cross on the planked Kaibab Suspension Bridge.

Historian Mike Anderson offered some thoughts as to how the Silver Bridge improved travel along the Corridor trails. For those ascending and descending to and from Phantom Ranch along the Bright Angel Trail, the Silver Bridge decreases their journey by a mile. Otherwise, they would have to follow the River Trail farther east to the South Kaibab Trail, take the South Kaibab down to and across the Kaibab Suspension Bridge, and walk a quarter mile west to get back to Bright Angel Campground and Phantom Ranch.

With two bridges, hikers can travel to the river from the South Rim without backtracking by coming down the South Kaibab Trail, crossing the Kaibab Suspension Bridge, then walking to the Silver Bridge to ascend the Bright Angel Trail—or vice versa. Because of the distance and elevation change, this is a multiday trip.

The bridges also create a two-mile River Trail loop that is promoted as a day hike from Phantom Ranch. This loop involves crossing one bridge, following the River Trail from bridge to bridge on the south side of the river, and returning to Phantom Ranch on the opposite side. Along with those benefits, the Silver Bridge offers an alternative route across the river in the rare instance of a rockfall on the trail or a dead mule or some other emergency on the Kaibab Suspension Bridge.

The Silver Bridge provides an observation deck of sorts to watch the river. Underneath, a small rapid called Bright Angel Rapid—rated 3 on the 1–10 scale—churns and spirals its way through a place where the Inner Gorge walls narrow. There, lucky hikers will find an opportunity to witness river trips pass under the bridge, thanks to its see-through grating. The bridge offers a chance for people on foot to peer into that alternate canyon traveler's world, and to dream of a canyon trip by boat rather than by boot.

⊶ ✢ ⊷

I am not the first person drawn to this river in the desert. All around me are signs of the people and lives that came before, drawn to the life force of water and the challenge of the Grand Canyon. On the dawning of an October day, I walk out to the river. I sit and watch from an excavated ruin located along the South Kaibab Trail on the north side of the river. I observe the stunted walls of the ruin, standing mere feet above the traditional high-water line. The foot-high walls frame out six rooms and a smaller room, probably used for storage.

The School of American Research dug out the walls in 1969, down to the floor. The excavation revealed some metates, or long flat stones used to grind corn. Studies show ancestral Puebloan sites such as this one date back to ad 1050, around the height of the ancestral Puebloan culture. Places such as Chaco Canyon in modern-day New Mexico's Chaco Culture National Historical Park and Mesa Verde National Park in Colorado thrived during this time. Discoveries that agriculture occurred at the inner-canyon sites suggest a seasonal living situation, where the people came down into the canyon during the longer—and hotter—days of the year. With this approach, they could take advantage of a long and fruitful growing season, with access to river water and many hours of sun.[16]

Douglas Schwartz, who worked on the site, commented, "These ancient people, who time and time again moved into the canyon country, lived on the edge of splendor and desperation."[17] Archaeologists found a burial site on the Bright Angel Creek delta. The burial involved a woman in her forties. Her bones suggest, even at her middle age, the onset of severe arthritis. The long days of labor, particularly of grinding corn against stone beneath the searing southwestern sun, might have contributed to such a problem. Other discoveries of burial sites have revealed deaths at younger ages, and death possibly caused by serious dental infections and other problems.[18]

Not far from the ruin stands another memorial. The grave of Rees B. Griffiths sits adjacent to the South Kaibab Trail. It is nestled in an alcove of granite, and most people walk right by it, unaware. The grave is aboveground, a pile of stones slightly longer and wider than a body. Geologist Wayne Ranney notes that solid rock just under the dirt prevents the digging of graves without a good amount of dynamite, hence the aboveground burial. On top of the stones, family members placed fused horseshoes designed to look like large flowers and a lasso.

Little is written about Griffiths other than some footnotes and a plaque that hangs over the site. The plaque reads: "REES B. GRIFFITHS Trail Foreman, National Park Service. Born Oct. 26, 1873. Died Feb. 6, 1922, in the Grand Canyon he loved so well. As a result of injuries received near this spot while in performance of his duty in the building of the [NORTH] KAIBAB TRAIL."

During an interpretive walk with a Grand Canyon Field Institute trip, Ranney noted that Griffiths is most likely the only Caucasian buried at Phantom Ranch. In recent decades, the National Park Service has banned burials and graves inside the Grand Canyon, though they've grandfathered in sites such as Griffiths's. I understand that the park regulation must exist to counter demands for burials from people who love the canyon and want their bodies there, but I appreciate the romantic notion of a burial in the canyon's depths. I often find myself stopping at the Griffiths site and thinking of all of the people who carry the Grand Canyon in their spirit, and who wish they could forever be a part of its legacy.

Not paying much attention to the dates, I once assumed that Griffiths worked with the Civilian Conservation Corps and died doing challenging and treacherous work on the River Trail. Only after visiting with Ranney on the interpretive hike did I realize the date of his death came more than a decade before the CCC company arrived. And, I learned that no one died building the River Trail—a strange truth despite all the dynamite, flying rock, and landslides involved.

I thought of this during a winter visit when I peeked into the alcove to see Griffiths's grave and thought of the kind of work he did improving the North Kaibab. Still, I caught myself looking across river at the line where the River Trail finds its way along the sheer schist and granite cliffs. I pondered the work and the lives of people that converged in this place and left the canyon's most permanent trail.

CHAPTER 8

THE RIVER TRAIL:
Carved into the Eons

My friend **Greg Good** and I descend most of the South Kaibab Trail on a late October hike to the bottom of the canyon. The day rings with perfection. Light winds swirl as the air temperatures in the inner canyon remain below seventy degrees. The sky is blue without interruption. Greg and I feel healthy, not a sore muscle, knee, or foot. Not a blister. Not a hint of exhaustion. Everything is going right. We embrace the canyon's cardinal rules: steady pace with occasional breaks, plenty of water, and salty snacks in the form of cashews and a can of Pringles.

Because of this, we feel no rush. We begin to meander. Greg stops to take photograph after photograph. This happens during almost everyone's first time in the Grand Canyon. Greg, fifty-seven, is from Morgantown, West Virginia, and is a tireless backpacker and former rock climber. But he's never made it to the Grand Canyon before. Not even to Arizona. I invited him to make the journey, a chance for me to repay his mentorship during my college years. We rekindle our rapport as we thread our way, with laughs and smiles, into the sacred body of the Grand Canyon.

With the trip going right, we choose to add a half mile to our trip by taking the River Trail—originally called the Colorado River Trail—to

CCC enrollees use jackhammers to break down rock during the construction of the River Trail, circa 1935. *Courtesy GCNPMC (#03973E)*

Phantom Ranch instead of following the South Kaibab Trail. We stay on the south side of the river. We walk into the fractured, cooked, and compressed madness of the Vishnu Schist and Zoroaster granite.

Through the chaos runs a line of order. A trail appears, blasted from the solid walls through 1,700-million-year-old rock, formed during an era of Earth's creation before the appearance of any complex life-forms. The men of the Civilian Conservation Corps created the trail, practically a sculpture blasted into stone. It could outlast nearly all human-made endeavors.[1]

Greg, who counts trail-building among his skills, marvels at the River Trail, at the formation of a path where no path should go, blasted from the sides of cliffs—built as if meant to carry a railroad along a mountainside. The trail is gradual, with no more than a 7 percent grade.

These two miles of Corridor trail came into existence with the CCC's arrived in 1933. For a little more than two years, CCC Company 818 worked on the River Trail during its winter assignment at Phantom Ranch. It spent summers on the North Rim, with Company 819 on the South Rim.[2]

While in the canyon, 179 men handled the assignment of connecting the Bright Angel Trail to the South Kaibab Trail via a path that parallels the Colorado River. Before the River Trail, travel along the Corridor offered few alternatives in the event of a washout from a flood or rockfall. The Bright Angel Trail in its full length functioned only as a trail to the river, ending at the confluence of Pipe Creek more than a mile east of Bright Angel Creek. Only the adventuresome dared to cross on small scows to reach Bright Angel Creek upstream.[3]

The Inner Gorge grants few places to walk parallel to the river for any distance. Walls of metamorphic and igneous rock rise vertically from the river along most of the gorge's length. Every surface appears jagged and steeply sloped. Nothing offers a natural walking path riverside—the way some might imagine—save for a few beaches and banks. Otherwise, following the river on foot is easier done several hundred feet above it, on the Tonto Platform. The River Trail itself follows an elevated trajectory along cliffs rising 150 feet above the river.

This CCC-built trail opened up the alternative of using the Bright Angel to access Phantom Ranch more directly, and it connected the Bright Angel and South Kaibab trails near the river so hikers no longer needed to use the Tonto Trail for this purpose.[4]

The ultimate benefits offered by the River Trail came from serious effort. More than 75 percent of the trail is blasted from granitic rock; less than a half mile runs through sand dunes, requiring limited trail work.[5] Well-documented records of supplies show the challenge of blasting the trail out of the Vishnu Schist and Zoroaster granite, the canyon's basement rocks:

Forty thousand pounds of explosive powder.

Ten thousand special drill bits.

Five air compressors.

Ten jackhammers.[6]

A historic photograph shows young men hanging from ropes along the cliff faces as they chisel out chunks of rock to sculpt the trail. Similar images appear in newsreels shown around the country to share the work of the CCC during the Great Depression. In these scenes, men hang from 150-foot lines secured to ledges above. They wear helmets and safety belts attached to a second rope. Showing sheer physical skill, they wield jackhammers while suspended. In some cases, it took several men working one shift to drill one hole for one blast.[7]

The precarious position of workers, the crash and roll of rocks and boulders, the isolation of the Grand Canyon, and the use of explosives suggest at least one man—if not several—would die. The park service initially named the trail the Colorado River Trail, but agreed with the CCC to officially name it after the first worker to die building it.[8]

In the construction work from late 1933 to early 1936, no one died working on the trail and only three men suffered serious injuries. For this reason, the trail retained its working name. Historian Mike Anderson makes note of one of the seriously injured, a man with the last name of Blake. If Blake had died of his injuries, the Blake Trail "would have become the only trail in Grand Canyon named for an African American."[9]

That no one died was likely a result of the experience of some of the CCC crew and abundant precautions taken by supervisors. Company 818 recruited hard-rock miners and assigned them to work with the inexperienced men on the project. Crew leaders grew sharply observant of signs of possible landslides. If they saw falling pebbles, observed dust stirred out of a fissure, or heard strange sounds, they evacuated the work site.[10]

Louis Purvis supervised trail construction and later wrote a book about it called *The Ace in the Hole: A Brief History of Company 818 of the Civilian Conservation Corps.* He tells of a day in 1934 when supervisor A. T. Sevey calmly requested the crew leader to order the workers to move back to where he was sitting.

When the men gathered around Sevey, he offered a smile and said, "Sit down, boys, and rest a few minutes." Within ten minutes and without warning, the cliff face collapsed and buried the trail where the men had been working.

"Okay, boys," Sevey said, "you may go back to work now."

Granite proved both difficult to drill and susceptible to caving in without warning. One amazing example shows the difficulty of the task: Workers spent two to six hours and used as many as sixty-five steel bits to drill an eight-foot hole in the granite. The hole was drilled in order to create a single blast in an attempt to create a minor trail segment.[11]

The workers packed the holes with twenty to forty sticks of dynamite and ignited the blast. After all their work, they would watch to see if the blast resulted in a bench that could function as a trail section. Sometimes the blast proved a good calculation that formed the desired trail. Other times the blast caused a landslide and left a sheer cliff hanging over the river. When the second result came, the crew needed to repeat the process.[12]

Hard labor, frustration, and long days challenged the members of Company 818. But the workers enjoyed their time off in the Grand Canyon. All of their activities appeared in a newsletter called "Ace in the Hole," a name that suggests pride in a top-notch CCC crew stationed inside of the Grand Canyon.[13]

The company leaders showed movies, which they projected on a screen not far from the Colorado River. The December 1935 edition of "Ace in the Hole" reported a first for inner-canyon film viewing. "Nov. 15, 'Romance in Manhattan,' Grand Canyon's first talking picture was enjoyed very much by one hundred and five (105) enrollees, officers and Phantom Ranch guest [*sic*]. The equipment was brought down by the Army's Seventh Pack Train and the projectionist was E. M. Kaylor of Flagstaff, Arizona. Due to the fact that motion pictures are the main recreational service we have, we hope to be able to furnish more good pictures in the future."[14]

They also created a small but popular library. The newsletter detailed new arrivals for the library, with such titles as *What Is American?*, *Famous Stories of Five Centuries*, *Story of Money*, *Story of Mankind*, *Treasure Chest of Song*, a Thomas Jefferson biography, and Spalding's series of sports guides. The newsletter also shared the "10 High of the Camp Library," a list of company members who read the most books. Frank Guy topped the list in the December 1935 newsletter with ten books read. Charles Baxter and William Masterson followed close behind with nine books each.[15]

At the company camp, bragging rights did not only apply to trail work, or the number of books read. Boxing and wrestling tournaments proved to be major events among the members of Company 818. Even with fewer than 200 men, boxing tournaments were broken down into eight weight classes. Sometimes the bragging rights extended beyond the company, and men of the South Rim Company 819 would come down and box the men of 818.[16]

But trail work was their main objective. In addition to the River Trail, Company 818 also constructed the Clear Creek Trail, that nine-mile route that heads off from the North Kaibab Trail up Bright Angel Creek from Phantom Ranch. It climbs up to the platform above the Inner Gorge, a place that features views of Phantom Ranch below, the South Kaibab Trail, the Kaibab Suspension Bridge to the south, and the Colorado River coming in from the east. From there, the Clear Creek Trail snakes its way east to the next major side canyon. The company also built a now-closed trail to upper Ribbon Falls, made smaller improvements to existing trails, and took on building projects around Phantom Ranch.[17]

Still, one of the masterpieces of the company—and of all CCC work at Grand Canyon National Park—was the River Trail. Alton Frost, who grew up north of the Grand Canyon and worked both as a forest service and park service ranger, completed trail construction in January 1936. He ignited the dynamite blast that connected two sections of the River Trail located a short distance east of the present-day Silver Bridge. This last blast completed the Inner Gorge route between the South Kaibab and Bright Angel trails.[18]

The CCC continued its efforts in the Grand Canyon after 1936, but assignments began to wane. "They worked in the Grand Canyon from 1933 to, you might say, 1940," Anderson notes. "But the CCC presence at the Grand Canyon dwindled after 1937, and it dwindled in the rest of the country. FDR's New Deal was done by 1936 or 1937, as it looked like the country was coming out of the Great Depression. Of course, they were wrong. There was another stock market crash. So the CCC was not completely eliminated until 1942, but it carried far [fewer] responsibilities than it had in that middle 1930s period."[19]

The end of the CCC era also signaled the end of trail creation in the Grand Canyon. After the two companies left, the developed trails of the inner canyon remained unchanged, save for maintenance and rehabilitation of existing routes. The staff at Grand Canyon National Park has put most of its time and money into trail work for the Corridor trails, with occasional work done on the Grandview and Hermit Threshold trails. A special grant allowed for rehabilitation of the farther-west South Bass and North Bass trails, but most other Primitive trails see few improvements.[20]

The lack of new trails and routes, the growth of visitation, and the focus on the Corridor trails created a steady hoof-and-foot highway running from the South Rim to Phantom Ranch and on to the North Rim. But Anderson thinks this is to the benefit of the Grand Canyon, as visitors are funneled into one area of the inner canyon and the rest of the gorge remains relatively protected.

For this reason, too, he expects to see no future trail expansion or development—such as a footbridge to connect the North and South Bass trails to create a second reliable cross-canyon corridor. "I think today they understand the impacts that would have to cultural and natural resources," he says. "They would not have the resources to monitor these places. They have realized if they keep people in the central Corridor, they can service them more economically and protect the resources in the rest of the park."[21]

Along the River Trail, that last pathway to be carved in the Grand Canyon, a rare drilling or blast mark appears. The signs of labor against rock offer reminders of the raw work needed to create a trail system that runs through the Grand Canyon, finding a way through difficult topography. At its western terminus, the River Trail reaches the Bright Angel Trail. The route to the South Rim turns south. It follows Pipe Creek, edging its way upstream. The trail follows the drainage—the easy way, where no route needed to be blasted from stone.

⇥ ✦ ⇤

On that western end of the River Trail, in the place where the Colorado River is left behind on an ascent of the Bright Angel Trail, I stop every time. During a December hike, when breaking daylight streams in at a sharp angle, I stop for fifteen minutes and watch the sun find this place. I give myself time to look at the Vishnu Schist and Zoroaster granite, to listen to the river—to watch it in relentless motion.

When I see rock without horizontal orientation or something close to it, I know time and other forces have conspired to alter it. I know many of these places reveal Earth in some of its most ancient times, long before single cells grew from primordial seas. In the case of the Grand Canyon's bottommost layers, they are born out of volcanic and violent events.

An outcropping of Vishnu Schist at the Bright Angel Campground near Phantom Ranch reveals a geologic history that dates back 1,700 million years. *Courtesy of the author*

"Around 1.7 billion years ago, we had these volcanoes . . . [in] this mountain chain [erupting] on this island," begins Wayne Ranney in a geology talk at Bright Angel Campground. Greg and I meet up with him on our late October trip. Ranney is leading six people on a Grand Canyon Field Institute backpacking trip. He points to a foreboding hundred-foot-high outcropping at the back of the group campsite where they are staying. "Eventually what happened is that there were sediments and volcanic rocks on the ocean floor. These two pieces of land approached one another and collided, and that's when these rocks were buried thirteen miles deep."[22]

He continues. "The rocks were folded like an accordion. The amplitudes of these folds are for miles. This is one of the limbs of the fold that was folded down thirteen miles," Ranney says as he puts his hand on the rock wall. "What you're looking at right here is original layering in the rocks. Those used to be sandstones and shales, and they used to be horizontal. They were buried deep enough that the sandstones and shales . . . turned into schist."

Ranney points out the layers of sand thinly visible in the dark gray rock of one of the layers. The layers are propped up nearly vertically, making the wall appear as a series of columns. Ranney puts a hand on each layer, showing how, despite the different form the rock has taken, it began as sandstone or shale. "If you were going to go five miles deeper down, those rocks melted," notes Ranney, explaining that the stone met with the intense heat of magma. "That's what this pink rock is," he says of the Zoroaster granite intrusions that appear within the columns. "It's melted schist that became so buoyant it forced its way up in here. The granite is about 15 to 20 million years younger. . . . The magma took advantage of the foliation [a layering that forms within metamorphic rock during recrystalization]. They followed the lines of weakness."

As Ranney talks, the six people on the trip all focus on the rock. One woman touches it. A man on the trip by himself looks closer at it, studying the layering. "I used to hate these rocks because I'm a sedimentary geologist," Ranney admits. "To me, sedimentary geology gives you a record of a surface of the Earth, but we did not have this story I'm telling you when I first started working here. . . . We now know that what happened here is a lot like what is happening under Indonesia today. [There're] probably Vishnu Schist– and Zoroaster granite–like rocks forming there, because Australia is moving toward Indonesia." This movement of the Indo-Australian plate creates what is known as a continental plate subduction, which is also responsible for a chain of volcanoes in Indonesia.

Among the group, an interest surfaces in rock age and how the Grand Canyon's oldest rocks compare with the oldest rocks found in other places. "This Vishnu Schist is the oldest [major layer of] rock in the Southwest, not the oldest in North America, but [in] the Southwest," Ranney notes. He adds that no older rock layers exist underneath where we stand. "We could keep going down into the Earth from here and this is the only rock we would see. We would not see any other type of rock."

He adds that some parts of North America feature rocks that are 2,500 million years old, and in some cases much older. "They have found a 4-billion-year-old rock in Canada, which is the oldest rock [yet found on Earth]," Ranney notes to the group. His explanation shows that the Grand Canyon does not hold honors for the oldest rock. Instead, the canyon sparks awe for the breadth of geologic time exposed, from 270-million-year-old rocks to 1,700-million-year-old rocks. It covers a span of nearly 1,500 million years—despite a gap of missing rock, the Great Unconformity.

The canyon also presents a complex puzzle to geologists who try to postulate how it formed. In one of Ranney's books, *Carving Grand Canyon*, he shares an array of theories. Some geologists postulate that a catastrophic flood caused by the release of a giant inland lake began carving the canyon. Others suggest that stream piracy, wherein the Colorado River took up a riverbed once occupied by a river going in a different direction, is the origin of the gorge.

This theory is known as headward erosion. With headward erosion, the river's flow in its upper reaches has more power to erode, because of the steeper slopes around it, than it does in its gentler flows downstream. This causes the river to erode back into the plateau near its headwaters, where it can then capture other streams and divert them into its flow.

What remains a constant is the river, as the Colorado flows and steadily erodes its way deeper into the earth.

☲ ✦ ☴

Early in the afternoon, Greg and I stop at the River Resthouse, near the end of Pipe Creek. It signifies a new beginning on the trail. We hear the trickle of the perennial stream as it runs clear through ginger, red, and white rocks, water-rounded stones that found their way downstream thanks to floods. We sit and watch the hikers going up and down the trail, none stopping to rest at our spot near the mouth of Pipe Creek, in a place that shelters us from the midday sun.

At the resthouse, I contemplate both the river and the River Trail. I have noticed how historic accounts of the trail speak of its construction in reverent tones, how the endeavor to create the trail is celebrated. I cannot think of the trail carved out of rock using muscle, jackhammer, and dynamite as a scar on the landscape, as a line that separates human-encroached landscapes from pristine wilderness.

But then I look below the River Trail and see the river. Without flood, it runs green. Ranney jokes that it could be named the Rio Esmerelda for its color, caused by Glen Canyon Dam, which releases clear, cold water into the Grand Canyon, and traps sediment behind its massive face. The dam, though built with its own challenges and careful engineering, altered the river forever. The ire this structure raises is mostly due to the fact that it submerged beautiful Glen Canyon, but many legal fights revolve around how the dam impacts Grand Canyon's ecology.[23]

In recent years, the Department of the Interior has attempted simulated floods in the Grand Canyon with giant releases of water from the diversion tubes of Glen Canyon Dam. As a reporter, I rode a bus with other journalists down to the base of Glen Canyon Dam, near Page, Arizona, in the fall of 2004. We traveled through a tunnel carved through the Navajo Sandstone to bring supplies to the base of the dam during construction. When we reached the bottom—under a muted sky flecked with raindrops—we heard the unholy roar of water launching from one of the diversion tubes. The water rocketed out into the river at 45,000 cubic feet per second, more than four times the usual flow.

Downstream, the Colorado blossomed with sediments deposited by the silty, soupy Paria River. Not far from the Paria confluence, a crew of U.S. Geological Survey scientists launched their boats into the rollicking flow of an excited river, energized like a zoo animal escaped from a cage. They looked to measure sediments and hoped to see new beaches built along the riverbanks, to witness signs of the river environment that used to be.

On the way back to Flagstaff, I stopped to observe the river 800 feet below the Navajo footbridge near Lees Ferry. It churned the color of a melted root beer float. It appeared angry and beautiful. Rain spilled across the span of the bridge. As I leaned over the rail to watch the river, the patter of the rain around me sounded like applause.

"We really don't have any pure, untouched systems," notes Rose Houk in an interview at her Flagstaff office. "So we have to do what we can do to restore it to a [certain] level. It's not so much the individual species but the processes. So with something like Glen Canyon Dam and the Colorado River, our job is not to restore parks to what they were like in 1492, but to restore those processes like floods, which were there before the dam and played an important role. So the processes continue to work and thrive, and the natural systems would presumably follow. Where it's all going to lead, it's hard to say. There is no end point. It's always a process."[24]

Although the impact of human encroachment has changed aspects of the canyon, Houk notes that other aspects of the canyon continue their movements and cycles. "The canyon is still eroding, and the processes are going on, and we ain't going to stop them. Thank God we have places like the Grand Canyon to observe these in a seminatural state."

I often think of this along the River Trail, watching the changed river channel its way down to the next reservoir. I think of human encroachment and how it is viewed and measured as I walk along a trail almost entirely created by human hands, machinery, and explosives. But nature persists, and the trails and the primary river of the Grand Canyon let us enter into it.

I ponder the flourish of epiphanies I have experienced walking into the open chaos of the Grand Canyon. Houk and I talk of that wide view. Our conversation turns to that journey of bold rock and bolder scenery, on the South Kaibab Trail.

CHAPTER 9

THE SOUTH KAIBAB TRAIL:
Defying the Topography

The first of October on the South Kaibab Trail. Sun broadcasts across the Grand Canyon. The sky is cloudless, a vaulted dome. The temperature at Cedar Ridge hovers around seventy degrees in the shade, of which there is very little.

The Supai Group cap of O'Neill Butte emerges into full view as I descend the trail on a day hike to Skeleton Point. I study the contrast of red earth against cool sky. The raw and the divine.

I've spent hours daydreaming about these kinds of days. The wind feels perfect on my skin. I find a hiking groove, one that will carry me as far as I need to go.

The trail levels out. O'Neill Butte stands at the center of the view. It's a minor butte in the canyon, but I like its shape, its position next to the South Kaibab Trail. It stands sentinel, watching over the travelers as they head into the depths.

Nearly two miles down the South Kaibab Trail, the view of the canyon spreads open before me. The trail follows a spine of rock as it threads its way toward Skeleton Point, then drops to the Tonto Platform and onto The Tipoff, where the Inner Gorge begins. By comparison, the bottom portion of the Bright Angel Trail is tucked away, hidden in an amphitheater, nestled in the walls of Garden Creek and Pipe Creek canyons.

The South Kaibab uncoils like a different species.

It is waterless.

It is exposed.

In the summer, the sun claims nearly every foot of the trail as its kingdom. The South Kaibab is the shortest drop to the Colorado River—less than seven miles compared to nearly nine on the Bright Angel—but the shorter, steeper distance takes its toll, killing knees on the way down, tearing calves and taxing lungs on the way up.

Still, a day hike to Skeleton Point makes for a satisfying morning. I cut left off the trail for a break at O'Neill Butte and find a place in the shade.

I lower my pack to the ground, prop my feet onto my backpack, interlace my fingers behind my neck, and stare up at the unblemished sky. The Supai Group, chiseled-looking blocks in earth-red hues stained with black, appears at the top of the expansive view. I focus on the line between the stone and the heavens.

Until something breaks the line.

Two California condors take flight from the upper edge of O'Neill Butte.

They spread their wings and coast into the open blue. With slight adjustments to their tail feathers, the condors bank into the wind. They glide without a flap of the wings, turn circles over the deep cut of a side canyon, drift effortlessly into the ether.

I study their tilts and slow turns. I suppress my envy. I ponder the nature of the condor.

They work as scavengers, carryovers from the last ice age and big mammal era. They neared the blade of extinction, their population decimated, in part by eating lead ammunition embedded in the flesh of animal carcasses left behind by hunters.

I know at first sight the two birds are condors and not vultures. Along with their greater size, they wear numbered tags clipped to their wings that identify individual birds. This is part of the condor recovery project.

I wonder if human intervention can save them. It has worked so far, as condors are thriving in the canyon. Thermals carry them across the gorge, and caves in high cliffs give them protection. Harsh desert conditions mean other animals are prone to die here. The dead animals provide carrion, the primary source of food for the condors.

⊰ ✦ ⊱

In the spring of 2005, I spent some time with Chris Parish, then the condor field project supervisor with the Peregrine Fund, while working on an article about the condor reintroduction program. Parish and I hurtled in a pickup truck along a snowmelt-softened dirt road that ran halfway between the top and bottom of the eastern flank of the Kaibab Plateau. Parish took me to a remote side canyon nearly twenty miles from U.S. 89A, the closest major road.

There, two California condors nested.

They displayed behavior that suggested they were caring for an egg. A single egg, as condors only lay one, every other year.

Parish has worked long and tedious—and low-paying—hours for the Peregrine Fund to support the California condor release program in Arizona. He has the build of a linebacker: six foot five, all muscle and mass. I imagine him working construction or some other heavy-labor job that he could handle with his build, not engaged in the tedious observations and long hours sitting still that are required of condor work.

He enlightened me about other aspects of his job. Regarding feeding condors soon to be released in the wild, he tells me, "I've had to carry still-birth calves in garbage cans [on my back]. . . . I've had to walk them three and four miles at night to drop them near the condors."

Not far from the nest site, we stopped at a muddy wash and spent two hours working to free Parish's assistant's pickup truck. At times, I needed to cover my nose and mouth, for we were working right next to the rotting carcass of a cow that had become stuck in the mud and died. I wasn't sure if the condors had found it yet.

Despite the long effort of rigging a winch and maneuvering our pickup at different angles to free the truck, most of the hours I spent with Parish that day involved staring at the nest site through a high-powered scope. When condors have an egg and it's in a place where nesting behavior can be viewed, the duty of Peregrine Fund field biologists is simply to observe. Some days, this means several hours of watching nothing. Other days, the nest site is a flurry of activity as the male and female condor take turns brooding the egg.

Small observations such as the timing of an exchange and how long each adult condor incubates the egg can tell biologists a great deal. If both condors leave, the egg most likely failed. The staff of the Peregrine Fund

The endangered California condor has a made a tremendous comeback from the brink of extinction, with dozen of condors flying free over the Grand Canyon, other parts of northern Arizona, and southern Utah. *Photograph by Chris Parish, courtesy of the Peregrine Fund*

watches for these things. And watches. And watches. Sleeps, eats, and watches some more.

Their work includes tracking, through the use of telemetry, radio signals emitted by devices attached to the birds. Grand Canyon visitors sometimes see Peregrine Fund employees and volunteers as they record the movements of individuals within the condor population using this method. But condors are viewed firsthand as well, in remote areas of the Grand Canyon such as caves—often several hundred feet above the base of a cliff—where Peregrine Fund staff members watch for nesting and other behavior.

The release of condors into the wild begins at a site at the top of the Vermilion Cliffs, north and east of the Grand Canyon. There, Peregrine Fund workers keep the condors in a pen to acclimate them before releasing them—thus the need to carry in calf carrion to feed the birds once they are released. Parish and others work to monitor the birds and keep them out of trouble, which proves challenging.

Condors are curious by nature, and are drawn to the colorful clothing, possessions, and movement of people. South Rim visitors often watch condors watching them. Parish has to beware of condors showing too much comfort around humans. In fact, several times condors have found their way into campers' tents.

While it proves to be a lot of work to keep track of California condors in such rugged country and it can be a challenge to keep the birds out of trouble, the hope is to have a self-sustaining population in Grand Canyon country in the near future.

⊰ ✦ ⊱

As I stare up at the aerial display of California condors circling over Pipe Creek Canyon and think of all the work that goes into helping these birds, I hear singing.

Young girls' voices rise from the land. They sing "Ave Maria." I stay reclined and listen for a moment, but I want to stand. I want to learn whether the voices really exist or are some kind of heat-induced hallucination.

I walk a few feet until I see the trail. There, a group of four girls—young teenagers—sings to O'Neill Butte.

They try to sing loud enough so their voices will echo from the face of rock. They come from a Catholic school in Southern California. They are hiking to Phantom Ranch, where they plan to stay in the bunkhouses as part of a long-planned trip.

Our lives intersect here, at this place. They keep singing, their voices rising and falling: "Ave, ave, ave Maria! Ave Maria, gratia plena. . . . Maria, gratia plena. . . ."

O'Neill Butte gets attention.

The condors keep gliding.

We all remain at the tawny heart of the moment.

I lift my backpack and slip it onto my shoulders. *This*, I think, *is why I will never stop coming to the Grand Canyon.*

It is the magic of happenstance.

It's a resonating scene where human meets uncompromised land. Where animals move and there are no human barriers. Where Earth is made whole again.

No other trail in the Grand Canyon offers the same kind of moments, the same kind of scenes that emerge along the South Kaibab Trail. The South Kaibab breaks the trends of all other canyon trails. Other trails follow side canyons and fault lines, the flat tops of mesas and esplanades. The South Kaibab defies such topography by dropping along a ridgeline and then plummeting down a series of seventeen switchbacks known as the Red and

Whites, all the time remaining a wide open trail. This, compared to the Bright Angel Trail, which falls into shadow on large swaths of its upper three miles in the winter, and plunges farther into darkness as it descends between narrow canyon walls.

A mile past the Red and Whites, the trail reaches the lip of the Inner Gorge. It does not enter the gorge via a drainage, the way the Bright Angel Trail does, the way the Hermit Trail does, the way the South Bass Trail does. Instead, it brushes by a place known as The Tipoff and zigzags its way to the river. It makes a 4,860-foot elevation drop—nearly a vertical mile—in 6.48 miles. This is the shortest route to the bottom in the central canyon, but with no water and little shade.[1]

Because of this different line, the South Kaibab Trail offers near-constant open views of the canyon. This is especially true after Cedar Ridge, a mile and a half down from the trailhead, which is located four miles east of Grand Canyon Village near Yaki Point.

The South Kaibab Trail features sections where the scenery of the canyon is a 360-degree spectacle. This is most prominent at a place called Skeleton Point, before the trail drops down the Red and Whites. The view extends upriver and downriver. A small path that runs west from the trail at Skeleton Point gives a glimpse of the Colorado and of Phantom Ranch. Such a scene is not offered on the Bright Angel Trail.

The South Kaibab Trail, in conjunction with the River Trail and the two bridges over the Colorado, provides a hiking circuit down from the South Rim and back up to the South Rim without stepping on the same trail twice. That two routes to the same destination on the same side of the Grand Canyon exist owes much to the interference of a man named Ralph Cameron.[2]

Cameron rose as a pivotal figure in Grand Canyon's early tourism development. He, his brother Niles, and business partner Pete Berry helped develop a prominent tourist route into the canyon on what became known

Formal portrait of Ralph Cameron, circa 1910. *Courtesy GCNPMC (#17700)*

as the Bright Angel Toll Road. In the early 1890s they loosely followed a Havasupai route from the rim down to Indian Garden. By 1903, they completed the Bright Angel Trail down to the river.[3]

The three men were part of an economic shift at the Grand Canyon. Seeing little money in it, prospectors stopped trying to mine in the massive canyon and instead turned to the enterprise of tourism. Tourists began appearing in larger numbers following the 1901 arrival of the Santa Fe spur line to the South Rim. It reached the rim a hundred yards from the Bright Angel trailhead. Cameron and his partners reaped the benefits by charging one dollar for passage on their "toll road." Then, Cameron turned an area with a spring that had been used by the Havasupais into Indian Garden Camp.[4]

Thanks to his questionable mining claims, Cameron held on to the trail and camp through several alterations in governmental oversight. First the U.S. Forest Service assumed responsibility of the Grand Canyon, in 1905. Then, a 1908 proclamation by President Theodore Roosevelt further protected the scenic lands by designating them Grand Canyon National Monument, still under the management of the U.S. Forest Service. This gave the place added protection that involved increased regulations, which led to the scrutiny of prospectors, their efforts to capitalize on tourism, and their questionable mining claims.[5]

At the center of this conflict stood Cameron. For more than a decade, he staved off efforts by the government, the railroad, and other entities to seize the Bright Angel Trail from his control. He kept partial ownership of the trail after 1912, but it reverted to Coconino County by law in 1920. That did not end what became a grudge between private interests at Grand Canyon and the expanding role of the federal government to protect and oversee the national monument turned national park (in 1919).[6]

By 1920, Cameron's political ambitions resulted in his election as a U.S. senator for Arizona. Coconino County had continued to run the Bright Angel Trail as a toll road, charging for descending mule trips even after

Congress designated Grand Canyon National Park and the National Park Service began to oversee it. The park service convinced county residents to sponsor a referendum that would transfer ownership of the Bright Angel Trail to the national park. In exchange, the park service would put up money to build a highway from Williams to the Grand Canyon. It went to a vote.[7]

"Ralph Cameron used all of the influence he could to get the citizens of Coconino County to vote down the referendum," historian Mike Anderson says. "And they did. That so incensed the National Park Service, because they really hated Ralph Cameron by that time. They immediately—and I mean the next day—began building the South Kaibab Trail. They had already picked out a place where they could build the trail. They were really prepped to try to have a central trail to get around the toll road and therefore obviate the need for anyone to go down the Bright Angel Trail. They quickly built that trail after the referendum in November 1924 and finished by June 1925."[8]

This gave the park service unfettered access to the interior of the Grand Canyon and the river, as well as giving the Fred Harvey Company access to its recently built Phantom Ranch. But the Fred Harvey Company declined to use the shorter, toll-free South Kaibab Trail at first, as the company and the Santa Fe Railway had their own disputes with the National Park Service.

"Formally, the park service had control since they came in 1919, but informally the Fred Harvey Company and Santa Fe Railway were investing in things on the South Rim, and they had been running things for eighteen years," Anderson explains. "And they owned the utilities. They did not want to be told what to do. It took the park service most of the 1920s to establish . . . informal control over what was taking place in the park."[9]

As the end of the 1920s neared, nearly complete control of Grand Canyon National Park shifted to the park service. Three years after the vote on the Bright Angel Trail toll road, Coconino County turned over possession of the trail to the park service—a decision made by county officials without a referendum. In that same year, 1928, the park service helped fund the highway (today's Arizona Highway 64) from Williams to the Grand Canyon. Workers finished the road in 1932.[10]

Riders paying toll at Cameron's Bright Angel Toll Road trailhead, circa 1910. *Photograph by the Kolb brothers, courtesy of GCNPMC (#04744)*

The South Kaibab Trail is known for its history as a "political trail," a phrase Anderson uses to describe how it came to be. It also is known for being a trail built with great speed, completed from top to bottom in seven months. Despite the short duration in which it was built, crews still managed to make it a four- and five-foot-wide trail, with efforts to reduce steep grades and make it accessible to mules.[11]

While the Civilian Conservation Corps receives much credit for its trail-building skills and work, the crews working for the National Park Service at Grand Canyon established the standards of modern trail work when they designated the route and created the South Kaibab. Although the South Kaibab's slope has an overall steeper grade than the other Corridor trails, the original design for the trail included grades that were typically less than 18 percent, a relatively workable slope for stock animals and people.[12]

Workers constructing the trail—first called the Yaki Trail but later renamed for the adjacent national forest—moved fast. Dynamite was used to blast out many sections of the trail. Crews did get one break when they reached the Inner Gorge. Dave Rust had created a trail known as the Cable Trail, which ran up from the river to the Tonto Platform. The Cable Trail connected to the Bright Angel Trail, and therefore Indian Garden, via the Tonto Trail; one simply needed to walk west along the Tonto Platform to get there. And, the Cable Trail had already received improvements from the park service after the creation of the swinging bridge in 1921.[13] So it was simply incorporated as the bottom portion of the South Kaibab.

Despite the fact that some of the trail was already developed, the South Kaibab project was "dogged by severe weather problems, financial difficulties, and continual construction delays," according to National Park Service records.[14] "Progress was slow due to countless miscalculations regarding rock formations, and the project rapidly exceeded its budget."

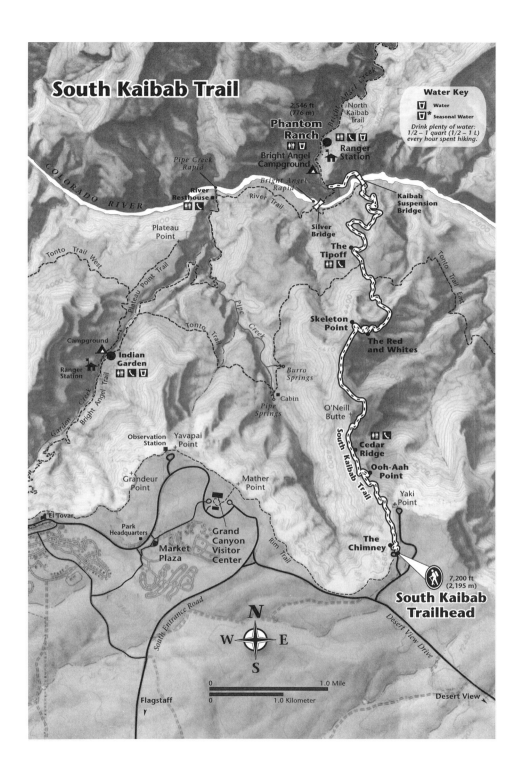

South Kaibab Trail

2,546 ft
(776 m)

North
Kaibab
Trail

**Phantom
Ranch**

**Ranger
Station**

**Bright Angel
Campground**

*Pipe Creek
Rapid*

COLORADO RIVER

*Bright Angel
Rapid*

**River
Resthouse**

River Trail

**Kaibab
Suspension
Bridge**

Plateau
Point

**Silver
Bridge**

Tonto Trail West

Plateau Point Trail

**The
Tipoff**

Tonto Trail East

**Skeleton
Point**

Pipe Creek

**The Red
and Whites**

Campground

Tonto Trail

*Burro
Springs*

**Ranger
Station**

**Indian
Garden**

Garden Creek

Bright Angel Trail

Cabin

*Pipe
Springs*

**O'Neill
Butte**

Observation
Station

Yavapai
Point

South Kaibab Trail

**Cedar
Ridge**

**Ohh-Aah
Point**

**Grandeur
Point**

Mather
Point

Yaki
Point

El Tovar

Park
Headquarters

**Market
Plaza**

**Grand
Canyon
Visitor
Center**

Rim Trail

**The
Chimney**

7,200 ft
(2,195 m)

**South Kaibab
Trailhead**

South Entrance Road

Desert View Drive

N
W   E
S

0   1.0 Mile
0   1.0 Kilometer

Flagstaff

Desert View

The South Kaibab Trail treats hikers and mule riders to a nearly never-ending panorama of the walls of the inner canyon. *Courtesy Grand Canyon Association*

This coupled with a lack of support for the construction of the trail. Employees of the Santa Fe Railway and the Fred Harvey Company went so far as to make fun of the trail. Such jabs made it into the local newspapers, and carried suggestions of imminent failure of the trail project.[15]

Even with all of the construction problems and ridicule, the National Park Service completed the trail in June 1925. It cost $73,000 to build, more than $30,000 over the original estimate.[16] Despite the cost and the opposition, the trail was dedicated and heralded by the park's then-superintendent, Miner "M. R." Tillotson. The trail, the Kaibab Suspension Bridge, and other inner-canyon infrastructure developed under Tillotson, who had a civil engineering background.[17]

The first mule caravan traveled up the South Kaibab Trail from Phantom Ranch on June 26, 1925, but the next few years would show relatively quiet traffic. As 1930 neared, the Fred Harvey Company began to soften its feelings against the National Park Service and took advantage of a trail much shorter—and less icy in the winter—than the Bright Angel Trail.[18]

Still, the South Kaibab Trail remains a maintenance challenge for the park service. The route it takes is beleaguered by rockfalls, steep sections plagued by runoff, and, despite the hard work of those who constructed it, sections of trail instability. A nonstop circuit of mule trains, loaded with weight, have rutted the South Kaibab Trail and abused it for much of its length. In recent years, the National Park Service has worked to upgrade it.

☿ ✢ ☽

To understand trail maintenance is to understand the nature of water. Water is an enemy to trails. In the Grand Canyon, it sloshes off the rim and down drainages in flash floods. Snowmelt eats trail. Freeze and thaw breaks down retaining walls. Water and gravity work to destroy trails just as they work to form the canyon, day by day, year by year, decade by decade.

When a summer monsoon storm breaks at night, trail field supervisor Rich Geopfrich struggles to sleep. He can imagine the runoff ripping through trails and walls. He might visualize a section of newly rehabilitated trail obliterated. He might get a call to assist with a pipeline break, the severed artery's flow eating out a part of the trail. Weather's violence and chaos can take out days and months and years of human work in seconds. All Geopfrich and his fellow trail crew can do is rebuild. And rebuild and rebuild.

After years of simply maintaining, simply responding to damage and repairing it, in 2009 the staff at Grand Canyon National Park took advantage of a federal funding boost to rehabilitate the South Kaibab Trail. Long battered by mule traffic and water and gravity, the South Kaibab needed extensive repairs. And, a better understanding of how to engineer trails in the Grand Canyon is giving crews a chance to improve the South Kaibab for the long term. It's not always just about fixing damage, it's also about making the trail better and safer.

It is the end of July, and Geopfrich and I hike down the South Kaibab Trail. We hike for less than a half mile to a section of trail that is receiving detailed rehabilitation attention. The two- to four-year project will not involve any major realignments and will work with the existing trail. But consider this: it will take two to four years to repair a trail that originally took seven months to build. The long time frame takes into account the process required to fix the trail right.

"This is a top section of trail that we have been working on for quite some time," Geopfrich says as he gestures to a length of trail. We stand to one side as hikers pass. "It was severely damaged, and [many things] made it severely damaged. . . . For one, it's a pretty steep section. It's about a 17 percent grade through here. It was failing because of no structure in the trail." He points to areas of new construction where stones are wedged together to form a walkway that will be buried with dirt. Juniper logs with rebar holding them in place are spaced out to give the trail additional support. "The original trail did not have these retainer bars or this riprap subsurface to hold back the dirt to prevent erosion in the trail. These liner rocks [rocks on each side of the path] were falling into the trail because of the lack of structure."[19]

To rehabilitate the trail section, the crew first measures out an average grade using a string line. They work to make a singular grade over the length of the segment of trail to create something more workable and stable. "If it's an overall 17 or 18 percent grade, they'll take this 14 percent and bring it up to a 16 percent and take this 18 percent and bring it down to a 16 percent. It's called pulling the grade. We try to give the trail more consistency, because it helps reduce erosion," Geopfrich explains.

He adds, "We can't change the trail alignment, because you would have to cut out so much and the amount of earth you would have to move would be very difficult [to move] with a shovel. So we have to build within the existing trail line. And it wasn't maybe totally thought out when it was first built. They were just looking for the natural breaks in the rock."

Along with pulling the grade, the trail crews use the most updated trail work science to determine how far to space out the logs, which are juniper harvested from a drought-damaged stand near Ash Fork, Arizona. The log placement is based on the steepness of the trail and how much erosion occurs in the area. When they run the string line, each log should be spaced out perfectly and evenly to further reduce erosion. Then, a drainage ditch is cleared on one side of the trail. Water must exit the slope without damaging the trail. This is done with rock "water bars" that channel the water down into the canyon.

It would seem like water events could cause the logs to suffer damage and rot, but Geopfrich said the logs, once buried in dirt, can last up to fifty years. The challenge is keeping dirt on the logs, especially with the mule trains. "As soon as it gets exposed, those mules' hooves work it. They're like little shovels. If you go down to Ooh-Aah [Point], you'll see where they have worn down the bedrock. Still, the logs are quicker to install, and they do last longer in the dry climate. Stone lasts [much] longer, but it shifts more easily. Ideally, you'd have one log across the trail with no joints."

This approach to rebuilding trail has evolved during the last twenty years as trail supervisors such as Geopfrich study the way water eats trail and where design approaches succeed and fail. "The technique isn't by any means perfected, because it is difficult to deal with erosion in the Grand Canyon. We battle erosion the way a firefighter fights fires. To do this, we're running string lines, tape measures, and line levels. We're pulling out all of these tools where we're really getting down to the inch. We're using riprap stonework, and the example of what we're doing here is what we're doing everywhere."

Modern Grand Canyon National Park trail crew shore up a rock retaining wall.
Courtesy NPS

While the work is measured in inches, it still requires labor and heavy-duty tools. The trail crew utilizes picks, shovels, firefighting rakes known as McClouds, long metal poles known as rock bars, and double-jack and single-jack sledgehammers. These manual tools are joined by a number of gas-powered tools, including chain saws to cut and shape the logs; a gas-powered drill used to bore holes in the logs, called by its brand name, Tanaka; and a pionjar, or stone drill. The drills in particular require specialized safety training, and all trail crew members regularly participate in rigorous safety retraining programs.

Trail crew work demands more than a typical job requiring physical labor, as workers must hone certain skills and adapt to the demands of the Grand Canyon both in its physical and logistical challenges. "An example of a skill required in Grand Canyon trail work is masonry. Dry-stone masonry is something all of our trail crew members need to know," Geopfrich explains. "They don't have to build a stone wall so perfect that it's a monument to themselves, but build it for the structural integrity that the trail needs. They also have to know the different trail features that go into the trail to make it functional. They have to know how to operate equipment. They have to know the different logistics the Grand Canyon calls for, such as packing mules and working around livestock as part of a job. They have to know how to work with the helicopters, which can be involved. And, along with all of those skills, they need the physical strength [to do] the work."

Employed trail workers—with all of their advanced skills and training—are often joined by conservation group workers or volunteers. In season, the work is handled by as many as forty trail crew employees of Grand Canyon National Park and thirty conservation group workers or volunteers. The two primary volunteer corps are the Coconino Rural Environmental Corps and American Conservation Experience. ACE teams are composed of volunteers from other countries who come on three-month work programs in national forests and parks. Although they work mostly as unskilled laborers, their contributions have helped with the unending task of maintaining the Corridor trails.

As we stand less than half a mile from the top, Geopfrich shares one of the great challenges of maintaining the Grand Canyon's trails, that is, the hike in and the hike out to a location before starting the work. Places like the one where we stand tend to get more maintenance attention because they are closer to the trailhead. Some areas closer to Phantom Ranch, where warmer temperatures allow trail crews to make repairs in the winter, also get attention. But the two to four miles in the middle are a different story. However, the 2009 injection of funding to upgrade the South Kaibab Trail is changing that.

Geopfrich explains how the trail crews have started to work from spike camps at places such as Mormon Flats, three miles down the South Kaibab Trail. "For the spike camps, we'll bring them in with a helicopter. We'll have camping gear and other supplies flown in and supplement their food and additional gear with the mules. So the crew will hike in the first day. We'll do a nine-day work tour with five days off, rinse and repeat. They'll have seven days to bust out as much work as they can get out in a day. Then, on the last day, they'll break down their camp and cache it real good and hike out. We leave everything down there for as long as the spike camp is down there. And that camp will be there for two months. This way, they are not spending a part of their work day hiking in three miles and hiking out three miles."

Only certain types of people gravitate to a career as a Grand Canyon trail crew worker. Hard labor, fierce heat, and long days toiling in the dust are all part of the challenge. As Geopfrich says, "It's not just a job. It's a lifestyle. [The trail crew employees] love what they do. It's about being where they are. They love the resource. They love to hike and stay physical and work with their hands. They love working on the trails and making it a better experience for the visitors."

The trail crew strives to rehabilitate and sustain paths into the Grand Canyon so people do not even think about them. The trails should have such a tread and such a grade that anyone on foot can pick their cruising speed and move into the canyon and not have to watch their feet. They can keep their eyes on the canyon around them. With a wide, easy-to-navigate trail in place, all manner of Grand Canyon explorer can enjoy the inner canyon—including the growing number of ultrarunners.

⊣ ✦ ⊢

Night is erased from the edges of the sky on a May morning. The sun prepares to transform the canyon. The bluer tones of dawn will soon lift and reveal the earthy colors soaked into the rocks. Into the soft morning light, six friends set off on the South Kaibab Trail. Among these friends are sixty-year-old Dan Williams of Lafayette, California, and forty-four-year-old Tamara Buckley Johnson of Pleasant Hill, California.[20]

They strike down the series of switchbacks in the Chimney at the top of the trail. They pick up a good pace as the trail straightens out for longer sections and heads toward Ooh-Aah Point. The group is on the move, one mile turns to three and four miles as morning erupts around them. They cruise in running shorts and shoes. They carry nothing more than a small daypack with a water bladder and some pockets for snacks.

They endeavor to run from the South Rim to the North Rim, then back to the South Rim. This accounts for forty-four miles of running, down and up the Grand Canyon twice. Like many rim-to-rim-to-rim runners, they begin their journey on the shorter and steeper—and hotter—South Kaibab Trail. With this start, they can reach Phantom Ranch in less than two hours, rest and grab water, then run the fourteen miles up to the North Rim.

Williams and Johnson run with Team Diablo, named for the Diablo Valley in the East Bay area of California, northeast of Oakland. The loosely affiliated team is made up of two dozen ultrarunners and trail runners.

They plan various runs and trips, and participate in running challenges, sometimes with distances reaching a hundred miles.

Those longer running events are usually assisted with water stations and support staff, but in the Grand Canyon, the runners are on their own. For most of the ultrarunners, running fewer than fifty miles of trail in a day—in as little as twelve hours—is not an overwhelming challenge. So the distance sparks little concern. The Grand Canyon's challenge falls in its waterless stretches, like the nearly seven miles of the South Kaibab Trail; the sometimes debilitating heat of the inner canyon; and the elevation loss, then gain, then loss, then gain of running from one rim to the other and back.

"I turned sixty, and I just needed to do it," Williams notes. "Most ultrarunners want to run the Grand Canyon at some point in their lives. I thought, *It may be now or never*, and this trip was coming together. Really, it's not something you should do by yourself. So it's good to get some nutty friends together for a three-day weekend to do it."[21]

Williams explains that the ultrarunning community—informed by magazine articles and friends and Internet networking—knows about the rim-to-rim-to-rim run. They often understand the logistics, the particular difficulties of the run, and have good judgment of how they will fair with the experience. Williams is friends with runners who have done it twice, and he joined a previous trip that ran to the river and back in Havasu Canyon, a thirty-six-mile round-trip.

That served as a primer for the longer and more difficult canyon run. Each year, hundreds and possibly as many as a few thousand people set off to run across the canyon and, in some cases, back the other way. The National Park Service has no clear idea of the number of people who make this accelerated journey, as no permits are required and they are not staying or eating at Phantom Ranch. But most rangers agree the number has increased year after year as more people take on the challenge.[22]

Two rim-to-rim-to-rim trail runners move up the North Kaibab Trail. *Courtesy of the author*

On multiple backpacking trips and multiple nights at Corridor campgrounds, I have talked to many campers who mention the runners they see or meet on the trail. The question that floats around these conversations is why. Why run through one of the greatest natural wonders of the world? One ranger jokes that it's like running as fast as you can through the Sistine Chapel.

"With the Grand Canyon, I would not backpack something that is easy to run in the sense that the trail is fabulous," Williams explains. "It's never narrow or hard to navigate, and it's mostly in good shape. Running the trail allows me to see a lot of the Grand Canyon in one day. I still enjoy it. I still look at all of the trees and plants, and I can soak it all in as I'm going by."

Williams and his running partners have emerged as a different canyon breed. Like river runners, who have created a lifestyle and mentality that revolves around two- and three-week-long trips, endurance runners arrive at the canyon with a different mind-set than the average visitor. Their trips prove to be the opposite of river trips. Instead of a trip measured in days, they want to measure their trip in hours.

"My answer is that I chose the right parents," jokes Williams when sharing why he is physically capable to take on such a challenging run and has the mental fortitude to do it. "I am genetically predisposed to being a long-distance runner; my max VO2 is much higher than average. I chose trail-running because I love the outdoors—and I am crazy. I like running hundred-milers, and that's a real sense of accomplishment. Physiologically, I can run. So I am drawn to it."

On their May run, the members of Team Diablo set their own pace and take on the Grand Canyon on their own terms. Williams chooses not to run to make his best time. Later, a trail runner friend's first question of Williams will be, "What was your time?" Not "How did you enjoy the Grand Canyon?"

"I was not going to run it as fast as I could," Williams says. "It could've been a once-in-a-lifetime experience. We spent an hour at Phantom Ranch just taking a break and enjoying it."

Still, one of the members of the trip experiences a difficult moment. Johnson is a longtime runner who in 2008 finished fourth place overall for women in the Angeles Crest 100-Mile Endurance Run in Southern California's San Gabriel Mountains. But as she runs down from the North Rim and passes Phantom Ranch for the second time, she turns ill and has to stop. She vomits a couple of times. "I was really challenged," Johnson admits, despite her training and stamina. "I wish I would have been a little more careful. The ranger thought I drank too much water. I felt like I was pretty good about salt and water. But there's too much sweating, and maybe I did not have enough water at the right time."[23]

Williams finishes his trail run on the South Rim, but he does not celebrate. "I was concerned about Tamara. . . . I thought [she would] catch up with me. I could not celebrate, because I was worried about her." Luckily for the members of Team Diablo, Johnson's sickness passes and she finishes her run. She joins the others in the observation of a major accomplishment—running back and forth through one of the planet's most challenging landscapes.

᚛ ✚ ᚜

The relative quality of the Corridor trails overall—and the trail infrastructure, shorter length, and alternative route of the South Kaibab Trail in particular—attracts another kind of Grand Canyon obsessive: the day hiker or backpacker who returns many times over to hike the Grand Canyon.

Gerd Nunner moved from Germany to the United States as an adult in 1990 and now makes his home in Santa Fe, New Mexico. He visited Grand

Canyon National Park in the nineties, but never thought to hike it until some friends suggested in November 2000 that he explore the Inner Gorge. He approached that first hike with all the experience of his youth climbing the mountains of Europe—including Mount Blanc in France and the Matterhorn on the Swiss–Italian border—and hiking the mountains around Santa Fe after moving to the United States. Nunner was overwhelmed with the majesty of the canyon on his first Grand Canyon hike, which he made at the age of forty-seven. "From that point, I just kept going back. After ten years of hiking the Grand Canyon trails, I have counted and I crossed the Colorado River 180 times."[24]

With Nunner's desire to cover as much ground as he can with each hike, he estimates that he chooses the South Kaibab Trail as his entry point 80 percent of the time. It's also his favorite trail in all of Grand Canyon. His favorite trail spot is also on the South Kaibab: Cedar Ridge—that rest area a mile and a half below the rim where great expanses of the Grand Canyon are revealed. He also embraces Skeleton Point, three miles down the trail, where the canyon views open up farther east and west and a short spur path reveals the first views of the Inner Gorge.

Nunner does not stay at these places long. He is a speed hiker who covers much ground. Not at the level of a rim-to-rim runner, he still manages to hike from the rim to the river on the South Kaibab Trail in as little as two and a half hours. What sets people like Nunner apart is the frequency with which they hike the canyon. In October 2009, following the completion of a dozen rim-to-rim-to-rim trips during the course of that year, Nunner completed a triple. He hiked from the South Rim to the North Rim, back to the South Rim, and then again to the North Rim. He completed this sixty-three-mile hike in twenty-six hours. The hike began at the South Rim at 7 am one morning and ended at 8:50 am the following morning on the North Rim.[25]

"It was just beautiful," Gunner recalls. "The night hiking was gorgeous because it was a full moon. I did a lot of hiking without a headlamp, and it was just incredible." He speaks of the joys and wonders of the hike but little of the difficulty. He only jokes, "Don't ask me if I'm going for the quadruple crossing."

He adds, "Really, after thirty-nine to forty miles of hiking, it is just . . . invigorating. I don't feel any pain. I don't get blisters anymore." Nunner has developed keen skills for knowing how much food and water to take, how much to eat and drink, and what seasons to hike. "I don't hike in the summers at all anymore," he notes. "It's just too hot and it's too crowded."

Friends and people he meets question his obsession with the Grand Canyon—actually one of two obsessions, as Nunner enjoys summiting Colorado's 14,000-foot mountains, known as the Fourteeners, in the summer. But he offers a plausible explanation. "One general thing is you might think I'm a nutcase. But the Grand Canyon, on any given day at any given hour, looks different. It has so many faces. And I'm planning my hikes in a way that the last two miles I hike in the sunset. I can't get enough of it. At that time of day, it looks like the canyon is going to sleep. As I hike it during that time, it feels like this is my canyon. It's so peaceful, it's unbelievable."

He adds, "People always ask me, 'Are you getting bored with this? Are you going to get bored with this?' I say, 'Never.' The Grand Canyon is always interesting—for the views, the animals, and for the people you meet out there."

When the hiking is over, Nunner travels to the community of Tusayan near the South Entrance to the park—mostly restaurants, hotels, and attractions—to sleep before traveling back home to Santa Fe. "At the Holiday Inn [Express], I always get the same room. I get room 338. It's like they've made it my room. At the pizza joint [We Cook Pizza and Pasta], I have a punch card. The canyon for me is home away from home."

Only one time did he sleep inside the Grand Canyon. He took a trip with his son, ten years old at the time, and they stayed at Phantom Ranch. Nunner likes to tell the story of how his son thought the Grand Canyon was so beautiful. He needed to spit but would not allow himself to because he thought the Grand Canyon was too beautiful to spit in.

Nunner prefers to keep moving in the Grand Canyon, to be awake in it and constantly watch its changing moods.

⊨ ✢ ⊫

On a November hike down the South Kaibab Trail, my friend Fred Calleri and I walk along the trail below O'Neill Butte. We descend steadily toward the leveled-out section of the South Kaibab known as Mormon Flats. We round a small corner, with Fred up front, and cross paths with an elderly man around nine o'clock in the morning. I know, moments ago, he hiked up the steepest and most demanding section, the Red and Whites. And yet he doesn't look winded. Instead, he moves with the energized spirit of someone younger than us.

"How's it going?" Fred asks.

"I'm fantastic!" he bellows and takes in a big breath. Without missing a beat he says, "Ask me how old I am."

"How old are you, sir?" Fred asks, with an attempt to match his enthusiasm.

"I am eighty-one years old!" he announces.

"Wow," Fred replies.

"Ask me how many times I have crossed the Grand Canyon this year," he commands.

"How many?" Fred asks.

"Forty-three and counting," he informs us.

Without any more prompting, he enters into a lecture. "People wonder how I do it. And I have a saying. It's 'Go light, go tight, and go right.' It's all about traveling with light gear and going with only what you need. It makes all the difference, especially in the Grand Canyon." Fred and I both nod, feeling foolish with big, bulky packs filled with forty pounds of gear— six pounds of mine is camera equipment. The elderly man looks over our packs, knows he preaches to the unconverted.

Then, as quickly as we meet him, he picks up his hike and moves along the red dust and rock of the trail. In moments, he disappears. Fred and I spend the next fifteen minutes talking about how old we feel meeting up with a man four and five decades our senior working on his forty-something hike across the canyon for the year. I know we just met the man, the legend whom everyone who knows the Grand Canyon talked about: Rim-to-Rim Maverick.

The early life of Laurent "Maverick" Gaudreau is known in small and varied increments. Allan Blair, a fellow hiker who joined him on several trips, says that Gaudreau served as an X-ray technician in the Army Air Forces in the West Pacific during World War II, earned a college degree to become a teacher to students with reading disabilities, and lived in Denver, Colorado, before moving to Grand Canyon National Park in his later years. His wife-to-be, Shirley Gaudreau, moved to the Grand Canyon from Fresno, California. Over time, the two became a well-known couple within the Grand Canyon Village community. Shirley worked for the Grand Canyon Association.[26]

Maverick ascended to canyon legend in many circles for both his hiking accomplishments and his age. He crossed the Grand Canyon more than eighty times one year. Unlike Nunner, his hikes usually involved an overnight stay, but nonstop hiking throughout the year from his late seventies until he was eighty-two caught the attention of many people. Phoenix news stations and metro newspapers in the Southwest often tracked him down to interview him for human interest and pure inspiration.[27]

Gaudreau entered rare company, the Grand Canyon hyper-hikers who rack up hundreds of miles in the gorge. Depending on how one measures hiking feats, he was only bested by a handful of people, the best-known being Harvey Butchart. Butchart, a Northern Arizona University professor who in his free time logged 12,000 pioneering miles in the Grand Canyon and made eighty-three summits, including twenty-eight first ascents up the canyon's temples, buttes, and mesas. He cataloged his forty-two years of adventures in a series of guidebooks and became the subject of an extensive biography, *Grand Obsession*, by Elias Butler and Tom Myers.[28]

Gaudreau had plans to co-author a book, as well as lend his name to energy drinks or nutritional supplements. His trajectory of becoming a celebrated and honored Grand Canyon figure—of becoming an esteemed part of Grand Canyon history—crashed on February 9, 2009.

The front page of the (Flagstaff) *Arizona Daily Sun* on the following day featured a story with these opening sentences: "Well-known Grand Canyon hiker Laurent 'Maverick' Gaudreau, 82, fired gunshots and called emergency dispatchers minutes before park rangers found him and his wife dead on Thursday, the Park Service said Monday. The investigation points to him as the apparent shooter of his wife, 73-year-old Shirley Gaudreau, before taking his own life, the Park Service confirmed Monday. Park investigators gave no motive. Nor would they discuss the contents of a call Maverick made to emergency dispatchers shortly before killing himself."[29]

In the period following the murder-suicide, friends, family, and longtime admirers of Gaudreau strained to piece together the tragedy. Many wondered how a man so upbeat and energized on the trail, a man known for a physical and mental fortitude that allowed him to cross the canyon hundreds of times in his old age, would kill his wife and himself. He was described by friends and family as being a kind husband, with no known history of abuse. Recognized almost wholly for his positive accomplishments, on track to be remembered for the physical efforts that defied his age, Gaudreau cut it all short and left a dark mystery.

His obsessive nature and restlessness might offer some clues. Newspaper reports following his death revealed that he carried on a struggle with alcoholism. He took "Maverick" as his name for Alcoholics Anonymous meetings during a time when he lived in Moab, Utah. Friends quoted him as using the phrase "If I was a drinking man, I'd drink to that." This combined with observations by friends that he was becoming senile. In the time leading up to the shooting, they noticed that he acted like he did not know certain people with whom he was well acquainted.[30]

After my first Maverick encounter, I met up with him one other time as I descended the South Kaibab and he ascended. The second time we met, he had just interacted with a recently retired couple hiking down for a stay at Phantom Ranch. His exchange with them sounded nearly identical to the one he made with Fred and me. And it happened only a short distance farther up-trail, closer to O'Neill Butte.

I saw Gaudreau two other times in addition to our meet-ups on the trail. The last was January 1, 2009, a little more than a month before he took his life and his wife's. On that date, he joined dozens of others for the May backcountry permit draw at the Backcountry Information Center. I hoped to schedule my rim-to-rim backpacking trip. He picked up the No. 1 ticket, which gave him an open calendar to schedule his rim-to-rims that month. I ended up with number twenty-eight. As soon as he lined up all of his trips, he walked quickly out and disappeared into the cold morning. When I talked to the backcountry employee, I asked about Gaudreau's dates. I hoped for a chance to meet him on the trail again, the only good place to interview a man such as him.

"I think you'll see him down there," the ranger told me with a firm nod and a smile.

≒ ✦ ≓

At 10:30 am my friend Greg and I rest at the point on the South Kaibab Trail known as The Tipoff during our October hike to the bottom. We sit on dirt studded with dark rocks near the hitching post for the mules. To our south rise the majestic walls of the South Rim. To our north, we see the walls and buttes that stand on the other side of the river.

"After a few minutes of hiking," I say to Greg, "we'll reach my favorite place on the South Kaibab Trail."

"Really?" he says. "Why's that?"

"Five things," I note, my speech well rehearsed from other trips. "First, it starts our descent into the Inner Gorge, and you enter a canyon within a canyon. Second, you really see the river and hear the river for the first time and realize that, seriously, there is a big river down here. Third, the geology is amazing. Fourth, you can look out and see a solid half mile of trail that cuts a long switchback through this red dirt. And fifth, the bottom is near; you can see it."

We see no one else, save for a French woman in her early thirties traveling solo. She takes a short break and moves on while we spend close to twenty minutes eating snacks and contemplating earth and sky. I ponder the different reasons I marvel at the South Kaibab Trail and share them with Greg. I note the short time it took to build a trail that barrels down to the river. I note, as everyone else does, the open views of the canyon, how it feels like an airplane descent into the gorge. I ascribe the South Kaibab with a killer instinct, the lack of water and exposure leading to the undoing of many canyon travelers on the hotter days.

I also add that, even traveling at a steady pace, with backpacks and plans to take the long way using the River Trail, we will arrive at Phantom Ranch by noon. "A Grand Canyon expressway," I say, although I'm not a fan of comparing trails to roads.

"A scenic bypass," Greg adds. And it's a perfect description.

We shoulder our packs and migrate to the bottom.

CHAPTER 10

THE BRIGHT ANGEL TRAIL:
Walking Highway

By 2:15 am on a Monday morning in August, Ty Modisette and Mark Minges have already rounded up twelve mules from the corral and have saddled each one. Two of the mules wear riding saddles, the others have on pack saddles. The sliding door to one of the stables rattles open, and the two mule handlers begin to lead the animals into the main part of the mule barn.[1]

Lead mule packer Jeff Pace steps into the barn, bleary eyed in the earliest hours of the morning. He looks over the food, gear, and supplies destined for Phantom Ranch. They are spread across the floor of the barn and loosely separated by weight. The food represents the majority of the load.

Pace, who works for concessioner Xanterra Parks & Resorts, surveys the food going down. It includes four gallons of red wine vinegar, a box containing two commercial-sized cans of peach halves, four gallons of pancake and waffle syrup, sixteen pounds each of chicken base and beef base, four boxes of frozen sausages, sixty pounds of frozen corn, 176 apples, and fifty pounds of pancake mix. Each box is marked with a "PR" for Phantom Ranch.

A string of pack mules carrying mail, trash, recyclables, and other material start out from Phantom Ranch bound for the South Rim. *Courtesy of the author*

Personal packages join the food. One delivery is a three-foot by two-foot cardboard box marked "Down to Phantom for Ross, no rush." Three backpacks and two duffel bags are in the pile as well, tagged with red labels. They belong to Phantom Ranch guests who have paid to have them carried down by mule so they can hike in with a lighter load.

Separate from the supplies for Phantom Ranch, five sets of saddlebags are lined up near the south barn wall. Each leather pannier holds a fifty-pound sack of alfalfa cubes. This is mule feed, carried down to Phantom Ranch so all of the mules can eat following the long trek to the bottom.

Modisette and Minges bring the mules out one and two at a time. The men's spurs click on the concrete floor, the bridles jangle, and the sound of clopping hooves fills the barn. The handlers tie the animals to a line and give each one a plastic feed bucket filled halfway. Pace looks over the mules in this two-part pack string: Blue, Cedar, Two-Step, Buffy, Simpson, Fooler, Reba, Bart, Jody, Cher, Shasta, and Holbrook. Nearly all bury their faces in their feed bucket. The exceptions are Cedar—who is chewing on her rope and getting into trouble—and Holbrook. Holbrook decides to gnaw on the wooden barn slats. After several minutes, the cold barn is warmed by the body heat and breath of a dozen animals.

Modisette loads Bart, Jody, Cher, Shasta, and Holbrook. Each of these mules will carry down two bags of feed. Modisette hoists a bag up and loops the handle onto a saddle post. He picks up a second bag and loops it onto the opposite side of the mule. He works his way along the row. Minges takes on the bigger challenge of loading up the mules with duffel bags and Phantom Ranch supplies. He needs to balance each load. On Simpson, Minges adds a weighted bag to one side just to get the balance right. If the load is uneven by more than a pound, the long, pounding ride down the trail might pull things too much to one side and cause a loss of cargo.

For each mule, Minges unfolds a sheet of canvas and pulls it over the supplies. He then secures the canvas with a rope, tossing it over and pulling it underneath each mule, all the while making a clicking sound with his tongue to get the animal to step one way or another.

As Minges finishes, Modisette begins to tie his five mules together to form a string. Although he recently started his job, Modisette works steadily and without hesitation. He possesses skills that all of the mule handlers possess. Modisette grew up on a ranch in New Mexico. He has worked around stock animals all his life. He, Minges, and Pace understand the nature of mules. They know their behavior. They recognize what the cock of an ear or the flip of a tail might mean. They can second-guess the animals' reactions to most situations. On-the-job training is not enough to turn someone into a top-notch mule handler. It takes years of collective experience around stock animals to ride and handle them with confidence, to navigate a string of mules and the 1,700 pounds of supplies they carry into the Grand Canyon.

⊰ ✢ ⊱

At 9:20 am on an early fall day, twelve mules—two saddled for riding, the others carrying supplies—arrive at Phantom Ranch. The wranglers take them behind the canteen and tie them to hitching posts. Jeff Pace has led the team down from the rim via Bright Angel Trail, serving as an alternate route for pack mules during South Kaibab Trail rehabilitation work. Five Phantom Ranch employees greet Pace and the mules and begin to unpack. One of the employees takes out a pencil and paper and begins to note every box or bag of food as it is unloaded.

The employees quickly carry off the perishable food and take it straight into the walk-in refrigerator/freezer known as the Montana Room. They stack the nonperishable food—from beets to potatoes to boxes of pancake mix—on a long table just outside the canteen's back entrance. The mules flick their ears and tails and one of them shakes his head as the wranglers lift the weight out of their pannier bags and stack it on the ground or hand it to one of Phantom Ranch's employees.

In fifteen minutes, the staff finishes the unloading and sorting. The employees move the nonperishable food inside and go back to other tasks, including laundry and cabin cleaning. Laura Tibbetts, the assistant manager, notes the staff's gratitude for the mules and their handlers. "The mules play a big part in keeping this place going," she says. "The only other alternative for getting supplies here is by helicopter, and we would not want to do that for daily deliveries because it's noisy and it can be dangerous."[2]

The helicopters do bring down supplies in rare circumstances. They sometimes deliver large items such as mattresses. But the mules carry down the bed frames. Tibbetts particularly loves to see the mules carry down Christmas trees, which happens each year at the start of the holiday season.

The work at the top and arrival at the bottom complete a supply mule and mule handler's day. Their efforts keep Phantom Ranch operational 365 days a year. But these are not the only mule trains that head into the canyon. Mules and wranglers also bring down visitors each day, year after year.

The tradition of mule supply trains and tourist trips into the Grand Canyon dates to the Bright Angel Trail's earliest days.[3] The Bright Angel served primarily as a mule- and horse-riding route for the first six decades of its use. From 1900 to 1910, Grand Canyon tourists rode down the Bright Angel Trail on horses, but the animals proved too skittish for the perilous descent into the canyon. Around 1910, Bright Angel guides switched to mules and helped establish the hearty animals' link to the Grand Canyon. "In the early days, people just did not hike," notes historian Mike Anderson. "There were no hikers or backpackers. The tourists rode. Everybody rode in America. Hiking was not a popular pursuit. So all of our early photographs of tourists are typically of them on stock."[4]

In the late 1960s and 1970s, the hiking and backpacking craze moved more people to take on the Grand Canyon by foot. From that point on, of the people who stayed overnight in the Grand Canyon, more hiked in than rode a mule. Mules stopped descending to the river from the North Rim by the 1980s; after that time North Rim mule trips were limited to the three-mile excursion to Supai Tunnel and back and to rides that stay on the rim.[5]

From the South Rim, families, retirees, and people of all ages and nationalities continue to ride mules into the Grand Canyon and down to Phantom Ranch for the sheer experience of it. "When you hear of something and know of something as deeply rooted in Americana as these mule rides, that's the draw," notes Steve Oredsen, a mule guide at Grand Canyon. We relax in the mule barn office on a well-worn sectional sofa that invites long sits with visitors. "Once that draw takes place, it stirs the inquiry. It stirs the imagination. Then people get the reality of actually sitting up and riding the mule and experiencing the canyon."[6]

He continues, "Riding the mule gives you the opportunity to have two experiences: the mule ride itself and the chance to look around and see the canyon in a way that's different from a hiker. A hiker has got his hands full, as his life is in his feet's hands. The mule rider can get the chin up and the eyeballs open in a way the hiker can't. The hiker has to stop to look around more. It's a whole lot different experience from that standpoint. But the mule rider doesn't feel the dirt under his feet. It's a whole different feel as far as I'm concerned."

No one can know how content or discontent mules might feel toward their work and all the gear they carry while descending and ascending the canyon's trails. But everyone who works with the mules senses some level of contentment—or sense of purpose—in the animals. "These mules are bred for working," Oredsen observes. "I don't think they stand around and reason and consider. But I do think there's something deep in their spirit that tells them they have a mission and a job to do. I think that gives them purpose. I have seen dogs, cats, and animals of all kinds without purpose. They seem to go flat mentally. We don't see these mules go flat. They are active in their mind and body all of the time."

The Bright Angel Trail and its nearly nine-mile descent from the South Rim to Phantom Ranch—including a portion of the River Trail—shares much history with the mules. Tourism ignited in the years following the 1901 arrival of the railroad line to Grand Canyon. It led to the growth of Grand Canyon Village. The Bright Angel Trail begins in the village, making it the most accessible of any of the trails. And while prospector, politician, and Grand Canyon businessman Ralph Cameron made improvements to the Bright Angel, it was originally a Havasupai route into the depths.[7]

"The Native Americans did everything on foot; they did not have stock animals," Anderson explains. "They picked places to go down into the Grand Canyon that were suitable to foot traffic. So, they could pick steeper routes. They even built ladders in places or leaned logs up against ten-foot cliffs so they could make a much more direct descent down into

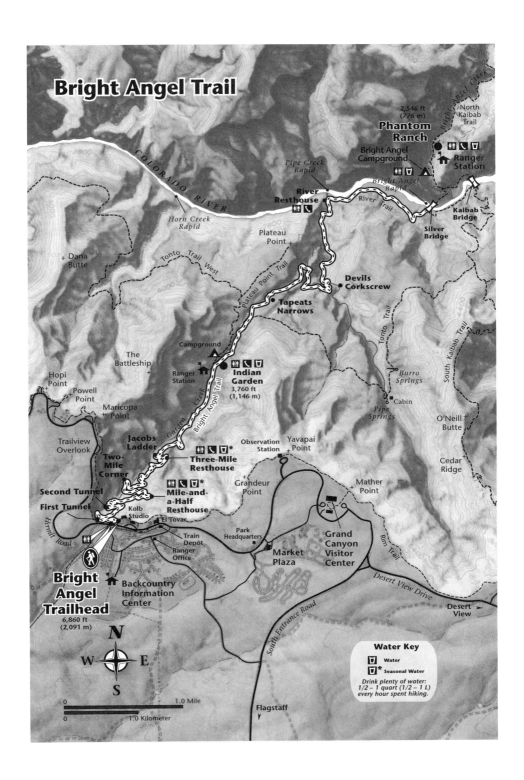

Bright Angel Trail

Phantom Ranch 2,546 ft (776 m)

North Kaibab Trail

Bright Angel Campground

Ranger Station

COLORADO RIVER

Pipe Creek Rapid

Bright Angel Rapid

River Resthouse

River Trail

Horn Creek Rapid

Kaibab Bridge

Silver Bridge

Plateau Point

Dana Butte

Tonto Trail West

Devils Corkscrew

Plateau Point Trail

Tapeats Narrows

Tonto Trail

The Battleship

Campground

Burro Springs

Hopi Point

Ranger Station

Indian Garden 3,760 ft (1,146 m)

South Kaibab Trail

Powell Point

Cabin

Pipe Springs

O'Neill Butte

Maricopa Point

Garden Creek

Bright Angel Trail

Jacobs Ladder

Observation Station

Yavapai Point

Cedar Ridge

Trailview Overlook

Two-Mile Corner

Three-Mile Resthouse *

Second Tunnel

Grandeur Point

Mather Point

First Tunnel

Mile-and-a-Half Resthouse *

Kolb Studio

El Tovar

Train Depot

Park Headquarters

Grand Canyon Visitor Center

Rim Trail

Hermit Road

Ranger Office

Market Plaza

Bright Angel Trailhead 6,860 ft (2,091 m)

Backcountry Information Center

Desert View Drive

South Entrance Road

Desert View

N W E S

0 — 1.0 Mile

0 — 1.0 Kilometer

Flagstaff

Water Key
Water
Seasonal Water *

Drink plenty of water: 1/2 – 1 quart (1/2 – 1 L) every hour spent hiking.

the canyon. And they did that. Every trail at the Grand Canyon except the South Kaibab Trail that I'm aware of follows a route Native Americans used before. But Native Americans did not build trail."

Anderson dispels the notion that prospectors and pioneers arrived at the Grand Canyon and simply began using paths created by Havasupais, who populated the canyon and migrated seasonally into the inner canyon to farm. Though Havasupais did use the route that became the Bright Angel Trail to access the area known as Indian Garden, where they used the springs to cultivate crops, they made no improvements to it. Prospectors, on the other hand, constructed trails, creating flatter grades and removing obstructions to accommodate pack animals.[8]

While Cameron and the county ran Bright Angel as a toll road during the early years, the park service finally gained control of the trail in 1928. Park service oversight led to great improvements. Right away the park service set aside $20,000 to begin construction of the newly acquired trail and sought to rebuild it to the standards of the brand-new South Kaibab Trail. From November 1929 to June 1939, National Park Service crews worked to reconstruct the trail as part of three different projects. During that ten-year period, the Civilian Conservation Corps arrived and built shelters and buildings along the trail, namely the Mile-and-a-Half, Three-Mile, and River resthouses, and structures at Indian Garden.[9] In the end, they had created what most park historians consider an entirely new trail from the one Berry and Ralph and Niles Cameron operated.

The reconstruction involved the ambitious rerouting of the Devils Corkscrew, a place where the trail climbs from the bottom of Pipe Creek and connects to the shallow canyon where Indian Garden sits. The new corkscrew bypassed a steep and relatively narrow route that nose-dived into Pipe Creek. A thin scar of trail to the north of the current trail shows the old way. The crew built the trail segment to a width of four feet and created grades of 16 percent or less. Much like the River Trail, crews needed to blast through granite to create the trail, though not as extensively. The one-and-three-quarter-mile the Devils Corkscrew formed an almost entirely new route from the old trail and cost $19,000 to construct.[10]

Little in the way of major construction took place between 1933 and 1938, but the third and final construction project was launched in February 1938 to finish the trail from Pipe Creek to the Colorado River. A park service trail crew constructed more of its standard four-foot-wide trail for the entire length of Pipe Creek below the bottom of the Devils Corkscrew. A reported 75 percent of this segment was carved into granite cliffs a few dozen feet above flood level. The crew completed the project in June 1939. While the River Trail, finished three years earlier, is considered the last trail built, the final work on the revitalized Bright Angel marks the last of the major trail realignments along the Corridor. In all of the years since 1939, trail work has focused on repair and rehabilitation.

᛬ ✛ ᛭

The Devils Corkscrew on the Bright Angel Trail. It sounds like the title of a country song.

Ascending this section offers hikers their first chance to put in some serious work, to begin toiling at the ascent from Phantom Ranch to the South Rim. The River Trail rises and falls in elevation for dozens of feet at a time, only offering a modest challenge. The trail up Pipe Creek to the base of the corkscrew gains elevation steadily as it moves up from the river but stays close to the side canyon's floor.

The corkscrew is a stairway.

Eight major switchbacks carry the trail from the bottom of Pipe Creek Canyon. The canyon floor serves as the point of liftoff. Progress is measured by how thin the trail running through Pipe Creek becomes. Water bars and stabilizers create small steps along the switchbacks. The corkscrew represents more than half of the 1,800-foot elevation gain from the river to Indian Garden. After the carved-out switchbacks, the trail uncoils for a long and steady ascent. It is a route notched in the Vishnu Schist and Zoroaster granite. It teeters along drop-offs and slips around tight corners. Each stretch opens new vistas.

On a rim-to-rim hike in May, I ascend the corkscrew in the 8 am hour. A canyon wren's call peals out from the drainage below. The temperature climbs while the sun makes its steady progress, now sitting on the lip of the rim high above. I keep up my pace to avoid the temperature spike I know is on its way. The nature of the high-pressure weather system promises to spare no one moving through the canyon.

I find solace in my pace. I can breathe. I can whisper to myself. I sing a song called "Go Places," the voice of Neko Case in my head. "Like Magic/ Play Aces/Stay with me/Go Places/Once more for the ages." As I trudge up the dark rock toward the sun, I imagine myself in the opening scenes of some epic fantasy movie. I can picture a dragon flying and clearing the cliff face above and swooping into the canyon below.

Instead, I encounter foot traffic. Two mule trains trudge down the switchbacks. I see them and hear them several minutes before they pass. Nine trail runners jog past during the time I am in the corkscrew, most wearing small water packs, silky running shorts, and ball caps. They breathe heavily and rush by. Most do not return my hello—they either nod or ignore me. Four teenagers talk loudly and, based on the limited amount of gear they carry and their conversation, I suspect they're going rim to river and back to the rim in a day. This, despite signs in multiple languages along the trail warning not to do this. The signs show a fatigued man and make emphatic use of exclamation points. Following the teenagers are three older couples looking prepared for at least a night at Phantom Ranch. Behind them and gaining fast are a college-aged man and woman. The man carries a dry bag on his shoulders—they're most likely meeting up with a river trip.

By the time I finish the corkscrew and enter into that shallow canyon that holds Garden Creek, I have passed all manner of trail humanity. I ponder whether to celebrate this. Too many days, the Bright Angel Trail feels crowded. It serves as the most traveled of all the trails descending into the Grand Canyon. Although the South Kaibab Trail provides a shorter distance from rim to river, it also requires forty minutes or more on a shuttle from Grand Canyon Village. At the South Kaibab trailhead, public parking is prohibited. The Bright Angel plugs right into the most visited area of the South Rim. It is visible from some of the viewpoints and is easy to find. Many visitors seem to have little awareness of the other trails into the inner canyon from the South Rim—South Kaibab, Grandview, Hermit, South Bass, Tanner, and New Hance trails among them.[11]

What further causes the Bright Angel Trail to stand apart from the others is that the park service recommends its use during the warmer months of the year, when most people visit the Grand Canyon. The Bright Angel, unlike the South Kaibab and others, offers more shade and more access to drinking water and creek water, helping adventurers stay cool and hydrated. Rangers such as Bil Vandergraff and others implore people to not even think about the South Kaibab in the summer, unless they do it as a night hike.[12]

But access remains the key reason for the Bright Angel's popularity. Hundreds of people descend at least part of the top mile of the Bright Angel each summer day. The number of people who walk even a short distance of the trail is hard to measure, but a good guess puts it in the hundreds of thousands out of the 4 million or more people who visit Grand Canyon each year. And the whole length of the trail becomes well populated with runners and people with more ambition from May through October, a period that includes the summer vacation season and the entire operating season of the developed North Rim.

Because of this, my early morning ascent from Phantom Ranch to Indian Garden feels like a parade. I find small, quiet moments to myself as I make a couple of Garden Creek crossings and listen to the clear water flow alongside the trail. But as I ascend further out of the notch in the earth and make the final half-mile approach to Indian Garden, I pass two families with pre-teen and teenage children and a group of seven women. All of them sound loud to me, chatting about topics from cell phone coverage in the canyon ("I wonder if we'll get any reception at all") to thoughts on other people not on the trip ("It's a good thing we didn't bring Shelly on this trip—she would have turned around a long time ago").

I suppress my desire to interrupt these conversations and sweep my arms across the view above us and the scene around us. To point to the cottonwood trees growing next to the pristine creek and say, "Forget about cell phone reception. Forget about Shelly." But I know people, including myself, are prone to small talk, caught in a cycle of chatting, expressing thoughts, and noting concerns about reception bars missing on cell phones. I remember moments on the trail with Wayne Ranney, who chooses to celebrate the people he sees on the trail. He notes that they are interested enough to break from the comforts of the rim and drop inside the canyon. That says something about them, far beyond the small talk.[13]

I still ponder quieter times on the Bright Angel Trail, at night or in the winter, when I can focus on the sheer beauty of one of the planet's most famous paths.

⊐ ✢ ⊏

February on the Bright Angel. Snow and ice cover the trail. The sky hangs, heavy gray, over the Grand Canyon, save for spotlights of sun striking locations in the distance. Dream fog hovers around the higher temples, such as Zoroaster and Brahma. Snow lies deep on the rim, and thins out at the edge of the Redwall layer, 2,000 feet below the rim.

I begin a solo hike, hazy with a head cold and a swirl of melancholy. I see no other hikers. Mule trains disappeared into the canyon long ago. I pick the Bright Angel Trail because it has better clearance than the South Kaibab Trail. The mules work like snowplows, breaking up the path and keeping it clear across its entire width. As of this writing, mules are not using the South Kaibab due to that trail's reconstruction.

I wear ice crampons and carry hiking poles for balance. I chug along, poles clicking and ice cleats digging in. I study the trail, a flat ribbon through slopes of deep snow, faint green from mule droppings. A storm moves in behind me, another low-pressure system riding in from the north Pacific. Depending on its track, it might mean another six inches of snow.

Some winters the snow near the rims piles pretty high. Trail crews had their hands full digging out the Bright Angel near the trailhead after a major snowfall in January 1949. *Photography by Eden, courtesy NPS*

I walk almost one and a half miles and pass no one going down or up. I suspect the snow and ice limit the number of day hikers. My timing—I started midmorning—might also serve as a factor. Most people going to Phantom Ranch or other deep canyon locations left much earlier, or chose the South Kaibab Trail for its shorter length and quicker drop below the snow line.

I finally pass two young men minutes before I reach Mile-and-a-Half Resthouse—a stone shelter built by the Civilian Conservation Corps with seasonal water and an adjacent bathroom. The men are saddled with seventy-pound packs and armed with step-in crampons, though they are wearing long-sleeved shirts and ball caps, not winter coats and hats. While the temperature stands at a shade above freezing, they are sweating. "Tried to go up . . . the North Kaibab," the blond man with a thin beard says. "It was waist deep at the Bridge in the Redwall. We turned around there."

I ponder this report, because the bridge is three miles down in south-trending, sun exposed Roaring Springs Canyon. Big winter has dropped on canyon country, with blizzards and other storms laying down as much as three feet of snow at a time. The South Kaibab and Bright Angel trails remained open and mostly passable despite this, with a few exceptions. "After the big storm," notes David Meyer of Phantom Ranch, referring to a weeklong record-setter that brought four feet of snow to the South Rim in January 2010, "there was a spot that developed just below The Tipoff, a slope of solid ice. Even the most experienced hikers were scared."[14]

Meanwhile, the North Kaibab Trail is more or less shut down beyond Roaring Springs.

Hikers and mules keep the two main paths from the South Rim open. But fewer backpackers in the campgrounds and fewer runners and ambitious day hikers on the trails make everything quieter. It is on this day in February that I hike the longest stretch of Grand Canyon Corridor trail in my life without passing a single person on foot or on a mule.

My solitude begins at Indian Garden, the halfway point between the South Rim and Phantom Ranch, four and a half miles from the rim. There, I wave goodbye to a woman waiting for her friend to finish using the bathroom. My solitude ends a little more than three miles later at the delta of Pipe Creek where it flows into the Colorado River. The pallor of the sky, the pecking of the rain, the turn of the switchbacks during the sharp descent in the Devils Corkscrew, and the darkness of the wet schist and granite make for a desolate stretch.

After close to an hour of hiking—through the shallow canyon of Garden Creek and down the corkscrew—I spot five hikers ahead of me, moving down the trail. The sighting makes me buoyant, and a feeling of order returns. After numerous hikes up and down the Bright Angel Trail during all months of the year, I expect to pass a person or a mule train with moderate frequency. Seeing no one for an entire segment of trail is rare, even in the wintertime.

I finish out the switchbacks to reach the bottom of Pipe Creek. I cross its small trickle and follow the trail on the eastern side of the stream. The nearly empty creek bed holds a wild tumble of boulders and thatch of shrubs and bushes thirsty for the creek's water. On the opposite canyon wall I spot a green strip of moss and other plant life a hundred feet high. At the top, a seep feeds the moss. I stop for a few seconds to appreciate it. To give thanks to the canyon's seeps and springs. I wonder if Pipe Creek earned its name from water figuratively piped here from different places: springs, the confluence with Garden Creek, seeps like the one before me, or perhaps the nearby transcanyon pipeline.

I only learn later it comes from a meerschaum pipe Ralph Cameron— the canyon entrepreneur who tried to maintain the Bright Angel Trail as a toll road—found along the trail. He supposedly carved a fake date in the pipe, a year in the early 1800s, as a hoax to convince friends that settlers had arrived long before them.[15]

I take a break to lash my hiking poles to my pack, given the lack of elevation gain or loss before me and no snow or bad trail. I walk with more of a bounce, my ice cleats shaking loose from where I strapped them to my pack. Their metal parts jangle. I close the distance to the river. I cross Pipe Creek two last times and see the resthouse near creek's end. Here, I cross paths with a young woman hiking solo.

"You're the first human I have seen since Indian Garden," I comment.

"That's a good thing, right?" she notes.

We pass each other. "More or less," I say with a shrug, "but kind of lonely when you're used to seeing people."

At the start of the River Trail, I run into the group of five I spotted from midway down the Devils Corkscrew. They are visiting from Columbus, Ohio. One man is retired and leads the other four, three of whom are schoolteachers taking advantage of the Presidents Day holiday and an administrative day, all together giving them a four-day weekend. They have an ambitious itinerary that involves catching a flight at 5 pm in Phoenix on the same day they wake at Phantom Ranch and hike out.

We stand and talk, and I point to the river. I explain how I seldom see it this way, filled with sediment from winter runoff, flowing red-brown. Rain dots the dark rock around us. I start off to continue my hike while the group of five strips off extra layers and uses the bathroom at the junction where the two trails meet.

Before I tread down the River Trail, I mentally give praise to the Bright Angel, its nine miles of winding glory—down into an amphitheater, through Indian Garden, through the shallow canyon of Garden Creek, down the Devils Corkscrew, and along the bottom of Pipe Creek.

Having walked nearly half the trail without passing a soul, I find myself meditating on the Bright Angel and the terrain it has led me through. In quiet times, in winter snow and rain, I cannot take the Bright Angel Trail for granted.

In a conversation with a work friend before one of my Grand Canyon trips, he scoffs at my plans to hike in and out on the Corridor trails. Like a number of outdoor-loving locals in Flagstaff, he calls them "tourist trails." He considers the routes boring and predictable, and suggests I get into the primitive backcountry—someplace like Nankoweap or the Bill Hall Trail or the trek to Royal Arch, all on the fringes and infrequently visited. In my work friend's mind, the Corridor trails—with their designated campgrounds with services, Phantom Ranch at the bottom, water stations, and emergency phones every few miles along the route—create too cushy of an experience.

The trip that follows that conversation proves otherwise. It shows that no matter the facilities offered to hikers, mule riders, and others, the power of the elements always rules in the Grand Canyon. And a nine-mile hike out of the great gorge is never cushy. On that October hike, steady rain betrays the Inner Gorge's arid soul. By our departure time the morning we are to leave Phantom Ranch, rain batters the canyon and turns relentless.

When my wife and our two friends Amy and Stephen cross the river on the Silver Bridge, we see below us roiling, creamy brown water specked with debris and swirling eddies. We make it to the other side, to the River Trail. My glasses become so fogged and wet that I have trouble seeing. A few times I take a moment to wipe the lenses clean with a handkerchief. With glasses clear, I spot a white thread from the Inner Gorge's rim to the river below. It is across the river and downstream.

A waterfall.

I marvel at it, releasing a small knot in my nerves, and breathe. But fear still drifts into my thoughts. We approach Pipe Creek, a major drainage. It is sure to be flooded. Ahead lies a swollen creek and its crossings. Decisions will have to be made.

Observe the flow.

Cross or wait?

Observe the flow.

Cross or wait?

The canyon feels closed in. I begin to view the place as one monstrous drainage system. When we turn the corner of the River Trail and walk into the mouth of Pipe Creek Canyon, we see it. The creek is swollen into a muddy churn. We do not have an easy way to get to the resthouse on the other side. I had hoped to enjoy a break from the rain in the shelter. Instead, we march on to the first creek crossing on the trail.

There, docile Pipe Creek has enlarged into a churning mess. It has expanded from a creek crossed in one big step to one a dozen feet wide.

I study the water for a few seconds. I see an eddy behind a rock. I figure the water is deep there, but slow. I take one step into the current and plant the next big step in the eddy. From there, the opposite creek bank is two more big steps away. I make it to the other side.

I turn back to my wife and our friends.

"It's fine," I yell. "Do-able."

With that, we hear the noise.

I think at first it is the rumble of thunder, but it remains constant and becomes louder. The sound fills the canyon walls and vibrates off of them.

A flash flood approaches.

I look to the water. The surface of the creek changes from longer waves to taut ripples, as if fish have launched into a feeding frenzy just below the surface. The creek widens and gouges out all of its safe passages.

My wife and I find ourselves divided.

She begins to cry.

"Don't cry!" I call out over the sound of the raging water, as a plea.

I've angered her because I crossed a flooded creek. I know it's dangerous. But I did not know, at that moment, that it would get worse.

I try to snuff my fears by noting the positives. We have escape routes on each side. I have a slope of rocks I could climb. Jane and our two friends could back out of the side canyon and onto the River Trail. I doubt we will need to take such drastic measures.

Mostly, we endure the pain of waiting. Of having our path severed by a flood.

Still, my fears linger. We stand inside a canyon with a flash flood coming toward us. I know what these things can do, how fast they change, how often they have killed.

Adrenaline pours into my blood.

Fight or flight.

But we can do neither.

Other backpackers and hikers gather on each side of the creek. Two men come up behind me, having just barely made the last crossing. "We'll just wait it out here," one man says to the other.

Three other backpackers fall in behind Jane, Amy, and Stephen. A small drama plays out as a college-aged woman with a large pack tries to climb a slanted rock to find a crossing place upstream. Twice she slips and nearly pitches herself backward into the roiling creek.

After several minutes of watching the liquid violence of the flood, I notice the tight ripples loosen in places. A chance for crossing looks to happen soon, should the water continue to slacken.

A trail runner comes up behind my wife and friends and all of the people on the other side. He skirts past everyone and makes a running leap into the creek. The current knocks him down but he keeps moving. He crosses.

We can do no such thing with large backpacks on. But the creek looks as if it is continuing to recede. Our friend Stephen—the least concerned of all of us—sees the stone that formed the eddy resurface. He crosses halfway to it and plants himself. "Okay! You can cross in front of me," he calls out.

This leads to a mass crossing of people on both sides. My wife and Stephen's wife go first. Stephen stays in the creek to help the others across, including the college-aged woman with the big pack and the two men on my side.

Jane and I hug and kiss.

She cries. She punches me in the chest.

I apologize.

More crossings of Pipe Creek await. With each one, we pick the best places to cross. Stephen accepts the mantle of creek sentinel. He plants himself in the creek each time and we cross in front of him.

As we make it to the Devils Corkscrew, we pass clusters of people. "How's the stream down there?" a teenage boy asks us.

"Running high," I say.

"Yeah, a bunch of us have been stranded by the creek up there." He points up toward Garden Creek.

I look to the sky, dark and pregnant with clouds. The rain retreats to a drizzle. I hope for a dry-out soon. Either way, I am glad to be moving out of the drainage. "C'mon, Hobbits!" Stephen yells as we hike out of the canyon. The rain, the mist, and the dark rock make it appear like a scene from *Lord of the Rings*. I imagine us hiking to Mordor. The rain picks up again. For the first time that morning, I welcome it. It keeps me cool as we vault up the switchbacks and reach the longer stretches of trail.

We hike a different canyon than I am used to. The rain washes away the memory of its bone-blanching nature. It feels lush, with tiny ribbons of waterfall running from its ledges. The sinister dryness is difficult to remember with the storm raking through. It makes me wonder about how Grand Canyon might look in another climate—in a temperate place. Would it have the same rocky dynamic? Or would much of its color and layers become muted by soil and loam and moss? Would people come to admire its views only to find the canyon socked in with rain and hidden under mist most days?

We trudge up the last leg of the Devils Corkscrew. We look over our right shoulders at the canyon below us. We make the last turn out of Pipe Creek Canyon and reach the shorter walls and intimate realm of Garden Creek's canyon. We handle a couple of crossings of the swollen creek, over our fears and impatience to reach our destination. The rain returns. This time, it pounds us. The water is determined to soak us through all our layers. My boots and wool socks turn heavy and soggy.

The approach to Indian Garden feels prolonged. We walk for fifteen minutes in the kind of rainfall that usually sends people running for shelter. We have no shelter to flee to. And our fleeing response is stayed by the thirty to forty pounds we each carry on our backs.

We reach Indian Garden as the rain recedes for a second time, this time diminishing from a downpour to a steady shower. The drops patter on leaves as we step over a pulsing stream of runoff and enter the campground. We drop our packs at our campsite.

Indian Garden Campground gives us one prime luxury: each site contains a ramada over a picnic table. Seeing the roof and dryness underneath makes us smile at one another. We no longer need to worry or care about the rain. I string up the rain fly from my tent to create a private spot where we can get out of our wet clothes. We take turns stripping bare and pulling on dry clothes from our packs. I change into my sport sandals, my cold and pale feet bare and my tendons stiff.

We use the rafters of the ramada to hang wet clothes and gear to dry. As we do this, the sky calls off the deluge. Within a half hour, we spot patches of blue and segments of rainbow in the distance.

I rub my arms through my long-sleeved faux-wool shirt to warm up and walk out to the wash that churned with runoff several minutes before. It has mellowed to a trickle. Winds pulse and pull around me. They carry off the fears and frustrations of the flash flood. We still have four hours of daylight yet to spend—to walk to Plateau Point, to wander under Indian

Garden's cottonwood trees, to stare off at the cliffs, buttes, and spires in the distance.

I return to camp, where my friend Curtis Anderson has arrived wearing a silly grin and a pack double the weight of mine. We met up along the South Kaibab Trail the day before and at Bright Angel Campground last night. Curtis is working as a guide for a group of men from India. For this reason, we have found little time to talk until now, at Indian Garden. Here, Curtis catches a short break. We talk of a night hike or a scramble on the old Bright Angel Trail.

I meet back up with Jane, Amy, and Stephen. A touch of hypothermia gives Jane the shivers. She climbs into her sleeping bag and I boil water and dump it into two water bottles, then tuck them in beside her. Her chills subside after about twenty minutes, and we opt for motion to keep ourselves warm. We vote to walk out to Plateau Point.

Stephen obsessed earlier about photographing a rainbow that arced above the whole of the canyon. We turn into rainbow hunters, determined to find that moment when the sun and rain paint the sky. The canyon is all beams and clouds and shadows. Mist drifts around temples. Spotlights of sun emerge and disappear.

We walk past fields of purple cacti and smoky-hued blackbrush. Despite the chill, I revel in the cloud cover. I know how hot most daytime walks to Plateau Point can be. We walk beneath a low roof of clouds, and I return to that reckoning place. Plateau Point.

The canyon appears calmer. Sublime. The pulsing arteries relax into trickles. The floods and waterfalls subside. Around our feet, dry spots appear on shelves of Tapeats Sandstone.

The Grand Canyon shifts back to its drier nature. We will wake up in the morning to a flawless sky. And, under it, plot our return home.

CHAPTER 11

INDIAN GARDEN AND PLATEAU POINT:
Magic in the Middle

I wake at noon after a second nap on a picnic table with my sleeping pad underneath me and a sack of clothes for my pillow. I stare at the beams and pitch of the small ramada above me at my Indian Garden campsite. I hear voices of people as they walk up or down the Bright Angel Trail, about fifteen yards away. I hear the conversations of other campers, some newly arriving and others who spent the previous night here.

On my May solo trip, the temperature hovers around a hundred. I am a refugee of the sun. I finished my hike from Phantom Ranch to Indian Garden by 9 am. I left behind the escalating heat of the Inner Gorge and timed the hike to mostly avoid the touch of sunlight. I struggle to break a restlessness that comes with arriving at Indian Garden this early and knowing only four-and-a-half trail miles to the rim lies before me. I could reach the top by the end of the lunch hour. Instead, I will spend the day ducking the sun and making use of my canyon time, and save the hike for the earliest hours of the next morning.

My camping permit for Indian Garden gives me another day in the canyon, another day of disconnecting from the upper world, and another day to observe bony rock and fleshy biology. Few places relax me into a perfect lull the way Indian Garden does. Towering walls of Redwall Limestone and the rock layers stacked above them cradle this halfway place between top and bottom. Cottonwood trees shade the campground, the picnic tables for day visitors, the mule corrals, and the small buildings that dot this oasis. In the understory, all manner of small trees and shrubs, even patches of grass, create a lush and pastoral realm.

To the west of the developed area runs Garden Creek, a few inches deep and five feet across in places. A small dam of stacked rocks holds back the creek, forming a two-foot-deep soaking pool. I get up from my nap and walk the five minutes it takes to reach this spot by the creek. On the other side, the Plateau Point Trail picks up and heads a mile and a half to the edge of the Tonto Platform. Another trail breaks from the Plateau Point Trail, the west Tonto Trail. It continues its fifty-mile east–west run through the Grand Canyon. When the east and west sections of the Tonto Trail are counted together, the trail stretches ninety-five miles from Red Canyon to Garnet Canyon.[1]

I sit at a picnic table and listen to the quiet talk of the creek as it finds channels to get through the stacked-rock dam. I might normally soak in the pool or wet myself down on such a hot day, but I have just changed out of sweaty clothes into dry ones and am sticking to the shade instead. With the slight breezes, I feel more warm than hot. I find equilibrium. I watch small brown birds flit around on the ground and along the creek. I hear more voices in the distance, but they stick to the Bright Angel Trail and to the benches and bathrooms next to it. I sit and think of Indian Garden as a crossroads. The Bright Angel Trail runs north to south. The Tonto Trail comes in from the east and exits to the west. The Plateau Point Trail unfurls to the north, a short distance west of where the Bright Angel follows Garden Creek down to the Devils Corkscrew.

For this reason, Indian Garden feels like a staging ground. Backpackers coming down into the canyon might use it as a relatively easy-to-reach first destination. Backpackers also use Indian Garden to break up the hike out. Instead of going nine miles from Phantom Ranch to the top, stopping at Indian Garden allows for a more manageable ascent over two days. In the cooler months, it provides a chance to spend more time at Phantom Ranch before beginning the climb to the halfway point. In the hotter months, it means not having to finish out a hike to the top in the heat of the afternoon. And anyone hiking out can relax at Indian Garden and make a late afternoon or evening trek out instead.

The campground also provides a way to break up eastbound or westbound hikes on the Tonto Platform. Backpackers can head out from Indian Garden in the morning to points west, such as Monument Creek, ten miles away. Or, they can hike down the Hermit Trail to the west, travel across the Tonto Platform, and spend a night at Indian Garden before ascending the Bright Angel—a trip usually done over three or four days. Some day hikers and backpackers hike down the South Kaibab Trail, pick up the Tonto Trail at the place known as The Tipoff, and hike westbound to Indian Garden before ascending the Bright Angel. Whether that's done as an overnight trip or a long thirteen-plus-mile day loop, Indian Garden provides the ideal resting point before the climb out.

It also creates a few other options. Some less-experienced backpackers—or those with limited time—can use Indian Garden as a closer destination from the rim. It gives them a chance to claim they backpacked the Grand Canyon. Two nights at Indian Garden offer an opportunity to backpack down and camp, with the option of a day hike to the river carrying less pack weight.

As I walk back from the creek to the place where two dozen people mill in the shade by the day-use restrooms, I suspect my fondness for Indian Garden grows from the fact that the campground has served most of the above-listed roles for me. It creates an entry point where the more ambitious arrive on an extended day hike or the more committed launch the start of a major trip. A number of people descending from the South Rim can reach Mile-and-a-Half Resthouse on the Bright Angel Trail. Another set of people can drop down to Three-Mile Resthouse and complete a six-mile round-trip hike with all of its elevation gain and loss, 4,200 feet all together. But a more adventuresome breed makes it at least to Indian Garden, committing to more than nine round-trip miles of trail and more than 6,000 feet in total elevation loss and gain.

They reach a place that looks like a narrow strip of green from Grand Canyon Village, where the thirty-foot-plus-tall cottonwood trees appear shrub-sized. The location of Indian Garden in the center of Bright Angel Amphitheater and its shock of green in the spring and summer draw the attention of visitors who wander the distance to reach it by trail. Seeing the green, knowing it must offer hospitality among the hostility, could lure anyone off of the rim and into the inner canyon.

⊰ ✛ ⊱

For several hundred years, ancestral Puebloans, Cohoninas, and Havasupais lived and worked at Indian Garden. Their work happened seasonally, most likely in the warmer growing season. The indigenous people of the Grand Canyon used the site below the rim because of its perennial springs and relatively level land for agriculture. They wore a footpath to the rim that generally follows what became the Bright Angel Trail, most likely with the use of ladders to ascend some rock outcroppings. At a place two miles below the rim—and near the top of the trail at a place known as Mallery's Grotto—you can see rock art, which appears to have been etched by the people who came before European settlers arrived.[2]

When Ralph Cameron made the choice to establish a camp for tourists at Indian Garden in 1903, he reached some unknown agreement with the Havasupais still living and working seasonally there. Historic records show the Havasupais were farming into the 1910s near Indian Garden. By the 1920s, they had mostly vacated the area, but the reasons for their departure remain debated. A Havasupai leader named Yavñmi' Gswedva—known as Big Jim to non-Indians—and another Havasupai named Burro tell a story of President Theodore Roosevelt arriving in 1903 and sharing with them his plans to create Grand Canyon National Monument. Roosevelt, they say, urged them to leave. Accounts also suggest that a man named Campbell (most likely Cameron) at one point asked the Havasupais to leave.[3]

Big Jim continued to travel to and farm at Indian Garden until he was eighty years old. This puts him at Indian Garden through the mid-1930s. He

Yavñmi Gswedva, 1903. Known as Big Jim to non-Indians, Gswedva farmed at Indian Garden through the mid-1930s. Here, he wears a top hat given to him by President Theodore Roosevelt and a medal presented to him by the king of Belgium. *Courtesy of the Autry National Center, Southwest Museum, Los Angeles, #19417*

is often portrayed as a figure helpful to settlers, assisting them in finding their way through the region in the park's early days. His ongoing presence and the fact that he continued the traditional lifestyle of the Havasupais made him a tourist curiosity. His family before him had long slept in wicki-ups near the springs, set fires to help improve the soil, and irrigated a plot of peach trees and vegetables.[4]

Indian Garden remained coveted from the time of the ancestral Puebloans through the pioneer era and into modern times for one key reason: the water. Few places south of the river and close to the South Rim feature perennial water. North-side drainages usually feature more-reliable water than those on the south side, and Indian Garden offers a rare perennial spring on the Tonto Platform.

The springs of Indian Garden produce not much more than 10 percent of what bubbles to the surface at Roaring Springs, but both rims of the Grand Canyon offer little to no reliable surface water.[5] Two years after the Utah Parks Company built its pipeline up from Roaring Springs, the Santa Fe Railway began construction of a water system at Indian Garden to supply water to the South Rim. The 1931 construction included the installation of a cable tramway—removed a year later—from the rim to a point a mile up-trail from Indian Garden. Accounts also reveal that the company transported a five-ton tractor to Indian Garden to facilitate construction.[6]

The water system included two pump houses built of native stone that, like the Roaring Springs operation, required sufficient hydraulic power to pump water up several thousand elevation feet—4,000 feet for Roaring Springs and 3,000 feet for Indian Garden. For the next three decades, the National Park Service struggled to keep up with the water demands created by tourists, who, by the 1930s, were arriving by car as well as by train. After World War II, Grand Canyon tourism expanded further, and the developed rims required even more water.

This ultimately led to the creation of the transcanyon pipeline. The start of its construction in 1965, the destruction of the pipeline work by a major flood in December 1966, and the reconstruction through to 1970 mark one of the last major inner-canyon building projects.[7] The work involved the use of Bell 47 helicopters to transport materials, and people who lived at the Grand Canyon at that time recall the constant overflights related to pipeline construction.

While most of the transcanyon pipeline is buried pipe, its prominent features include the Roaring Springs pump house; the Silver Bridge, carrying the line over the Colorado River; and the pump house at Indian Garden. The Indian Garden facility is in a square, twenty-foot-tall building. Its appearance is much different from Indian Garden's mule barn and corrals, the modest house that serves as the ranger station, and the cabin that currently serves as Indian Garden's small library and interpretive center.

Still, it remains a part of Grand Canyon's historic development. The pumps and hydraulics of the system speak to the power of engineering, for they work to send water up to the South Rim. The pump house also represents the work required to overcome the natural barriers to water on the rims of the Grand Canyon, where most visitors spend their time.

⊰ ✦ ⊱

Early afternoon arrives at Indian Garden on one of my solo rim-to-rim trips. Michelle Lin, the young woman traveling with Omar Martinez on the Four Seasons guided adventure whom I met at Bright Angel Campground, hangs out at the benches where most day hikers stop to rest. She photographs and shoots video of the rock squirrels. The animals aggressively harass people for food. Two of them attempt to get into hikers' unzipped packs. I toss small stones and wave my hands at them, but they are undaunted.

A Grand Canyon rattlesnake, an extremely rare sight in the inner canyon, near Indian Garden. *Courtesy of the author*

Five feet back from the benches and up a slight slope toward the bathrooms, I spot another rock squirrel acting strangely. It runs up to a designated spot, kicks up a bunch of rocks, runs away from the spot, then repeats this odd pattern of behavior. I hear it making sharp squeaks. I wonder what's going on, then I notice another creature nearby. It's a Grand Canyon rattlesnake, striped with a tawny pink. I point it out to Lin.

"Oh my God, look at that," she says. We watch as the squirrel runs up to within inches of the snake, kicks up dirt and pebbles, and runs away from it. The snake holds its mouth open and fires off its rattle in short bursts. I notice that its long, sleek body has a bulge in it. I point it out to Lin.

"Maybe the snake ate his friend or something," Lin says. She zooms in with her camera and shoots some video: rock squirrel versus canyon rattlesnake. Lin jokes about posting the video on the Internet, how it might be the next big thing to go viral. And, as hikers pass, it does go viral. We point out the action to everyone, and a small crowd gathers, watching and wondering if the snake is going to bite the squirrel. "I think he's going into a food coma," I note, given that the snake is rather obviously trying to digest whatever he just ate.

As we watch, the snake makes occasional, halfhearted lunges at the rock squirrel, who is still determined to harass the viper. Each lunge brings a gasp from someone in the crowd, but the snake does not appear to be in a position to strike. Instead, it mouths the air and flicks its tongue, most likely smelling the squirrel bothering it. Slowly, the snake begins to turn away from the place where the squirrel stands its ground.

"Go squirrel!" Lin says.

"Might be a mother squirrel protecting her nest," I suggest.

We watch the natural drama as others come and go. Lin and I joke about how entertaining the squirrel-versus-snake reality show turned out to be, captivating us for a good twenty minutes. We talk about how, if anyone spends enough time in the Grand Canyon, he could find all kinds of entertaining nature shows that rival television. Between the people, the mules, and the wild animals, we could create a Corridor Network rich with programming.

I leave Lin, the day hikers, and the rock squirrels and head to the small cabin that functions as the library and interpretive center for Indian Garden. In recent years, interpretation has expanded here. This means more books, information, and seasonal ranger talks. The move by National Park Service staff to bring additional materials and programs to Indian Garden is tied, in part, to encouraging people to spend more time here. As ranger Pam Cox notes, a visitor waiting for the heat of the day to wane can pick up a book or check out a ranger talk instead of rushing to get back on the trail and continue the steep hike out. And along with interpretation, the rangers have a chance to offer smart hiking tips while they interact with visitors.[8]

I enter the small room, about ten feet by twelve feet, at the front of the cabin. I look at a framed map titled "The Heart of the Grand Canyon." I find it difficult when looking at any Grand Canyon map not to study its features and figure out where I stand among them. I also study old photographs of Indian Garden and browse the titles of books on a shelf. Among them, I spot Rose Houk's *An Introduction to Grand Canyon Ecology*. After watching squirrel versus snake, I feel inspired to read it. Instructions typed on a piece of paper and taped to the book suggest leaving it in my campsite's ammo can—a container mainly used to prevent animals from getting at food— before leaving. The same instructions are printed on decks of cards provided by the library.

I stroll back from the cabin to my campsite and sit at the picnic table under the ramada. Determined to avoid sunburn and too much sweat, I stretch out across the top of the picnic table again. I alternate between reading and writing, closing my eyes and observing. The day moves from early to mid-afternoon. I sense the slow tick toward the transformation, the quiet hours of evening descending. I plan to use them to hike the three miles for the ultimate final reward of a last full day in the Grand Canyon—the views from Plateau Point.

⊨ ✛ ⊨

I stand at Plateau Point, the center of a geologic universe. On the teetering edge of 525-million-year-old rock.

I turn around in circles. I try to ingrain it in my memory. The North Rim and the South Rim. The buttes and temples and mesas. The flat wideness of the Tonto Platform. And below, the Inner Gorge and the Colorado River.

I return to the word *temple*. I write it down. *A land of temples. Of sentient rock forms.*

I raise my digital camera and take a picture of the temples above and the river below.

I look at the display image on the small screen. I frown. It appears flat, drained of the drama I see on the other side of the lens. It is a postage stamp of a window trying to capture a canyon that unfolds, unfolds, unfolds, reaches, and drops.

At Plateau Point, the canyon is 360 degrees of expansive views.

A camera, I think, *does nothing here. Even if it has a super-wide-angle lens with panoramic view and video capability.*

I need to etch the place into my memory.

I stop taking photographs.

I have watched the ritual, time after time, year after year. Millions of tourists—most these days with digital cameras—snapping photographs of the Grand Canyon. What becomes of the pictures? The millions and millions of them saved on computers, printed and pressed into albums or put in boxes? For most people, the Grand Canyon exists as memory and a handful of photographs. It lives at the edge of their consciousness. It remains obscure and unfathomable. We know and don't know what it holds.

The canyon is a place where geology is scraped raw and the sun bakes everything. A place where people whisper their secrets into the wind. Where people engage, awaken. And their eyes are wide again.

As I muse on the Grand Canyon, I hear a sound like clicks on metal. I turn around from where I sit—on a stone bench with a view into Pipe Creek Canyon and the river.

A raven has landed on the metal railing behind me. His black feathers reveal purple glints in the light. He caws softly into the wind. I want to take his picture. To capture the scene with the raven and his curious eyes. Instead, I only watch.

The raven and I are alone. I wait to see if he might tell me a secret. If he might tell me things about the Grand Canyon only a raven would know. The raven, I suspect, walked the life–death line. A scavenger, the raven senses death coming on an animal's breath. He might even detect cancer in a body.

The raven lets out a second caw. He takes off to the east. I imagine what his caw means. *You will live, for today.*

In the fading light, I stare out at the buttes, temples, and mesas. They become subtle and unreal, like the distant background of a painting. In the pale. I know my camera cannot register this light the same way my eyes do. So I only watch.

I walk the wide Plateau Point Trail back to camp at Indian Garden. I look to the South Rim. A camera's flash blinks from the edge. Either the photographer is watching a sunset show that is out of my view or he is simply firing off shots and hoping for the best. The sun is gone. Night sets in.

I collapse into my tent and turn my camera on. I click through the photographs of the day. I delete the ones that have not turned out well or are repetitive. I study the stunning images that remain. I feel a small pinch of guilt for looking at my video screen slide show. I should be outside, in search of the first stars of the evening.

I think, too, of Ellsworth and Emery Kolb. More than one hundred years before, the brothers from Pittsburgh, Pennsylvania, arrived at the Grand Canyon to photograph it. Their images, like all Grand Canyon photographs, only hint at the magnitude of the place. Still, the Kolb brothers hungered to capture the canyon both in photographs and motion pictures.[9]

I know the Kolbs hiked down here, to Indian Garden. They produced their photographs using the cool, clean waters of Garden Creek. They built a darkroom here. Instead of mining minerals, they mined images from paper coated in silver nitrate.

Most men tried to make money in the West through mineral and timber extraction. An average man would have tried to find copper. But the Kolbs knew of other riches.

The train and the camera brought people to the Grand Canyon. The ride from almost anywhere in the country to the canyon proved long and expensive. It took images to inspire people to travel West. In photographs, people saw the truth of the canyon. It was no painter's exaggeration. No railroad company hyperbole. It was wide. It was deep. It had a river.

What Ansel Adams did for Yosemite Valley, the Kolbs did for Grand Canyon. More showmen than artists, the Kolbs climbed ledges, lassoed trees, and dangled from ropes to get just the right photograph. In 1911 and 1912, they were the first to create motion picture footage of running the Colorado River by boat from Wyoming through the Grand Canyon. East Coast skeptics could no longer deny its majesty.

I shut off the camera's viewer and go outside. I prep my stove and make some peppermint tea to soothe my stomach. I clutch my plastic mug and walk out of the campground.

I look east for the moonrise. It's too early. Above, clouds begin to close up the sky. I do not see a star.

As I have done many times before, I look up toward to the South Rim. This time, I think again of the Kolb brothers. I imagine them in their

Ellsworth (left) and Emery Kolb during their historic run through the Grand Canyon from Wyoming to Mexico. Ellsworth later wrote a book about the adventure, and Emery showed the resulting film footage on the South Rim for 61 years. *Courtesy GCNPMC (#17171)*

edge-of-the-canyon studio. I can picture Ellsworth and Emery poring over the photographs of the day.

I think, too, of how hundreds of millions of people have seen the Grand Canyon, at least in a photograph or video. But they still come here, in some cases from the other side of the planet. Over and over. The canyon is still worth more than its image, more than any photograph could ever contain.

Since 1892 tourists have traveled to Plateau Point, to that 360-degree view embedded in the heart of the Grand Canyon. Tourism operator Sanford Rowe, with an agreement from Ralph Cameron and Pete Berry, guided guests of his South Rim camp down the Bright Angel Trail to Plateau Point, then called Angel Plateau.[10] For all tourists, the point offers a chance to see the river below and the geologic wonder it helped create.

I return to my campsite. I take one last look at my pictures of the river from Plateau Point, many shot downriver, suggesting the more than one hundred miles of canyon that keep going beyond. In the photographs, the canyon appears both viscerally real and mysterious. I let an image linger before turning off the camera and walking around Indian Garden in the freshly cooled evening.

Although the hour is later, I am reminded of the time at Indian Garden when the toy action paratrooper drifted down from the sky in the quietude of the waning day. I think of the paratrooper again, the strange and surreal moment when I watched the messenger from the South Rim finish its half mile–plus drop into the Grand Canyon, completing in minutes a trip that will take me more than three hours of hiking tomorrow.

The thoughts of the paratrooper combine with my observations of a flash that pops along the rim, despite the fact that the vast canyon is cloaked in darkness. I walk back to the campsite, where dinner plans involve a stowed-away pot, camp stove, and freeze-dried refried beans. My accommodations come in the form of a tent. Others' already appear as glowing domes while people nestle inside with their flashlights and headlamps.

I wake at Indian Garden during a March group backpacking trip. The early sky holds thick, gray clouds. A fine mist of rain falls. It doesn't matter. The hike up and out from Indian Garden to the South Rim marks our last of five days in the canyon, the trip a Hermit–Tonto–Bright Angel loop.

I walk out of the campground to a place where I can see El Tovar Hotel lights, the ones that shine on the American flag. I look for the places where the Bright Angel Trail clings to the outcropping of land along the cliff face. I squint. In the dull light, they do not appear.

A storm gathers around the edges of the canyon. Although morning, the sky darkens instead of lightens as the minutes pass. I return to camp and boil water with the last of my camp stove fuel. I empty two packets of oatmeal into the hot water. I add some trail mix and dried mango. I eat my last Clif Bar. The only food I have left for the hike out is a few handfuls of cashews.

"Think it's snowing up there?" I ask Wayne Ranney, who serves as the expert geologist on a Grand Canyon Field Institute trip I have joined.

He cranes his neck to look up at the rim. "If it's not, it will be."

I nod. I want snow. I want to walk into a land transformed, to step into the quiet beauty of it.

Two days before, I sat at a beach near the Colorado River's Granite Rapid. I wore sandals and shorts. The temperature neared seventy.

I clean out my cook pot and finish packing my gear. I wear only pants and a thin Capilene top over a T-shirt. The cool, damp air gives me a chill. But in minutes, I'll accelerate my blood flow. I'll be hiking uphill with thirty pounds on my back, a lighter load than normal because most of my food is gone and I'll carry only the water I need to get out.

One person in our crew of five wakes early and leaves before the rest of us. Ranney stays with a woman on our trip named Marcy Hardy of St.

Gabriel, Louisiana, who plans to take it slow. That leaves Nick Moulton—who traveled from his London home to visit the Grand Canyon—and me to stick together for companionship as we hike out.

The trek from Indian Garden to the South Rim begins easily. The trail crosses a wash and moves along the slopes below the looming cliffs. The elevation gain is steady, and soon, looking back, the trees of Indian Garden lower and the vista reaches over them and past Indian Garden, out to the edge of the Tonto Platform.

As we walk, the rain falls in a steady rhythm. I high-step over the water bars in the trail. In the big ascent up the Bright Angel, I think of the footprints that marked the trail before mine. The millions of hiking boots, the endless progression of mule hooves. But Grand Canyon's nature is to claim the path. Floods devour sections that then require rebuilding. Rockfalls take out layer after layer of switchback. In just a few years, a neglected trail will begin to break up and, in some cases, turn impassable. Not because it is buried by the loam and plants of a lush climate, but because it is battered away by sudden water and erosion.

The sky lightens with the expanding day, but still appears the color of slate. I narrow my eyes and look at the tops of the highest cliffs for signs of snow. I see nothing, save for isolated patches of white from the previous week's storm.

The Grand Canyon takes on a different kind of foreboding under a stormy sky. The colors of its rocks become muted. The canyon appears Draconian, mystic. Most visitors see it under cloudless conditions, when the canyon has a different kind of perilous feel, a sense that hiking it could cause a person to bake alive under the relentless sun. Has a sense that a body could turn from flesh to blanched bones in weeks.

I follow Nick up the trail for the first serious climb. It is named Jacobs Ladder, after the ladder to heaven in the Book of Genesis. Every few hundred feet we make a hairpin turn to the right or the left. We do this over and over, a dozen times, until we reach Three-Mile Resthouse. I stop, remove my pack, eat cashews and take sips of water.

I look up for the top of the cliffs, for the end of the trip. I take time to wipe the rain from my glasses with my shirt. I rub my hands and feel five days' growth of beard. It reminds me of the shave and hot shower that waits for me at home.

I glance to the rim one last time before shouldering my pack. After five days, the pack has become a comfort, a reassuring weight. I clip my waist belt, and the load balances between my hips and shoulders.

I stare at the view into the canyon and the places directly below us. Indian Garden now appears only as a cluster of trees among cliffs. When I trace the scene up to the top of the canyon walls, I notice gray specters drifting down from the clouds.

Snow.

I follow Nick for the next leg of the hike. I revel in it. With each step away from Three-Mile Resthouse, I move closer to the halfway point between Indian Garden and the South Rim.

We step into the rusty red realm of the Supai Group. It is the rock saturated with iron, like blood, turned red from the oxygen in the water and air. I daydream of iron as a connecting mineral. It is in the earth and it is in us.

The ascent becomes more gradual. Here, the switchbacks are longer. We make the steady climb toward Mile-and-a-Half Resthouse. The drizzle turns intermittent. We pass our first wave of day hikers and Phantom Ranch guests on their way down. Part of me wishes I could turn and follow them, forever looping through the Grand Canyon's interior, never surfacing at the rim. But the rest of my life waits above.

At the second resthouse, I drop my pack. My stomach gurgles from too much water or too many cashews. I use the bathroom. The water spigot is shut off because the cold temperatures could freeze the pipes, and I am nearly out of water.

My legs and back ache and my stomach hurts, but my thoughts remain buoyant. My hike of thirty miles winnows down to less than two. Foot traffic from the rim coming down increases. We hear the first clops and calls of a mule train descending. We will finish our hike in a little more than an hour.

Nick and I reshoulder our packs and travel with rhythmic creaks. A short elevation gain from the resthouse, we cross the rain–snow line.

The drizzle picks up an icy mix. After a few more switchbacks, small flakes spiral from the sky. They hit the ground and melt on the wet earth.

We walk to a tighter set of turns, where we make a left or right every hundred feet. The coiling of the trail leads up to the lower of two tunnels blasted out of the rock where the trail moves out of the Coconino Sandstone and into the Toroweap Formation.

As I follow Nick, I notice it. A magic moment. Every day in the Grand Canyon has one, or many. Each time Nick turns to the next level of trail, I see the loose outline of his body where the snow melts in the air. His body heat lingers where he has passed. It warms up the space in that partial degree change from snow to rain. With each switchback that he navigates, I see this outline.

It appears like a ghost.

By the time we reach the tunnel, the heat spirit is gone. I say nothing to Nick. I want it to be more than a quirky phenomenon, more than a "hey, neat" moment. I want to think of it as meaning something, perhaps that part of ourselves floats off into the canyon, remaining there after we leave. I want it to be a reminder that our place in the canyon is temporary—or that miracles are always lingering.

CHAPTER 12

UPPER BRIGHT ANGEL TRAIL:
Grand Entry and Exit

In the earliest hours of an August morning, three white touring vans pull into the parking area at the Bright Angel trailhead. From the vans emerge twenty-six people. They prepare for a hike to the bottom of the Grand Canyon and back. Without an overnight stay and with the heat of the summer, it will prove a difficult—and not recommended—endeavor. Still, they ready themselves with high spirits for the daunting task ahead of them.

The trip will not only involve going from the South Rim to the Colorado River and back in one day, it will also serve as an incredible feat for the entire team, especially one man. The group of mostly college-aged students from eight different nations plans to assist Juan Martin Botero in his journey to the bottom of the Grand Canyon. Botero, a paraplegic, suffers from a degenerative neurological disease called Friedreich's ataxia. The onset of the genetic condition came seven years before. After two years of the disease, he required a wheelchair.

For Botero, the loss of the use of his legs in his late twenties did not slow him down. A determined man, Botero emigrated from Colombia to the United States, eventually earning a PhD in anthropology from Harvard and settling in Boston, where he became a software engineer. He chose not to let the disease deter him from what he wanted to do. "The only obstacles are in your mind," he says.[1]

He soon learned about Alpenglow Adventures, a nonprofit organization based out of Carrollton, Kentucky, which is an extension of an Easter Seals camp there. Botero met the organizer and founder, Jim Ebert. Some people who know Ebert have described him as a determined man, one who is a positive and unflappable force. "If it's in his power to do it, he is always willing to try," notes Jim Watkins, a longtime friend and coworker. "He knows it takes a lot of effort, but his energy is so contagious."[2]

In December 2008, Ebert organized a trip and team to take Botero to the top of Mount Kilimanjaro in Tanzania, Africa. Thanks to the staff of Alpenglow Adventures, Botero summited the tallest mountain in Africa. "Right after doing Kilimanjaro with Jim, we said we had to do the Grand Canyon trip," Botero recalls.

Botero and an Indiana woman named Gina Nelson—also a paraplegic, in her case as the result of a gunshot from a domestic violence incident—came out to Grand Canyon together. Both went down into Havasu Canyon with the team to see Havasu Falls, finishing that trip the day before the one down the Bright Angel Trail. Nelson experiences some medical problems causing her pain that would be magnified by the Bright Angel Trail descent. So she does not go down that trail. She stays behind in the van to rest with some other team members.

In order to get Botero to the bottom, the team loads him into a device called a Kilicart. The elaborate four-wheeled chair features places where seven different people can help push, pull, or steer the cart. It has a retrofitted hydraulic hand brake to aid in the descent. Going down, the device can be handled by as few as two people. Going up, as many as seven people work to move it along the trail. Botero weighs 120 pounds. The cart weighs close to eighty pounds.

In the minutes after dawn under a sky piled with clouds, Botero, Ebert, and the rest of the team set a steady pace that takes them down the Bright Angel Trail a little less than a mile per hour. Their backpacks are loaded with water and snacks. The downhill work proves relatively easy, save for log water bars that create as much as a one-foot drop where the trail has eroded away. Above, clouds remain temporary blessings. Moisture from Arizona's summer monsoon storms mixes with a weak weather disturbance. The clouds linger and keep the sun exposure patchy.

After ten hours, they reach the Colorado River and stop at the resthouse where the Bright Angel Trail ends and the River Trail begins. They rest for thirty minutes, though some celebrate, wade in the river water, and take pictures. Ebert keeps everyone encouraged. This marks his third excursion to bring a disabled person down the Bright Angel Trail. In October 2008, he and a crew brought Sarah Service, a twenty-two-year-old quadriplegic who lost the use of her arms and legs in a car accident at the age of sixteen, down to Indian Garden. A month later, he led a team of four transporting a thirteen-year-old girl named Skylar Canon to the bottom. She suffered from spinal muscular atrophy. "Those trips gave us a start knowing what we could and could not do," Ebert says.[3]

The team working with Botero returns to the Bright Angel Trail for the ascent after a few hours of resting. They find relatively little trouble until reaching the Devils Corkscrew. From there, a steady rotation of the team works the Kilicart or takes on the role of support members—handing out drinks, snacks, and encouragement—to keep the forward momentum.

The real challenge, though, comes after Indian Garden. The same is true for everyone who hikes the trail. The first half mile above Indian Garden proves a moderate ascent. But from that point, the start of the top four miles proves brutal. Nearly 3,000 feet of climbing must be accomplished here, 750 feet up for each mile hiked. In some places, the climb is steeper than others. For Botero and the team, the added challenge comes with those log water bars.

Ebert and the supporting members keep the encouragement flowing despite their fatigue. At 2 am the morning after they started down from the South Rim, they arrive at Mile-and-a-Half Resthouse. Following a trip under clouds with occasional drizzle or steady rain, the sky opens up for a rare middle-of-the-night summer storm. That cools everyone off and reinvigorates them. They complete the mile and a half and get Botero from the resthouse to the rim in one hour and twenty minutes—less than twenty-two hours after their 6 am start.

Botero shares thoughts on the trip a month later, in an interview from his Boston home. "When I reached the bottom, I thought everything was worth it. But we stayed for so little that shortly my mind was set in getting back. Going down, everything was new, so I was wondering always what was behind the next corner. Going up, I was retracing my steps and sort of thinking, *It's still a long way from here.* But ascending mostly during the night gave it a different flavor; sort of mysterious and lonely, nice. . . . When I reached the top I was wet, cold, and exhausted. So I was happy it was over, but it felt good—a real sense of accomplishment."[4]

⊣ ✦ ⊢

In the case of someone like Botero, traveling down into the Grand Canyon along the Bright Angel Trail resonates as a symbolic journey. To a lesser degree, the same is true for many others. In overhearing conversations between hikers or talking to them at the resthouses along the Bright Angel Trail, I've learned that some have planned a Grand Canyon trip all their lives. New empty-nesters take the trip to celebrate their freedom and reconnect. Divorcees try to regain perspective on their lives. Some celebrate a birthday or a personal milestone. Still others just arrive and follow gravity into the canyon and check another must-do off their life list.

For backpackers, ambitious day hikers, or Phantom Ranch overnighters moving from North Rim to South Rim—or down the South Kaibab and up the Bright Angel Trail—the upper section of the Bright Angel serves as the punishment and the reward. The work against gravity, step after step, mile after mile, with the rim looming above and only getting fractionally closer, brings pain. Even healthy people feel it in their leg muscles, in the creak of joints and the work of the heart and the lungs. Climbing out of the Grand Canyon, against the grade, to an elevation that well exceeds a mile above sea level, can be a torment. Only by selecting a comfortable pace, where one can breathe and talk and stay upright, does the hike out not resemble torture.

The reward arrives with the end of the journey. "I would say most people's reactions are a sense of accomplishment, when we talk about people doing this endeavor for the first time," notes Wayne Ranney, who has guided many rim-to-rim hikes. "Their greatest emotive response is they can't believe they did it. . . . They are very jazzed when they get to the top of the Bright Angel Trail. I have pictures of people at the top, and their smiles are as big as the canyon. The next thing is they are so glad they got to see it from the bottom and understand in a real way what it looks like from the bottom."[5]

With the sense of accomplishment aside, there remains the pure wonder of the natural scenery along the trail. "I had an opportunity to hike the Bright Angel Trail when the trail was closed because of a landslide," explains historian Mike Anderson. "Hiking it all on my own, I was struck by how that is the most beautiful trail corridor in the whole park. Why it struck me so forcibly then was because I had never been able to concentrate on it. There's always a million-and-a-half people on it, walking, complaining, yelling, and moaning. When I could just take in the views and hike down to Indian Garden and be at Indian Garden with no one else there, it was such a lovely, lovely trail corridor to be hiking on."[6]

On most days and in most people's experiences, the people along the Bright Angel Trail in the upper section become a part of the experience. The true number of people who set foot on the Bright Angel Trail cannot be measured. The National Park Service is able to keep statistics on the number of backpackers who camp, the number of guests at Phantom Ranch, and the number of people who depart from or meet up with a river trip. But no one knows for certain how many people step on the trail, if only to walk for five minutes in order to say they hiked the Grand Canyon.

With 4 million to 5 million people visiting Grand Canyon National Park each year, 90 percent of them visiting the South Rim and Grand Canyon Village, many are bound to find the Bright Angel Trail. It is the most-traveled inner-canyon trail because of its access to the main population of visitors and to facilities. Unlike the South Kaibab Trail, it is one that people can drive up to and park near no matter the season. In addition, anyone staying at Bright Angel Lodge or another nearby hotel can walk over to the trailhead and, without fanfare, begin a descent into the Grand Canyon.

The number might be 500,000 people a year, equal to the population of a medium-sized city such as Albuquerque, New Mexico, a half-a-million man march into the glory of the Grand Canyon in search of a connection to the place, or simply for something to do on vacation. For this reason, the top mile of the Bright Angel Trail turns into a parade of humanity during the summer. The parade features people from all over the world, speaking multiple languages—from Mandarin to German to Arabic. Those speaking English have multiple accents and dialects: British, Scottish and Irish; Boston accents, New Jersey accents, southern accents, and midwestern accents among them. Some of the day hikers make it as far down as two or three miles, drawn into the canyon in search of more scenery. Or a magic moment.

Along those top miles of the Bright Angel Trail, I often find a specific scene that reminds me why people are hiking the trail, why the Grand

Canyon is amazing to so many. It is an event such as an animal encounter or the canyon emerging from the clouds of a storm or the first beam of sunlight to reach the inner canyon. Whatever it is, it reminds me that everyone can be moved by the landscape. Suddenly, the air turns electric, and I take in the blessing of witnessing it.

One of my favorite moments comes on a mid-July hike into the soft light of dawn. I stand by the stairs leading up to Mile-and-a-Half Resthouse. I am taking a break from my ascent up from Three-Mile Resthouse, where I day hiked. I make small talk with three hikers on their way to the bottom to join a river trip.

A sudden movement draws my attention. And I see him—a desert bighorn sheep with a full curl of horns. The others turn, and we watch in silence. The bighorn clops steadily up to the puddle of water that forms under the faucet, about fifteen feet from where I sit. He stands between me and the backpackers as we snap away with our cameras.

I hear the voices of young women as they come down the trail. I slip up the path to ask them to be quiet so they too can see the bighorn. They look at me skeptically, the one woman twisting up her mouth and furrowing her eyebrows. Then, they see him. They take perhaps two dozen pictures each as the bighorn saunters away from the water and down the trail.

"Amazing," one of the young women says to the other. "No doubt," the other responds.

What also cannot be measured is the impact of Grand Canyon on visitors. On the hike back up after the bighorn encounter, I walk behind the two women who saw him. They do not make small talk about what to have for lunch or cell phone reception. They talk about the bighorn sheep, about their luck.

What also cannot be measured, in my experience, is the feeling of finishing a hike or backpacking trip in the Grand Canyon—the feeling of taking all of those experiences and memories back to the surface.

At 8:45 am on the last day of a May backpacking trip, I cross the threshold.

Out of the inner canyon and onto the South Rim.

From trails angling upward to flatness.

From being engulfed by canyon walls to seeing only cliffs below.

From being inside of it all to looking down into it.

My first thought is to look to the North Rim, where I began. It appears far and hazy in the distance; it's a dream to imagine I started on that side of the canyon, ten air miles away. I look down again to the inner canyon and the twenty-four miles of trail I passed through. Beautiful walking. Incredible passage. I study, too, the way-down-below of Indian Garden. I walked up from it in less than four hours. Now I return to normality, reality. A different day begins.

Days of the week become lost inside the Grand Canyon. They carry no importance. Days fall into sunrises and sunsets. Into night skies swirled with depth and meaning and day skies bathing the canyon in light. I had situated my brain somewhere in the final dozen switchbacks. At the top, I think, *It's Wednesday. I have meetings and interviews and a planned lunch.*

I drop my backpack. I pull out a dry T-shirt, underwear, and hat. I slip into the portable bathroom not far from the trailhead and change. I take my backpack down to Bright Angel Lodge and drop it outside, behind the long bench under the gift shop window. Because I did a rim-to-rim trip, I did not leave a car at the South Rim. I must wait for my ride on a shuttle that will return me to Flagstaff. I walk into the lodge's restaurant for breakfast. I clutch my journal with pens clipped to it.

"One for breakfast?" the hostess asks. I see from her name tag she's from Arizona. I guess she is Navajo. I stand there, scruffy and not wearing deodorant, as the hostess searches for a table where she can put me. She locates a two-seater toward the back of the restaurant.

She smiles at me. "Enjoy," she says.

I order blueberry pancakes and a double latte. The latte arrives in a glass mug with a handle. I stare at it. It is the color of caramel, with a frothy cloud of steamed milk on top. After four days of walking along dusty trails through the Grand Canyon; sleeping on the ground, surrounded by the perfect chaos of nature, underneath the Big Dipper at night and a quarter-moon in the morning; eating freeze-dried food prepped by pouring boiling water into its pouch, the latte appears extravagant and wildly unnecessary.

The stack of half-inch-thick blueberry pancakes arrives. I scrape every speck of butter out of small plastic containers—the whole idea of small plastic containers seeming odd to me—and smear it over the entire surface area of the pancakes. I smother them in syrup. I eat them in heaping mouthfuls. I stop only briefly to drink my water or my latte.

The restaurant is full of clean, seemingly well-rested people. They chatter away, with two sets of recent retiree-aged couples sitting closest to me. I listen to them and their plans to move on to another national park—I hear Zion mentioned—or a place such as Sedona. One couple thumbs a text message to their daughter about the mule ride they took yesterday.

I leave the restaurant. I load up my backpack again and walk twenty minutes to the mobile home of a friend. There, I find the small blue duffel bag I arranged to have dropped off. It holds a change of clothes, shaving cream and razor, deodorant, and toothpaste. I shave off four days' growth of beard. I relish a hot shower. I return to feeling human. I set my watch alarm and sleep for an hour. I wake feeling as if I've surfaced from a coma.

Emergence. I write down the word in my journal.

The canyon trip is behind me.

I miss it too soon.

It is a place where hard, visceral reality fuses with dreamscape.

A heaven built of rock.

I jot down a few more sentences in my notebook before I leave for my first meeting.

I tell myself I will return to walk inside the Grand Canyon.

Nearly one month to the day after my solo rim-to-rim, I drive my Jeep Cherokee to the edge of the South Rim, into the Bright Angel trailhead parking lot. I arrive with my daughter, Grace, who has recently turned one. My wife, Jane, stays at home, ill, but I go ahead with the trip to the Grand Canyon, where I am to attend a wedding reception later in the afternoon.

The wedding reception is for Wayne Ranney, who, along with his wife-to-be, Helen Thompson, invites me to stop by and gives me another excuse to visit the canyon on a day trip. They choose to exchange vows at the edge of the Grand Canyon during summer solstice, at a place Ranney discovered more than twenty-five years before. On a new day, two loves are shared: Ranney's ongoing love for the Grand Canyon and his love for his new wife, who also feels a deep connection to the canyon.

I bring Grace to meet some people at the wedding reception, but I also revel in having an opportunity to hike down with her into the Grand Canyon. I step out into the midday heat of a late-June day. It reaches eighty-five on the South Rim, and I conjure the thought of the temperatures in the Inner Gorge—105, 110—in places with no shade.

I feed Grace a snack of cheese cubes and blueberries. I change her diaper and load her into a framed baby backpack. She fusses until I hoist her onto my shoulders. With her harnessed on my back, our movement and direction joined, she coos and repeats the same syllable, "Da da da da da da."

We maneuver through the South Rim's summer crowd. I guess Grace is studying the people and the faces, as she always does. I think of how we humans focus on one another's faces. How watching only faces is an elemental form of people-watching. And the South Rim is a people-watching place.

I turn off of the Rim Trail and head down the Bright Angel Trail. The smell of mule dung conjures memories. I wonder if Grace and I might see a mule train. I hope we do, to marvel my daughter.

On our hike, we are not traveling far. I plan to turn around after thirty minutes, given our schedule and the desire to minimize our exposure to the heat of the day. Today I am part of that different population of Grand Canyon hiker. I join the throngs who venture down the Bright Angel Trail for a short distance in order to say, "I hiked the Grand Canyon." This is my first time in the canyon with my daughter. Although it is a short hike, down a couple of switchbacks on the Bright Angel, it means something to me.

We mingle among the masses. Dozens of people head up or go down. I see a Japanese man wearing dress slacks, a button-down shirt, and loafers talking in his language on a cell phone. He waves his arms in sweeping gestures as he talks. I do not know if he speaks about the Grand Canyon or about something else. Another man with a sleeveless Harley-Davidson shirt and tattoos down the length of both arms also talks on his cell phone. He doesn't talk about the Grand Canyon, but about some job that causes him to unleash a cascade of profanities.

A couple and their teenage son head down the trail. He runs up to the edge and fakes like he is going to jump. His father snaps at him.

"What do you think you're doing? Trying to get yourself killed?"

"Jeez, I was joking!" the son yells back.

"What, you think accidents don't happen?" the father asks.

A group of ten people, all wearing yellow T-shirts, walk by us as we pause in a shady spot. The shirts show the face of a man named Boris and announce his fiftieth birthday.

On the hike out, we pass a Hispanic family with a son who is about five years old. He wears a Junior Ranger outfit. The woman takes a picture of her husband and son. They both grin, and the son giggles. We pass a dozen other people, cameras out, snapping pictures of their hike under the midday sun. We gingerly step between pairs and groups of people. A young teenage boy points to Grace, who rides in her carrier. "That's the way to go," he says.

Two grandmotherly women with their husbands smile at us as we ascend. One of the husbands nods to me. "Start 'em young," he says.

We make one more stop, and I huddle against a Kaibab Formation rock face for shade. I turn to see Grace's small hand as she reaches out to touch the rock. She pats it, the way she often pats the cat. As if to say, "Good rock." I think the same thing.

We step off the Bright Angel Trail and onto the rim. I walk along the Rim Trail for a short distance before I find a bench for the two of us. I sit her down and look out into the canyon. Most of her attention remains on a raven chortling from a nearby juniper tree and the occasional person who walks near our bench.

I point to the Grand Canyon and tell her about my hikes, about the Corridor trails. I tell her about the animals I have seen along the trail—bighorn sheep, California condors, mule deer, rock squirrels, rattlesnakes, and mules. I tell her about the geology in simple terms, the different rock layers and how the trail passed through them. She gets fussy, so I pick her up and hold her.

Time moves fast; the reception will start soon. I hold Grace as I let my gaze linger on the canyon's interior, on all of the buttes and rock walls, layers, and other Grand Canyon features within my view.

I take a deep breath and, in mind and heart, plot my next trip into that great wonder that lies below. I also daydream of a future where a backpacking trip includes my daughter—at a time when she is old enough to know the geology and the stories, and can comprehend the sheer miracle of the Grand Canyon.

EPILOGUE:
Safe Journeys

It's late summer at lunchtime, and I sit along the side of the parking lot at the South Kaibab trailhead after a day hike. A family of five and three retired couples from Alabama traveling together wait for the Kaibab/Rim Route shuttle. It leaves Grand Canyon Visitor Center and heads eastbound, taking people to and from Yaki Point and the South Kaibab trailhead, among other stops. It is the shuttle taken by most hikers and backpackers using the South Kaibab Trail, save for those who are early enough to catch one of the direct-route Hikers' Express shuttles from Grand Canyon Village. I took the 7 am direct shuttle that morning.

The twelve of us board the shuttle, already one-third full. This starts a forty-five-minute trip that involves transferring at the Grand Canyon Visitor Center to catch the Village Route shuttle through Grand Canyon Village. From there, I will stay on for more than a half-dozen stops before we reach the place where I parked my car at the Backcountry Information Center.

The hum and whine of the bus hydraulics and the chatter of the riders lull me into a relaxed state. I look passively at the view of the head of Pipe Creek. The driver pulls over and picks up two more people from the shuttle bus stop. I look toward the back of the shuttle and study the faces on the riders and wonder about where they are from and what brought them here at this point in their lives. I wonder how long they plan to stay at Grand Canyon and what they will do with their time.

With five more minutes of shuttle riding before the transfer, I look to the public service messages that line the top of the inside of the bus. They are rectangular, interchangeable placards, and I have seen most of them on previous trips. The maps of shuttle routes, warning signs about feeding wildlife, and advertisements for the Grand Canyon Association bookstores are included, but my attention falls on one message in particular.

The sign explains how more than 300 people are rescued from the Grand Canyon every year, and how most of them look like "this guy." The guy in question is young and handsome and looks fit, with a clenched and chiseled jaw. My wife and I once made fun of this sign, as it could be construed to suggest that the Grand Canyon has suffered from a spate of handsome male models requiring evacuation. It seemed like a strange epidemic.

Our joking aside, we did get the point. The male model doesn't necessarily represent people with chiseled good looks, but people confident, in shape, and feeling ready to take on the Grand Canyon. Such people can suffer at the hands of their own overconfidence. Poor choices in hiking, backpacking, or running the Grand Canyon can result in serious suffering, medical problems, and death. For example, Margaret Bradley, who became the center of a public service campaign for Grand Canyon National Park, ran in the Boston Marathon. She was a twenty-four-year-old medical student who was in shape. She collapsed and died while running in the inner canyon in the summer of 2004.[1]

Bradley did not bring enough water and underestimated the extreme heat and difficult terrain of her planned twenty-seven-mile trip. She separated from a running companion, who nonetheless managed to find help and get out of the canyon alive. Bradley died near a place called Cremation Canyon, where park service staff estimated the temperature exceeded 120 degrees that day.

Other Grand Canyon hikers have suffered similar fates. In July 2009 Northern Arizona University college student Bryce Gillies took off on a solo backpacking trip in the Thunder River and Deer Creek area west of the developed North Rim. He died from heatstroke and dehydration, according to the Coconino County medical examiner's autopsy report. The book *Over the Edge: Death in Grand Canyon* highlights numerous fatal hiking trips much like these. So, as you can see, the ad campaign with the young male model carried truth. The canyon is capable of killing anyone, no matter how young or how fit.[2]

The canyon conspires to contribute to such deaths due to six of its features: lack of water, lack of shade, steep trails, extreme summer heat, low humidity, and the fact that the uphill part of the hike comes last. Even the well-traveled, well-developed Corridor trails, complete with emergency phones and some available water, can offer extreme hazards and prove a miserable experience that can turn into a medical emergency.

In 1997 the National Park Service staff launched an initiative they call Preventative Search and Rescue, or PSAR for short (pronounced "peace-r"). The program involves volunteers and rangers interacting with visitors along the trails and checking on their plans, how much water and food they have, and asking them questions to determine how prepared they are. Following visitor interaction, the PSAR volunteer or ranger might give advice or suggest people scale back an ambitious itinerary.[3]

The volunteers and employees of the National Park Service stress the following. First, they instruct people to carry plenty of food and water. In the summer, water consumption should be measured in quarts, as in a quart for every two or three miles of planned hiking. Food should include salty snacks, which when eaten in balance with water intake restore salts and minerals lost in sweating and prevent hyponatremia. Hyponatremia is the result of flushing precious minerals from the body through drinking lots of water but not eating enough and through sweating. Hyponatremia can also be avoided by consuming electrolytes found in sports drinks.

Second, the park service advises people to consider the length of their hike. Everyone is cautioned about hiking to the river and back in one day. It sounds like a noble achievement to tackle, but down the Bright Angel Trail this becomes a sixteen-mile round-trip commitment, more than eighteen miles if you go all the way to Phantom Ranch. Down the South Kaibab, it's nearly a fourteen-mile round-trip commitment, along a trail with no water and virtually no shade in the summer.

Third, the park service emphasizes timing. Hiking at the wrong time of day or wrong time of year can be the worst choice people can make. A typical error is to wake up on the South Rim during the hot summer months and start a hike down the South Kaibab Trail at 7 am. It's an easy mistake to make, because at 7 am, among the shady pines of the 7,000-foot South Rim, it might be fifty degrees. The high temperature for the day on the rim might be eighty degrees. But down in the Inner Gorge that day, it could well exceed one hundred degrees.

Hiking the Grand Canyon in November proves a more pleasant experience than hiking it in June. As ranger Bil Vandergraff says, only fools and rangers hike the Grand Canyon in the summer. The rangers are only there to save the fools.

Experienced canyon hikers know to begin a summertime trip (though most would avoid the summer) at 3 am, or even as early as midnight if they were going down to Phantom Ranch. They might reserve such night hiking for full-moon nights as well.

Along with heat, summertime brings another serious danger: flash floods. Flash floods typically occur during the Arizona monsoon, a season identified by the National Weather Service as June 15 through September 15. During this time of year, severe thunderstorms can threaten the Grand Canyon. These storms have the potential to produce flash floods, which have killed hikers and backpackers in the Grand Canyon. Storm systems during other times of the year also can create flash floods. Be sure to check the forecast and the Backcountry Information Center for more information.

A fourth factor involves the exercise of good judgment. When planning any hike or backpack, you should think of the above three areas, make the right decisions, and adjust decisions as needed. If a planned hike to Indian Garden and back begins to feel like it might be too long, for example, good judgment calls for shortening the trip. If it takes longer than expected to arrive at a destination such as Indian Garden, one might consider a long break there and a later hike out, when the Bright Angel Trail has more shade. This judgment should also include preplanning and preparation, such as checking the weather report and talking with the Backcountry Information Center (South Rim) or the Backcountry Office (North Rim) rangers either the day before or the morning of the trip. They can share information about trail conditions, trail closures, and water availability, and offer thoughtful advice.

Before anyone attempts a major hike or backpacking trip in the Grand Canyon, training and exercise should be part of the preparation. The staff at the Backcountry Information Center can offer some ideas on how to accomplish this based on an individual's fitness level. Someone with limited hiking experience will want to attempt a variety of day hikes and consider other backpacking experiences with easier terrain first. Also, Grand Canyon backpacking trips do not require that you go all the way to the river. A night at Indian Garden, a nine-mile backpacking excursion, is a great first trip to get initiated.

As a note, the Internet age has produced a lot of information about the trails in Grand Canyon on various Web sites and hiker chat rooms. It's important that you not rely solely on this information, though it might be well-intentioned. For example, the Grandview Trail hike to Horseshoe Mesa has been described as "a great day hike" on a couple of sites. But six miles round-trip on one of the steepest trails from the South Rim to a mesa with lots of sun exposure might not be such a great day hike in the hot months, and it certainly will not be an appropriate day hike for all people of all abilities. A stop at the Backcountry Information Center can help eliminate any misconceptions.[4]

Above all, I hear one message on a constant loop from the National Park Service at Grand Canyon: individuals are responsible for their own safety. Too many people may take on the Grand Canyon believing that the park service will take care of them and/or rescue them should they run into any problems. While the park service conducts rescues in serious medical emergencies, their ability to rescue is based on daylight, where a helicopter can land, availability of staff, and whether or not other, more severe emergencies are happening in the park.

Finally, an August 2010 article in the *New York Times* reported on the growing trend of national park visitors to rely heavily on technology while in the backcountry. For example, visitors can overuse personal satellite message systems. This includes one instance reported in the article in which a Grand Canyon hiking group summoned help because their water supply "tasted salty." While technology might help people in serious trouble, it should not be used as a substitute for education, experience level, skill, and common sense.

When someone is interested in moving beyond being a day hiker, permits for camping inside the Grand Canyon can be obtained from the Backcountry Information Center. The permits carry a small fee, but prove well worth the cost for the experience of spending the night in the Grand Canyon and for breaking up any hike into or out of the gorge. Permits for a given month become available four months in advance (June 1 for October permits, for example). Permits list backcountry rules, and the trip leader must sign the permit acknowledging that he or she has read the rules and pledges to abide by them.

Backpacking brings its own added factors to consider. The single biggest factor, after the ones mentioned above, is the weight of your pack. While everyone wants to be prepared, leaving the tent behind if there is no call for rain and paring down your gear list to the essentials can make for a more comfortable experience. The general rule is that a pack should never weigh more than 25 percent of the weight of the person carrying it—and, if possible, it should be lighter than that. A hike down and back up with a heavy pack can prove difficult. Rangers agree that the heavier packs reduce the fun.

Backpackers also should take in added considerations regarding distance. A rim-to-rim hike with a backpack proves most comfortable when broken up into two or three nights. Some backpackers are known to spend only one night at Bright Angel Campground near Phantom Ranch, when a night at Cottonwood and Indian Garden campgrounds creates a more leisurely, more comfortable experience.

Good judgment and careful planning make the difference between a spectacular Grand Canyon hike and a miserable and potentially deadly one. For anyone who chooses to hike smart, Grand Canyon will offer a transcendental experience.

BIBLIOGRAPHY

Abbott, Lon, and Terri Cook. *Hiking Grand Canyon's Geology*. Seattle: The Mountaineers Books, 2004.

Aiken, Bruce. Artist. Interview at his studio in Flagstaff, Arizona, July 2009.

Aiken, Mary. Interview at Bruce Aiken's studio in Flagstaff, Arizona, July 2009.

Aiken, Mercy. Interview in Flagstaff, Arizona, December 2009.

Aiken, Shirley. Interview in Flagstaff, Arizona, October 2009.

Aiken, Silas. Interview in Flagstaff, Arizona, August 2009.

Aitchison, Stewart. *Grand Canyon's North Rim and Beyond*. Grand Canyon, Ariz.: Grand Canyon Association, 2007.

Alden, Peter, and Peter Friederici. *National Audubon Society Field Guide to the Southwestern United States*. New York: Alfred A. Knopf, 1999.

Anderson, Michael F. *Living at the Edge: Explorers, Exploiters and Settlers of the Grand Canyon Region*. Grand Canyon, Ariz.: Grand Canyon Association, 1998.

———. *Polishing the Jewel: An Administrative History of Grand Canyon National Park*. Grand Canyon, Ariz.: Grand Canyon Association, 2000.

———. Interview at his home in Strawberry, June 2009.

Berger, Todd R. *It Happened at Grand Canyon*. Guildford, Conn.: Twodot, 2007.

Botero, Juan Martin. Interviewed from his Boston, Massachusetts, home, January 2010.

Butler, Elias, and Tom Meyers. *Grand Obsession: Harvey Butchart and the Exploration of the Grand Canyon*. Flagstaff, Ariz.: Puma Press, 2007.

Civilian Conservation Corps Company 818. "Ace in the Hole" newsletter, 1935.

Cole, Cyndy. Reporter for the *Arizona Daily Sun*. Articles from February 2009 regarding Laurent Gaudreau, July and August 2009 articles on Bryce Gillies, and articles on Grand Canyon habitat restoration, 2008–2009.

Cox, Pamela.Grand Canyon interpretive ranger. Interview by phone from Cedar Breaks National Monument, Utah, July 2009.

Ebert, Jim. Director of Alpenglow Adventures. Interview by phone from Carrollton, Kentucky, August 2009.

Geopfrich, Rich. Trails supervisor. Interview at Grand Canyon, Arizona, August 2009.

Grand Canyon National Park staff. "National Register of Historic Places Nomination Forms for the Corridor Trails," March 1988.

Henry, Marguerite. *Brighty of the Grand Canyon*. Fullerton, Calif.: Aladdin, 1953.

Houk, Rose. Naturalist and writer. Interview at her office in Flagstaff, Arizona, November 2009.

Hirst, Stephen. *I Am the Grand Canyon: The Story of the Havasupai People*. Grand Canyon, Ariz.: Grand Canyon Association, 2006.

Johnson, Tamara Buckley. Interview by phone from her home in Pleasant Hill, California, July 2009.

Leavengood, Betty. *Grand Canyon Women*. Grand Canyon, Ariz.: Grand Canyon Association, 2004.

Lee, Katie. *All My Rivers Are Gone*. Boulder, Colo.: Johnson Books, 1998.

Lin, Michelle. Interview at Bright Angel Campground and Indian Garden, Arizona, May 2009.

Martin, Tom, and Duwain Whitis. *Guide to the Colorado River in the Grand Canyon: Lees Ferry to South Cove*, 4th ed. Flagstaff, Ariz.: Vishnu Temple Press, 2004.

Meyer, David. Manager at Phantom Ranch. Interview at Phantom Ranch, Arizona, February 2010.

McDermott, Mike and Sue. Interview at Bright Angel Campground, Arizona, May 2009.

McConnell, Tayloe. "The Brothers Grand: How the Kolb Brothers Found Adventure and Art in the Grand Canyon," *Northern Arizona's Mountain Living Magazine* (July 2007): 14.

McNamee, Gregory. *Grand Canyon Place Names*. Boulder, Colo.: Johnson Books, 2004.

Muller, Seth. "From Canyon to Canvas," *Northern Arizona's Mountain Living Magazine* (January 2006): 12.

———. "Woman of the Canyon, Woman of the River," *Northern Arizona's Mountain Living Magazine* (March 2007): 18.

Nunner, Gerd. Interview by phone from his home in Santa Fe, New Mexico, February 2010.

Oltrogge, Maureen. Grand Canyon public information officer. Interview at Grand Canyon, Arizona, August 2009.

Oredsen, Steve. Mule handler with Xanterra Parks & Resorts. Interview at Grand Canyon, Arizona, July 2009.

Osborn, Sophie A. H. *Condors in Canyon Country: The Return of the California Condor to the Grand Canyon Region*. Grand Canyon, Ariz.: Grand Canyon Association, 2007.

Price, L. Greer. *An Introduction to Grand Canyon Geology*. Grand Canyon, Ariz.: Grand Canyon Association, 1999.

Purvis, Louis. *The Ace in the Hole: A Brief History of Company 818 of the Civilian Conservation Corps*. Columbus, Ga.: Brentwood Christian Press, 1989.

Pyne, Stephen J. *How the Canyon Became Grand: A Short History*. New York: Penguin Books, 1998.

Ranney, Wayne. *Carving Grand Canyon: Evidence, Theories, and Mystery*. Grand Canyon, Ariz.: Grand Canyon Association, 2005.

————. Interview at his home in Flagstaff, Arizona, July 2009.

Reisner, Mark. *Cadillac Desert: The American West and Its Disappearing Water*. New York: Penguin, 1986.

Sadler, Christa. *Life in Stone: Fossils of the Colorado Plateau*. Grand Canyon, Ariz.: Grand Canyon Association, 2006.

Sheidler, Dennis and Pat. Interview at Bright Angel Campground, Arizona, May 2009.

Silcock, Kim and Neal. Interview at Bright Angel Campground, Arizona, May 2009.

Sjors. Grand Canyon National Park volunteer. Interview at Phantom Ranch, Arizona, May 2009 and February 2010.

Slater, Matt. Grand Canyon interpretive ranger. Interview at Phantom Ranch, Arizona, May 2009.

Steinbeck, John. *Cannery Row*. New York: Penguin, 1992 edition.

Streit, Jon. General manager for Xanterra Parks & Resorts, Grand Canyon National Park. Interview, Grand Canyon, Arizona, May 2009.

Swanson, Frederick H. *Dave Rust: A Life in Canyons*. Salt Lake City: Univ. of Utah Press, 2009.

Thybony, Scott. *Official Guide to Hiking Grand Canyon (Revised Edition)*. Grand Canyon, Ariz.: Grand Canyon Association, 2005.

————. *Phantom Ranch, Grand Canyon National Park*. Grand Canyon, Ariz.: Grand Canyon Association, 2001.

————. *South Kaibab Trail Guide*. Grand Canyon, Ariz.: Grand Canyon Association, 2006.

Tibbetts, Laura. Assistant manager at Phantom Ranch. Interview at Phantom Ranch, Arizona, May 2009.

Vandergraff, Bil. Grand Canyon park ranger. Interview at Cottonwood Campground, Grand Canyon, Arizona , May 2009.

Watkins, Jim. Alpenglow Adventures volunteer. Interview at Grand Canyon, Arizona, August 2009.

Williams, Dan. Ultrarunner. Interview by phone from his home in Lafayette, California, July 2009.

Wunner, Mark. Grand Canyon Backcountry Information Center. Phone interviews and e-mails, March 2010.

* Although some books appearing in the bibliography do not appear in the notes, they became important cross-references or guidebooks for the author during the writing of the book.

NOTES

Introduction

1   The celebrations of anniversaries and birthdays by people were discussed in interviews with geologist and Grand Canyon guide Wayne Ranney, in an interview in July 2009, and with David Meyer, manager at Phantom Ranch, during a February 2010 interview at Phantom Ranch. Ranney also talked about how people call him every so often, as many as ten and fifteen years after a Grand Canyon trip.

2   Grand Canyon National Park Staff, "National Register of Historic Places Nomination Forms for the Corridor Trails," March 1988 (Received from Michael F. Anderson, who co-authored the nomination submissions), 7

3   Michael F. Anderson, *Living at the Edge: Explorers, Exploiters and Settlers of the Grand Canyon Region* (Grand Canyon: Grand Canyon Association, 1998), 157.

4   Ibid., 73.

5   Jim Ebert (director of Alpenglow Adventures, Carrollton, Kentucky), in discussion with the author by phone, August 2009.

6   Dan Williams (trail runner with Team Diablo), in discussion with the author by phone from his home in Lafayette, California, July 2009.

7   Anderson, *Living at the Edge*, 73.

8   Information provided by Xanterra Parks & Resorts from their offices in Denver, Colorado, and from Jon Streit, general manager for Xanterra at Grand Canyon National Park.

9   Ibid.

10 Based on Grand Canyon National Park Backcountry Information Center estimates.

Chapter 1

1   Wayne Ranney (Grand Canyon geologist and author), in discussion with the author at Ranney's home in Flagstaff, Arizona, July 2009.

2   Lon Abbott and Terri Cook, *Hiking Grand Canyon's Geology* (Seattle: The Mountaineers Books, 2004), 232.

3   Stewart Aitchison, *Grand Canyon's North Rim and Beyond* (Grand Canyon: Grand Canyon Association, 2007), 24–25.

4   Ibid., 11.

5   Lon Abbott and Terri Cook, *Hiking Grand Canyon's Geology,* 227.

6   Based on reports and records by the National Weather Service, Bellemont, Arizona.

7   Aitchison, *Grand Canyon's North Rim and Beyond*, 31.

8   Ibid., 8.

9   Members of the trail-running group Team Diablo referred to the rim-to-rim-to-rim run as this in discussion with the author, and said it was a common title for the run among the trail-running community.

10   Aitchison, *Grand Canyon's North Rim and Beyond*, 63–64.

11   Ranney discussion.

12   Aitchison, *Grand Canyon's North Rim and Beyond*, 11, 13–15.

13   Michael F. Anderson, *Living at the Edge: Explorers, Exploiters and Settlers of the Grand Canyon Region* (Grand Canyon: Grand Canyon Association, 1998), 115.

14   Ibid., 115.

15   Ibid., 115–116.

16   Michael F. Anderson (Grand Canyon historian and author), in discussion with the author at Anderson's home in Strawberry, Arizona, June 2009.

17   Frederick H. Swanson, *Dave Rust: A Life in Canyons* (Salt Lake City: Univ. of Utah Press), 44–52.

18   Anderson discussion.

19   Aitchison, *Grand Canyon's North Rim and Beyond*, 31–33.

20   Ibid., 29–31.

21   Anderson, *Living at the Edge*, 154–157.

22   Anderson discussion.

23   Aitchison, *Grand Canyon's North Rim and Beyond*, 31.

24   Anderson, *Living at the Edge*, 155.

25   Aitchison, *Grand Canyon's North Rim and Beyond*, 32.

26   Anderson discussion.

27   The history and idea of environmental disruption has surfaced in a number of articles by reporter Cyndy Cole at the *Arizona Daily Sun* on whether or not controlled floods in the Grand Canyon worked to restore beaches and habitat. Most of the articles ran in 2008 and 2009.

28   Betty Leavengood, *Grand Canyon Women* (Grand Canyon: Grand Canyon Association, 2004), 45, 51.

29   Anderson discussion.

30   Ibid.

Chapter 2

1   Lon Abbott and Terri Cook, *Hiking Grand Canyon's Geology* (Seattle: The Mountaineers Books, 2004), 10–14.

2   Ibid., 15–60.

3   Christa Sadler, *Life in Stone: Fossils of the Colorado Plateau* (Grand Canyon: Grand Canyon Association, 2006), 27, 45.

4   Rose Houk (Grand Canyon naturalist and author), in discussion with the author at Houk's office in Flagstaff, Arizona, November 2009.

5   John Steinbeck, *Cannery Row* (New York: Penguin, 1992), 46.

6   David Williams, *A Naturalist's Guide to Canyon Country* (Helena, Mont.: Falcon, 2000), 63.

7   In a story the author was asked not to attribute, a river guide related to the author an experience that he and another guide shared with datura wherein ingestion of the plant left the two blind for several hours.

8   Michael F. Anderson, *Living at the Edge: Explorers, Exploiters and Settlers of the Grand Canyon Region* (Grand Canyon: Grand Canyon Association, 1998), 123, 125.

9   Ibid., 123.

10   Ibid., 146.

11   Frederick H. Swanson, *Dave Rust: A Life in Canyons* (Salt Lake City: Univ. of Utah Press), 33.

12   Grand Canyon National Park Staff, "National Register of Historic Places Nomination Forms for the Corridor Trails," March 1988 (Received from Michael F. Anderson, who co-authored the nomination submissions), 1

13   Ibid., 1.

14   Ibid., 1.

15   Ibid., 1.

16   Anderson, *Living at the Edge*, 156–157.

17   Betty Leavengood, *Grand Canyon Women* (Grand Canyon: Grand Canyon Association, 2004), 8–12.

18   Anderson, *Living at the Edge*, 46.

19   Swanson, *Dave Rust*, 32–33.

20   Abbott and Cook, *Hiking Grand Canyon's Geology*, 233.

21   Ibid.

CHAPTER 3

1   Information on Roaring Springs flow provided by U.S. Geological Survey spring flow data.

2   Michael F. Anderson, *Polishing the Jewel: An Administrative History of Grand Canyon National Park* (Grand Canyon: Grand Canyon Association, 2000), 17, 27.

3   Michael F. Anderson (Grand Canyon historian and author), in discussion with the author at Anderson's home in Strawberry, Arizona, June 2009.

4   Ibid.

5   Rose Houk (Grand Canyon naturalist and author), in discussion with the author at Houk's office in Flagstaff, Arizona, November 2009.

6   Seth Muller, "From Canyon to Canvas," *Northern Arizona's Mountain Living Magazine* (January 2006): 12.

7   Seth Muller, "Woman of the Canyon, Woman of the River," *Northern Arizona's Mountain Living Magazine* (March 2007): 18.

8   Bruce and Mary Aiken (residents of Roaring Springs for more than thirty years), in discussion with the author at Bruce Aiken's studio in Flagstaff, Arizona, July 2009.

9   Muller, "Woman of the Canyon."

10   Ibid.

11   Ibid.

12   Ibid.

13   Shirley Aiken (second daughter of Bruce and Mary Aiken), in discussion with the author in Flagstaff, Arizona, October 2009.

14   Ibid.

15   Silas Aiken (son of Bruce and Mary Aiken), in discussion with the author in Flagstaff, Arizona, August 2009.

16   Ibid.

17   Ibid.

18   Mercy Aiken (first daughter of Bruce and Mary Aiken), in discussion with the author in Flagstaff, Arizona, December 2009.

19   Ibid.

20   Bruce and Mary Aiken discussion.

CHAPTER 4

1   Bil Vandergraff (Grand Canyon park ranger), in discussion with the author at Cottonwood Campground, Grand Canyon, Arizona, May 2009.

2   Bruce and Mary Aiken (residents of Roaring Springs for more than thirty years), in discussion with the author at Bruce Aiken's studio in Flagstaff, Arizona, July 2009.

3   The couple did not offer their last names for use in the book, but were comfortable with being included using their first names.

4   Because of the situation being a medical emergency, the man asked that he and his son not be mentioned by last name but agreed to the author using their first names for the book.

Chapter 5

1   Grand Canyon National Park Staff, "National Register of Historic Places Nomination Forms for the Corridor Trails," March 1988 (Received from Michael F. Anderson, who co-authored the nomination submissions), 2.

2   Ibid., 2.

3   Ibid., 2.

4   Ibid., 2.

5   Ibid., 2.

6   General information on the nature of flash floods provided by the National Weather Service, Bellemont, Arizona.

7   Gregory McNamee, *Grand Canyon Place Names* (Boulder, Colo.: Johnson Books, 2004), 96.

8   Marguerite Henry, *Brighty of the Grand Canyon* (Fullerton, Calif.: Aladdin, 1953), 52.

9   Bil Vandergraff (Grand Canyon park ranger), in discussion with the author at Cottonwood Campground, Grand Canyon, Arizona, May 2009.

10   David Meyer (manager of Phantom Ranch), in discussion with the author at Phantom Ranch, Grand Canyon, Arizona, February 2010.

11   "National Register of Historic Places Nomination Forms for the Corridor Trails," 2.

Chapter 6

1   Laura Tibbetts (assistant manager at Phantom Ranch), in discussion with the author, May 2009. Laura explained that most of the supplies come down by mule, save for appliances and items such as mattresses. Tibbetts also shared her story about the flash flood and various facts and thoughts about Phantom Ranch.

2   Grand Canyon National Park Staff, "National Register of Historic Places Nomination Forms for the Corridor Trails," March 1988 (Received from Michael F. Anderson, who co-authored the nomination submissions), 3.

3   Michael F. Anderson, *Living at the Edge: Explorers, Exploiters and Settlers of the Grand Canyon Region* (Grand Canyon: Grand Canyon Association, 1998), 149.

4   Information provided by Xanterra Parks & Resorts from their offices in Denver, Colorado, and Jon Streit, general manager for Xanterra at Grand Canyon National Park.

5   Tibbetts discussion.

6   Frederick H. Swanson, *Dave Rust: A Life in Canyons* (Salt Lake City: Univ. of Utah Press, 2007), xii–xix.

7   Ibid., 32–33.

8   Ibid., 146–149.

9   Ibid., 88.

10   Michael F. Anderson (Grand Canyon historian and author), in discussion with the author at Anderson's home in Strawberry, Arizona, June 2009.

11   Anderson, *Living at the Edge*, 103–104.

12   Anderson discussion.

13   "National Register of Historic Places Nomination Forms for the Corridor Trails," 3.

14   Ibid., 4.

15   Ibid., 4.

16   Sjors (longtime volunteer worker at Phantom Ranch), in discussion with the author, May 2009. Although his last name has appeared in other articles and published materials, he made a specific request to the author his last name not be included in the manuscript. This request is being honored.

17   Ibid.

18   Ibid.

19   Official information on Preventative Search and Rescue provided by public information officer Maureen Oltrogge of Grand Canyon National Park, August 2009.

20   The video of the removal of the mule was posted on the video-sharing site YouTube, April 2009.

21   Matthew Slater (inner canyon interpretive ranger), in discussion with the author and observed during his ranger talk, May 2009.

22   Pam Cox (inner canyon interpretive ranger), in discussion with the author by phone while she was at Cedar Breaks National Monument on work detail, July 2009.

23   Kim and Neil Silcock (backpackers), in discussion with the author at their Bright Angel Campground site, May 2009.

24   Dennis and Pat Sheidler (backpackers), in discussion with the author at their Bright Angel Campground site, May 2009.

25   Sue and Mike McDermott (backpackers), in discussion with the author at Bright Angel Campground, May 2009. Some additional information received via e-mail, June 2009.

26   Michelle Lin (backpacker), in discussion with the author at Bright Angel Campground, May 2009.

27   Tibbetts discussion.

Chapter 7

1   The information comes from Powell's notes regarding the 1869 expedition, in which he wrote grand and detailed descriptions of Redwall Cavern.

2   This has been expressed in several of Katie Lee's books, including in *All My Rivers Are Gone* (Boulder, Colo.: Johnson Books, 1998).

3   Marc Reisner, *Cadillac Desert: The American West and Its Disappearing Water* (New York: Penguin, 1993), 120

4   Ibid., 121.

5   Ibid., 120.

6   Based on user statistics from Grand Canyon National Park's Backcountry Information Center, 2008.

7   Frederick H. Swanson, *Dave Rust: A Life in Canyons* (Salt Lake City: Univ. of Utah Press, 2007, 48–49.

8   Ibid., 98–99.

9   Michael F. Anderson, *Living at the Edge: Explorers, Exploiters, and Settlers of the Grand Canyon Region* (Grand Canyon: Grand Canyon Association, 1998), 109, 149.

10   Ibid., 109.

11   Grand Canyon National Park Staff, "National Register of Historic Places Nomination Forms for the Corridor Trails," March 1988 (Received from Michael F. Anderson, who co-authored the nomination submissions), 4–5.

12   Ibid., 4–5.

13   Ibid., 4–5.

14   Anderson, *Living at the Edge*, 157.

15   Grand Canyon National Park Staff, "The Historic Nominations for the Bright Angel Trail," which includes some information on the Silver Bridge, to be submitted to the National Register of Historic Places.

16   Scott Thybony, *Phantom Ranch, Grand Canyon National Park* (Grand Canyon: Grand Canyon Association, 2001), 17.

17   Ibid.

18   This information comes from notes and discussion presented by Wayne Ranney during a Grand Canyon Field Institute trip he led in October 2009.

Chapter 8

1   Grand Canyon National Park Staff, "National Register of Historic Places Nomination Forms for the Corridor Trails," March 1988 (Received from Michael F. Anderson, who co-authored the nomination submissions), 10.

2   Michael F. Anderson (Grand Canyon historian and author), in discussion with the author at Anderson's home in Strawberry, Arizona, June 2009.

3   "National Register of Historic Places Nomination Forms for the Corridor Trails," 8.

4   Ibid., 8.

5   Ibid., 9.

6   Ibid., 10.

7   Ibid., 10.

8   Ibid., 10.

9   Anderson discussion.

10   Anderson discussion.

11   "National Register of Historic Places Nomination Forms for the Corridor Trails," 9.

12   Ibid., 10.

13   The December 1935 edition of "Ace in the Hole," the newsletter for Civilian Conservation Corps Company 818, Grand Canyon National Park Museum Collection, 1.

14   Ibid., 5.

15   Ibid., 6.

16   Ibid., 8.

17   "National Register of Historic Places Nomination Forms for the Corridor Trails," 3, 4, 7.

18   Ibid., 10.

19   Anderson discussion.

20   Ibid.

21   Ibid.

22   This information comes from notes and discussion presented by Wayne Ranney during a Grand Canyon Field Institute trip he led in October 2009.

23   The legal fights have appeared in newspapers, including the *Arizona Daily Sun*, which has detailed suits between environmental groups such as the Grand Canyon Trust and the Department of the Interior regarding how they have handled the management of the endangered canyon fish known as the humpback chub.

24   Rose Houk (Grand Canyon naturalist and author), in discussion with the author at Houk's office in Flagstaff, Arizona, November 2009.

CHAPTER 9

1   Lon Abbott and Terri Cook, *Hiking Grand Canyon's Geology* (Seattle: The Mountaineers Books, 2004), 114–115.

2   Michael F. Anderson (Grand Canyon historian and author), in discussion with the author at Anderson's home in Strawberry, Arizona), June 2009.

3   Michael F. Anderson, *Living at the Edge: Explorers, Exploiters and Settlers of the Grand Canyon Region* (Grand Canyon: Grand Canyon Association, 1998), 90–91.

4   Ibid., 86, 87.

5   Ibid., 90–91.

6   Ibid., 94.

7   Anderson discussion.

8   Ibid.

9   Ibid.

10   Ibid.

11   Anderson, *Living at the Edge*, 107, 147.

12   Ibid., 107.

13   Grand Canyon National Park Staff, "National Register of Historic Places Nomination Forms for the Corridor Trails," March 1988 (Received from Michael F. Anderson, who co-authored the nomination submissions), 6.

14   Ibid., 6.

15   Ibid., 6

16   Ibid., 7.

17   Ibid., 6.

18   Anderson discussion.

19   Rich Geofprich (trail field supervisor at Grand Canyon), in discussion with the author, August 2009.

20   This information comes from the Team Diablo Web site, *www.team-diablo.blogspot.com*, in May 2009 following a run at the Grand Canyon by six members of the trail-running group.

21   Dan Williams (trail runner with Team Diablo) in discussion with the author by phone from his home in Lafayette, California, July 2009

22   Based on 2009 conversations with ranger Bil Vandergraff and volunteer Sjors, who have noticed the uptick in runners on the trails during their time working in the inner canyon.

23   Tamara Buckley Johnson (trail runner with Team Diablo), in discussion by phone with the author from her home in Pleasant Hill, California, July 2009.

24   Gerd Nunner (avid Grand Canyon hiker), in discussion by phone with the author from his home in Santa Fe, New Mexico, February 2010.

25   Ibid.

26   In articles written during the week of February 8, 2009, in the *Arizona Daily Sun*, reporter Cyndy Cole interviewed friends of Laurent Gaudreau who shared information on his background. The articles also reported on the information then available about the murder-suicide.

27   Before Laurent Gaudreau's passing, he hosted a Web site that included newspaper articles and two news segments on Phoenix news stations.

28   Elias Butler and Tom Meyers, *Grand Obsession: Harvey Butchart and the Exploration of Grand Canyon* (Flagstaff, Ariz.: Puma Press, 2007), 1–9.

29   February 8, 2009, *Arizona Daily Sun* articles.

30   Ibid.

CHAPTER 10

1   Based on interviews and observations made during and after the packing of mules on a late August 2009 morning.

2   Laura Tibbetts (assistant manager at Phantom Ranch), in discussion with the author, May 2009. Laura explained that most of the supplies come down by mule, save for appliances and items such as mattresses. Tibbetts also shared her story about the flash flood and various facts and thoughts about Phantom Ranch.

3   Michael F. Anderson (Grand Canyon historian and author), in discussion with the author at Anderson's home in Strawberry, Arizona, June 2009.

4   Anderson discussion.

5   Based on the author's observations and observations of the Aiken family, who noted that the mules stopped traveling past their home in the early 1980s.

6   Steve Oredsen (mule handler), in discussion with the author at the South Rim mule barn offices, July 2009.

7   Anderson discussion.

8   Ibid.

9   Grand Canyon National Park Staff, "National Register of Historic Places Nomination Forms for the Corridor Trails," March 1988 (Received from Michael F. Anderson, who co-authored the nomination submissions), 14.

10   Ibid., 21.

11   Backcountry Information Center reports suggest the use of Threshold trails such as Grandview and Hermit receive many fewer hikers and backpackers than the more prominent Corridor trails. Primitive trails such as Tanner and Hance receive even fewer people, given their distance from Grand Canyon Village.

12 The "don't use the South Kaibab Trail in the summer" message surfaced a number of times with inner-canyon rangers, who assert that sun exposure and the lack of water on the trail pose serious problems for hikers.

13 Wayne Ranney (Grand Canyon geologist and author), in discussion with the author at Ranney's home in Flagstaff, Arizona, July 2009.

14 David Meyer (manager of Phantom Ranch), in discussion with the author at Phantom Ranch, February 2010.

15 Gregory McNamee, *Grand Canyon Place Names* (Boulder, Colo.: Johnson Books, 2004), 92.

CHAPTER 11

1 Scott Thybony, *Official Guide to Hiking Grand Canyon (revised edition)* (Grand Canyon, Ariz.: Grand Canyon Association, 2005), 42.

2 Michael F. Anderson, *Living at the Edge: Explorers, Exploiters and Settlers of the Grand Canyon Region* (Grand Canyon, Ariz.: Grand Canyon Association, 1998), 74–75.

3 Stephen Hirst, *I Am the Grand Canyon: The Story of the Havasupai People* (Grand Canyon: Grand Canyon Association, 2006), 83.

4 Anderson, *Living at the Edge*, 75–77.

5 Grand Canyon National Park Staff, "National Register of Historic Places Nomination Forms for the Corridor Trails," March 1988 (Received from Michael F. Anderson, who co-authored the nomination submissions), 2.

6 Ibid., 14.

7 Ibid., 2.

8 Pam Cox (inner canyon interpretive ranger), in discussion with the author by phone while she was at Cedar Breaks National Monument on work detail, July 2009. She talked of improvements in interpretive ranger presence at Indian Garden.

9 Tayloe McConnell, "The Brothers Grand: How the Kolb Brothers Found Adventure and Art in the Grand Canyon," *Northern Arizona's Mountain Living Magazine* (July 2007): 14.

10 Anderson, *Living at the Edge*, 86.

CHAPTER 12

1 Juan Martin Botero (paraplegic carried down Bright Angel Trail), in discussion with the author from his Boston, Massachusetts, home, January 2010.

2 Jim Watkins (staff member with Alpenglow Adventures), in discussion with the author, August 2009.

3 Jim Ebert (director of Alpenglow Adventures, Carrollton, Kentucky), in discussion with the author by phone, August 2009.

4 Botero discussion.

5   Wayne Ranney (Grand Canyon geologist and author), in discussion with the author at Ranney's home in Flagstaff, Arizona, July 2009.

6   Michael F. Anderson (Grand Canyon historian and author), in discussion with the author at Anderson's home in Strawberry, Arizona, June 2009.

Epilogue

1   This information comes from a poster that has been displayed in the Backcountry Information Center and a story that appeared in the *Arizona Daily Sun*.

2   The *Arizona Daily Sun* reported in July 2009 on the death of Bryce Gillies. This also happened to be a summer where three teenage boys drowned trying to swim across the Colorado River near Phantom Ranch.

3   Information on Preventative Search and Rescue provided by the Grand Canyon National Park Public Information Office, August 2009.

4   The Backcountry Information Center, located in Grand Canyon Village adjacent to Maswik Lodge, has staff members who can query and get background on a hiker before he or she heads into the canyon. They also can describe what trails are the best to hike at certain times of the day and year.

INDEX

Page numbers in *italics* refer to photographs

N

National Park Service: construction of South Kaibab Trail, 154–56; Preventative Search and Rescue program, 96–97, 233; reconstruction of Bright Angel Trail by, 184; taking control of Bright Angel Trail, 184; taking over management of Grand Canyon, 10, 28

Navajo Indians, 9

Nelson, Gina, 220

night sky over Grand Canyon, 109

North Kaibab Trail, xviii, 5, 15–16, 17, 19–77, 80, 117, 130; 1966 flood of, 40, 41; closure of upper portion due to snow, 190; development of, 10, 27–29, 70–71; elevation change, xv; map of, 23; on National Register of Historic Places, 29; route of, xv

North Rim developed area, xviii–xix, 2, 6–7, 14, 16–17; annual snowfall, 6; development of, 10–11; elevation of, 6; getting to, 5, 7. *See also* Bridle Trail; Grand Canyon Lodge

Nunner, Gerd, 169–72

O

O'Neill Butte, 145, 146

O'Neill, William "Buckey," 34–35

Old Spanish Trail, 9

Ooh-Aah Point, 162, 165

Oredsen, Steve, 181, 182

Over the Edge: Death in Grand Canyon, 232

P

Pace, Jeff, 177, 180

Packer's Cabin, 94–95

Parish, Chris, 147–49

Peregrine Fund, The, 147, 149

Perkins, Marc, 116, 117

Phantom Canyon, 72

Phantom Ranch, xviii–xix, 13, 31–32, 40, 67, 81–110, *82, 88,* 119–20, 121–22, 154; accommodations at, 85–87, 117; breakfast at, 112; canteen, 72, 81, 83–85, 87, 89–90, 102, 122; construction of, 83; delivery of supplies by pack mule, 177–80; dinner at, 83–85, 89–90; pay phone at, 87, 122; ranger station, *95*; swimming pool (since decommissioned) at, 94; temperatures at, 96, 113

Pipe Creek, xvi, 115, 142, 146, 185; flash flooding of, 193–96; naming of, 191

Plateau Point, 197, 198, 209–11

Plateau Point Trail, 200, 210, 213

Potterfield, Peter, 106

Powell, John Wesley, 118

Pratt, Parley, 9

Preventative Search and Rescue program, 96–97, 233

Purvis, Louis, 135

R

ranger talks: at Phantom Ranch, 98–100, 101

rangers: at Cottonwood Campground, 57–59, 61, 63–66, 66–67, 77; at Phantom Ranch, 98–102

Ranney, Helen (Thompson), 228

Ranney, Wayne, 1–5, *4,* 22, 129, 140–41, 142, 188, 214, 223, 228

Red and Whites, 150–51, 172

Redwall Cavern, 116, 118, *118*

Redwall Limestone, 20, 21, 28, 29, 36, 37, 55, 200

Ribbon Falls, 72, 73–77, *75*; day hike from Phantom Ranch, 72, 74–75

rim-to-rim hike: first known, 27

River Ranger Station, 95

river rats. *See* river runners

River Resthouse, 142, 184

trail runners, 165–69, *167*

train: first to arrive at Grand Canyon, 33–35, *34*, 153, 182. *See also* Santa Fe Railway; Union Pacific Railroad

transcanyon pipeline. *See* Roaring Springs, water system originating at

Tusayan, Ariz., 171

U

U.S. Forest Service, 28, 153

U.S. Geological Survey, 94, 95. *See also* Matthes, Francois, U.S. Geological Survey of 1902–1904 led by

Underwood, Gilbert Stanley, 10

Union Pacific Railroad, 10–11, 29

Utah Parks Company, 10, 40, 204

V

Vandergraff, Bil, 57–59, 61, 63–66, *67*, 76, 234

Vaseys Paradise, 118

Vishnu Schist, 20, 21, 70, 72, 132, 133, 138, *139*

W

Walhalla Plateau, 15

Watkins, Jim, 220

White Creek, 33

White, Georgie, 13, 120

Widforss Trail, 16

Williams, Ariz., 34, 154, 155

Williams, Dan, xvi, 165, 166, 168–69

Willow Marsh, 73

Wohleber, Shelby Earls, 121

Woolley, Edwin Dilworth "Uncle Dee," 10, 27, 91–92

X

Xanterra Parks and Resorts, 85, 177

Y

Yaki Trail. *See* South Kaibab Trail

Young, Brigham, 8–9

Z

Zion National Park, 11, 53

Zoroaster granite, 21, 70, 72, 132, 133, 138

ABOUT THE AUTHOR

Seth Muller was born in New Jersey, grew up in Florida, and later lived outside of Harpers Ferry National Historic Park in West Virginia. But he truly fell in love with the Southwest on his first visit in 1997. He moved to northern Arizona in 2001, and his work as an award-winning journalist has led him to write numerous articles related to the Grand Canyon. He also is author of a young-reader fiction series called *Keepers of the Windclaw Chronicles*, set on the Navajo Nation. He lives in Flagstaff, Arizona, with his wife and family.